EDMUND RUFFIN
SOUTHERNER

EDMUND RUFFIN

EDMUND RUFFIN
SOUTHERNER

A STUDY IN SECESSION

BY

AVERY CRAVEN

LOUISIANA STATE UNIVERSITY PRESS
BATON ROUGE

ISBN 0-8071-0104-4
Library of Congress Catalog Card Number 32-8631
Copyright © 1932 by D. Appleton and Company
Manufactured in the United States of America
1976 printing
Reprinted by arrangement with the author

TO

MY MOTHER

MARY ELIZABETH PENNINGTON CRAVEN

PREFACE

THE writer of this volume has no illusions regarding the place of Edmund Ruffin in American history. The man has, perhaps, been slighted by the political historian and too briefly noted by those interested in things economic. Yet it is more as a type than as an individual that he deserves detailed study. The Old South that rose to completion in what are called ante-bellum days held no figure that better expressed her more pronounced temper and ways than did this Virginian. He was unique, of course, even among his own kind. All Southern gentlemen were. Yet as the greatest agriculturist in a rural civilization; one of the first and most intense Southern nationalists; and the man who fired the first gun at Sumter and ended his own life in grief when the civilization that had produced him perished on the field of battle, his story becomes to a striking degree that of the rise and fall of the Old South. It is from this viewpoint that this work has been undertaken.

Historians have been too much inclined to gain their understanding of great crises from the study of prominent politicians, who, after all, seldom control the forces that precipitate final action. In studying the Old South they have too often overlooked the fact that it was Yancey and Rhett and Ruffin who had their way in 1860-61 and that Davis and Stephens took charge only when the damage had been done. The radicals, or, as they have been called, "the fire-eaters," played a part in creating the idea of Southern nationalism and in producing the struggle to establish an independent nation which was all out of proportion to their numerical strength. They had emotion on their side, and they believed implicitly in the justice of their cause. They presented a force quite distinct from that of the politicians in their appeal to the Southern masses, who were highly dependent on leadership and who lacked adequate means for securing reliable information. They profited by all the apprehensions and distrust that Northern radicals raised and in periods of uncertainty took charge to make Southern ways into "a peculiar civilization" to be saved only through force.

Edmund Ruffin, though thoroughly typical in both his personal characteristics and his social outlook, was one of the lesser radicals. He was not as well known as either Rhett or Yancey nor was he so great a force in the development of the Southern movement. Yet he does afford, because of the great amount of writing he left behind, a better opportunity for detailed study than either of the others. It is believed by the writer that he offers an approach to Southern secession which is unique and sound; that by tracing out the development of his attitudes we may come nearer to a true understanding of the South that was, and of its point of view in the secession struggle, than has yet been achieved. The effort has been thought worth while in spite of the great difficulties of combining a personal biography with the study of a great national crisis.

The author is under obligations to many persons for assistance with his task. The descendants of Edmund Ruffin have been more than generous in permitting the use of private papers remaining in their hands. Especial thanks are due Dr. and Mrs. Kirkland Ruffin, Mr. Julian Ruffin, Mr. Edmund Sumter Ruffin, Miss Janie Ruffin, and Mr.

Braden Vandeventer. Without the aid of these persons this work would have been impossible. "Colleagues," both at the University of Chicago and elsewhere, have given generously of their time and knowledge. Professors M. W. Jernegan, R. D. W. Connor, J. G. de R. Hamilton, and Bessie L. Pierce have read the entire manuscript and made valuable suggestions. Professors W. E. Dodd and William Casey have given much valuable advice and saved the writer from many errors by their keen understanding of the problems involved. Miss Esther Aphelin has typed the entire manuscript and corrected errors in spelling and punctuation. Those who have worked in the Manuscripts Division of the Library of Congress will understand the debt owed to Doctors J. Franklin Jameson and Thomas Martin. As a Research Associate I have had access to the rich collections in the Henry E. Huntington Library, which have both extended and altered my earlier work on this volume. To the trustees, to Mr. Max Farrand, and to the Library staff I am under deep obligations. To all of these, thanks are due for merits in the work; to the author alone the faults are to be charged.

A. C.

CONTENTS

EDMUND RUFFIN
SOUTHERNER

CHAPTER I

A GENTLEMAN OF THE OLD SOUTH

THE first gray of an April morning silhouetted Fort Sumter against the eastern sky. While night yet darkened the waters of the bay, a signal gun flashed from the mortar battery at Fort Johnson on the southern shore, and a "bomb-shell rose in a slow high curve through the air" to burst above the walls of the grim old fortress.[1] A few moments of silence—then the roar of cannon broke. The people of Charleston, who had gone to sleep with this alarm set for rising, poured out upon the "beautiful promenade" of the Battery to witness the struggle "with palpitating hearts and pallid faces."[2] The long and bitter contest between North and South had been transferred from the field of discussion to the field of battle; the conservative had been thrust aside by the radical; emotion had triumphed over reason.

On this morning, when the drums at Morris Island had roused the men of Steven's Iron Battery, an old man of sixty-seven years, his long white locks hanging down upon the shoulders of a homespun coat, had taken his place by the side of the "64 pound Columbiad" that had been selected to fire the first official shot of the fight. Four days before, recently arrived from his native Virginia, he had packed his carpetbag, obtained a musket from the commander of the Citadel, and hurried across to join the forces of attack. As the signal gun flashed, his gray eyes answered, and he pulled the lanyard to loose the storm on Sumter knowing that the object of years of effort was being realized, the repressions of a lifetime lifted, and that a citizen long out of step with the dominant forces in Southern society had caught stride and was swinging forward to meet whatever Fate held for a "peculiar civilization." A man and a newborn nation had sown the wind.

* * *

Edmund Ruffin, fifth in America to bear that name, was a descendant of one William Ruffin who had, in 1666, "seated" in Isle of Wight County, Virginia. The family early prospered and became prominent in a region where broad acres and negro slaves gave place and power and where intermarriage tied important families into ruling cliques. The Ruffin acres widened from generation to generation, and the menfolk, with a startling number of second wives taking the place of those laid to rest in family graveyards, gave to their children the blood of the Cockes, the Blands, the Shipwiths, the Roanes, and the Lucases. With increasing wealth came also political duties. At various times from 1777 to 1787 the paternal grandfather served his country in the Virginia House of Delegates; in 1787 he became county lieutenant, and in 1797, as was a gentleman's right, county sheriff.[3]

The father, George Ruffin, has been described as a "typical wealthy planter."[4] His estate, "Evergreen," at Coggin's Point in Prince George County, looking north across the broad sweep of the James River, was reckoned in importance only below "Shirley," "Westover," the "Brandons," "Curle's Neck," and the other great plantations of the tidewater region. Of the man himself little is known beyond the fact that he married twice and became the father of seven children. His lot seems to have been that of the ordinary planter—a life consumed in toil and procreation. Even these limited activities were cut short by an early death in 1810, and the task of wringing from his acres a living fit for a gentleman's family passed on to others.

Thus well sired, Edmund Ruffin had begun life on January 5, 1794. His mother, Jane Lucas of Surry, is a shadowy figure; she soon passed from the scene, like so many of her kind, leaving the rearing of her only child to a quickly acquired stepmother in the person of one Rebecca Cocke. What effect the birth of half brothers and sisters, at intervals never wider than two years, had on this sensitive lad in the days that followed we do not know. Nor can we do aught but guess as to the treatment he received or surmise the unrequited yearnings for love that rent his heart. We must be content with the meager information that as a youth he was frail of health and restless of spirit, reading much of whatever came to hand and growing up in almost complete ignorance of the practical agricultural tasks to which his life was to be largely devoted.[5]

Parents or private tutors undoubtedly furnished him with elementary schooling, for he left home for the first time when, at sixteen years of age, he went down to Williamsburg to enter William and Mary College. His career there was short and unprofitable. His time was seemingly spent in large measure upon affairs outside the classroom, one of them, evidently, a love affair, for he returned home shortly to wed Susan Travis, the comely daughter of a prominent

Williamsburg family, and to answer his country's call as a private in the War of 1812. He saw no actual campaigning in that struggle, but endured the hardships of intensive drill and inadequate quarters at Norfolk, boasting in after years that those of "gentle blood" evidenced superior capacity for taking hard knocks to those of "lower origin." After six months of military routine he was mustered out, immediately to assume, "by the easy indulgence of a guardian, the 'possession and direction' of his property which consisted of the Coggin's Point farm." He had begun the career of a Virginia gentleman.

And being a gentleman in the Old South meant something quite well defined—a type in the very absence of conformity to pattern, yet with certain rather clear-cut qualities. He was ever an individualist, a man of will and honor with license to peculiar bents and a willingness to accept the responsibilities involved. He took on a certain show of aristocracy, which approached reality in paternalistic notions of government; of culture, which manifested itself in the love of books; and of that sort of poise which those surrounded by dependents are apt to develop. Yet the homespun was upon him. The pattern was borrowed from the Old World, but the poundings of a rural life, which generally included some economic pressure, were too insistent for the individual not to be shaped to his section. In the end a lovable tyrant appeared, with some tradition of leisure and culture amid the pressing realities of acres and slaves and large families and southern weather—any one of which was enough to humanize even a gentleman.

*　　*　　*

Of the personal characteristics of the young man who thus

assumed the responsibilities of family head and plantation proprietor we know all too little. It is impossible, with existing records, to disentangle the youth from the mature man whose qualities were fixed or to follow the changes and developments that took place under experience. Our picture must represent completion, not beginnings. When he thus emerges, he was slight of build, standing five feet eight inches in height and weighing scarcely one hundred and thirty pounds. His health was ever bad. He suffered much from bilious colic, and spells of serious illness were frequent to the end of his life. Yet his form was erect, his activity ceaseless. On his sixty-third birthday he walked a distance of three miles across the frozen James in fifty-five minutes and returned immediately in sixty. His spirit rose above physical weakness though he never escaped the handicap.[6]

In personal appearance Edmund Ruffin was striking. Poor health sharpened his features, emphasizing a high, well-rounded forehead crowned with an abundance of dark hair which soon turned gray and was thrown back to fall in long, free strands upon his sloping shoulders. His steel-gray eyes were deep-set, looking out keenly from under heavy brows. A sharp, well-formed nose sent deep lines down to give firmness to a large, straight mouth and a square, well-set chin. It was a face to be noticed—one which suggested positiveness and determination toward well-understood ends.

There was a seriousness about the man that ran to the point of complete exclusion of any sense of humor. In the thousands of written pages that have come down to us from his pen there are only a few faint suggestions of levity. Once when, amid the crowd that jostled in the halls outside the Democratic Convention at Baltimore in 1860, the hoop skirts of a fair maiden pressed his legs and revealed the fact that she too possessed such appendages, he was moved to sprightly comment; when a weary or puzzled typesetter transformed a high-flying agricultural orator's reference to Lord Bacon's work on inductive philosophy into the phrase, "lard, bacon, pork or inductive philosophy," he clipped it for his files with evident relish. But these constitute nearly the whole of such pleasantry, and for the most part a man who took himself and life with dreadful seriousness stalked about, expecting others to realize the importance of the work in hand and to appreciate duly all efforts directed at setting things right.

He was, however, humorous in his overseriousness. In a period of great personal and family grief he once confided to his diary the shame he felt "of becoming fatter, and that it should be generally observed." He was really serious when, late in life and long after he had become a widower, he commented thus upon his feelings toward two charming young girls: "I should even fear that my attraction was allied to love, the most foolish and reprehensible of all— that of an old man for a young woman, if there was only one of them." Since there were two he felt safe, yet he added the comment that if only selfish feelings and inclinations were considered, "I might be as great a fool as most other old men, and seek to marry a blooming young girl."

As might be expected in one so serious, there was always something of the reformer about Ruffin—an urge which kept him moving from one bitter experience to another. Seemingly, deep in his nature, giving bent to his reactions, there was an abiding spirit of rebellion against incompleteness and restraints which must have lain as much inside the man himself as in the environment. He could not remain quiet or move along in sweet, indifferent accord with men and affairs—not that he was abnormal in any sense, but he was intensely alive in a world of common, plodding folks and stubborn realities. He was superior in mind and feelings to the average man and he knew it, but the world was slow to recognize the fact. And yet he might be inferior too! He did not gain the public approval he so much desired; he could not do well many things that men seemed to think good and worthy of reward and esteem. He was forever meeting rebuffs, failing to strike the popular chord. And his emotions, in spite of mental certainty of the unsoundness of men's judgments and the fickleness of their approval, told him that in his world these things were important.

This was nowhere better shown that in the matter of public speaking. Tradition said, in the Old South, that the gentleman should control. But it made leadership depend largely on personal influence and the ability to think and express thoughts to the conviction of hearers. It had a weakness for oratory. Eager as Ruffin was for public contact and control, he never acquired the ability of free and forceful speech. His self-consciousness and desire to do well and impress others only led to confusion and remorse for having tried. Sometimes, under intense feeling, he forgot himself to achieve an effectiveness quite out of the ordinary, but as often to be suddenly checked in disorder at the realization of himself so out of character, and to end in fluster. Yet he never ceased to try, and he seldom refused an invitation to appear, glorying in such success as came, bemoaning failure, but a bit puzzled by it. For, mingled with an apparent envy of those who could sway audiences, there was a faint suspicion of some trick by which it was done, some cunning, perhaps, which made it part of the mysterious political influence that escaped him.

*　　*　　*

Perhaps it was this failure that gave him so much zeal with his pen—though it must be admitted that Southern gentlemen were, as a class, much with "pen in hand." "Nothing suits me so well . . . as writing," he says, "and when so engaged . . . there is no employment so pleasant and engrossing to me. . . . I can, with pleasure, write rapidly for twelve or more hours in the day or night and until it is necessary to rest my cramped right hand." His pen shed ink in an almost constant flow, early and late, upon matters great and small, personal and public, in private correspondence, diaries, newspaper articles, pamphlets, and books. Few men have written more.[7]

One further characteristic of the man needs to be noticed. He was extremely sensitive to criticism, a quality accompanied, strangely enough, by a tendency to frank, open, and cutting expression of opinion. A man casting the sharpest shafts, himself vulnerable to the highest degree! Always subjective, he apparently derived his greatest satisfaction from the approval of others, reproducing in his diary every compliment offered and, on the other hand, evidencing the deepest despair, with resolves to try no further, when criticized or misunderstood. The failure of all men in Virginia properly to appreciate certain reform efforts that he made to improve agriculture brought an early retirement from public activities with the wail, "My former and, I will presume to say, great services rendered to my native state (however praised and complimented by very many of the public) have been returned mostly by slighting neglect and ingratitude." He confessed himself "soured" toward his country-men and resolved to decline any "honor and any renewal of service to the public of Virginia, in any way." He moved in this spirit from Prince George County, leaving "few friends" and "many enemies," though the county joined in a great banquet in his honor, and regretting that the retention of property and friends there necessitated even an occasional return.

Such attitudes invariably led to the denunciation of critics and enemies as "self-seekers," "schemers," or even "politicians," for the very envy of whom he adopted this opprobrious classification. It became with him something of a conviction or duty to be constantly in arms against those who reached place and approval. Late in life he invoiced his faults with special emphasis on his "vanity and love of notoriety" but more on the "simple credulity" which had caused him to be used "by persons of very inferior minds" to his own "in every power except cunning, common sense and a correct perception of self-interest." Even the gallant fight he waged in Virginia against "the despotic ruling power of this country" in the person of the banks was motivated in part by the fact that "the banking gentry" were "annoyed" by his efforts. He confessed it an expensive "amusement" but was consoled by the fact that "other men spend their money or time and labor in hunting, shooting, fishing, &c., or in pursuit of office and honors" while he, with "no fancy for any of these very common pleasures," could afford to amuse himself "with hunting banks and bank directors and enjoying their anger & malignity thus excited. . . ." [8]

But human beings defy classification, and Southern gentlemen ever rise above it. When all is said, Edmund Ruffin remains a strange bundle of contradictions. Kind and loving with his children, generous to the worthy who needed, strong and loyal in friendship, he could hate with equal power, until his own blood estranged could be viewed with complete indifference and friends of long standing instantly turned into enemies to be forever afterward passed by. Slow to anger, his "resentment," when aroused, was "implacable"; deliberate and malicious "aspersions" were "rarely forgiven," lapse of time, separation from the offender, or even death never operating to "alter the feeling" or "abate the hatred." [9] Thus there was packed into the same personality so much that was rich and unselfish and so much that was petty and vindictive that one cannot escape the feeling that childhood experiences or physical limitations had lodged in the man, of really great qualities, a vague sense of an unfair deal which must somehow find vent against convenient realities.

*　　*　　*

The personality of Edmund Ruffin was clothed with the accretions that were apt to become part of the habits and viewpoints of the class to which he belonged. In early life, in a region where the custom "of drinking was universal," he was "drawn into the habits of the company" he kept and "for some years" drank "every day to the extent of intemperance." But "good sense, . . . considerations of the probable consequences," and a regard for reputation and family soon brought a halt and, in early manhood, a resolution to complete abstinence. And resolutions, with Ruffin, were made to be kept. He also used tobacco in these youthful days, as was the custom in the great home of the "filthy weed." But bad dreams and bad health dictated to a man ruled by reason the wisdom of reform, so this "consolation" likewise passed out of his life. Thereafter no Puritan of New England ever set reason more sternly to watch over appetites than did this son of the Old Dominion. Where was there another who suspended eating for days at a time simply because hunger did not press with sufficient pain? Where another who would not accept the physician's advice as an excuse for his toddy? [10]

But "temperance" did not extend to the matter of reading. Reared among books, as were those "born to the manor" in the South, Ruffin gathered a collection of well-thumbed volumes so large that the astonished "Yankee soldiers" who plundered it in war days could describe it as the largest library they had ever seen.[11] He roamed widely in his interests. Newspapers from London, New York, Charleston, and Richmond; periodicals as varied as *Blackwood's Magazine*, *Russell's Magazine*, the *Living Age*, the *Southern Literary Messenger*, and *DeBow's Review;* books which ranged from the classics to the latest scientific works of European scholarship and the last volumes from Southern pens, such were the materials that entered into his day-to-day reading from youth to old age. He had read all of Shakespeare's plays before he was ten years old. He tells of reading, "for the pleasure they afforded," the four-volume English *Complete Body of Husbandry* and Bordley's *Husbandry* by the time he was fifteen. In later years he was as familiar with the writings of Davy on chemistry or Lyell on geology as he was with the novels of Scott, Thackeray, or Dickens. In one period of a few months he read Pepys' *Diary*, Dana's *Two Years Before the Mast*, Boswell's *Johnson*, Prescott's *Philip II*, Smith's *Wealth of Nations*, Irving's *Life of Washington*, Schiller's *Wallenstein*, the *Memoirs of Sidney Smith*, and the *Life of Charlotte Brontë*. When the war came on and he was driven from his own books, he read even *Webster's Dictionary*, a volume ever before avoided as the "embodiment of the Yankee language and authority for Yankee deviations from Standard English." To his surprise, in spite of a rather frequent change of subject matter, he enjoyed it, finding these preconceptions wrong, as he might have found others had opportunity permitted.

But in the main he did not engage in indiscriminate, uncritical reading from habit or to pass the time—though he did assert that he "would rather read the lightest and more trashy tales, on the score of profit or intellectual improvement," than to play chess, which was "entirely unproductive to any good effect, except of present amusement." "Began to read *Hansford*," he writes, "but after seventy pages gave it up. This is the fourth new Virginia novel that I have attempted to read within the last few years, and neither [*sic*] of which I could finish. Yet all have been greatly praised. The others were *Alone, The Hidden Path,* and *The Virginia Connections*. It is said that of *Alone* several editions and even one or more translations have been published in Europe. If so, it shows that there is more bad taste there than here." [12]

Of history he read much. His quaint observation on historians, after reading Macaulay and pondering the question of that master's religion, reveals a rather keen understanding of the historical mind and method:

> I doubt whether he has any good claim to be either a
> sectarian or a Christian. I believe that there is from the
> nature and manner of their studies and habit of investigation, a tendency of the most profound historians
> to skepticism. I do not speak of mere compilers and

abridgers of voluminous annals and other materials—but of historians who closely scrutinize and weigh the probability of every recorded fact, and admit or reject them according to the rules of evidence and upon sound reasoning. They thus learn to judge of sacred or religious history by the same rules of evidence by which they would test the alleged incidents of profane history. Of course no sacred or religious history can stand the test. Its reception must be upon faith. . . . Whether I suppose the right case or not, it is certain that a large majority of the greatest historians have been supposed skeptics or total and avowed unbelievers. Such were Robertson (though a Christian divine and preacher), Hume and Gibbon. And even Prescott, raised and continuing in New England, the land of puritanical hypocritical observance (where every decent man, if not a Christian, pretends to be one, for his reputation's sake)—I suspect that even Prescott is a skeptic.[13]

As the struggle over slavery grew in intensity, he took pains to study every aspect of the problem, reading practically every book and pamphlet in that bitter stream which poured out in attack and defense of Southern institutions. From *Uncle Tom's Cabin* to *The Impending Crisis,* from the *Pro-Slavery Argument* to *Types of Mankind,* he knew the literature of the struggle and with meticulous care builded his own defenses and launched his own attacks. History yielded backgrounds; science gave authority for racial alignments; the thinkers of all time furnished proof of the superiority of Southern political institutions and practices. His appeal was to reason: what logic upheld was a right beyond question!

Here again is the planter type. The Southern gentry possessed an average of intelligence and an ability to think, write, and talk which has seldom been equaled on so extensive a scale among any other people. They "met in convention" on the slightest provocation, and there men unknown outside a limited neighborhood would rise to speak, one after another, their information abundant, their logic clear-cut and convincing, their phrases loaded with classical references, and their English pure and correct. It was learning and logic, not ignorance or refusal to think, that ruined the Old South. John C. Calhoun, right in his thinking, wrong in his understanding, was only the greatest of a type common in his section.

But acquaintance with learning was not all that went with culture in the Old South. The planter also enjoyed, or pretended to enjoy, both music and art. A dilapidated melodeon or a few family portraits hanging above the well-stocked sideboard might be the full extent to which the passion ran, but even that was sufficient to indicate the non-Calvinistic attitude of "the Master" and to express a general set of values that supposedly inhered in those fit to dominate the social order. Ruffin, true to form, had a real love for music and, ideas at least, on art. For his own amusement he fingered his "harmonican" and sang simple airs that ran, in origins, back deep into the life and experience of Anglo-Saxon folk. The music teacher was an essential part of his household; his children, gathered at evening about the fireside, delighted him with their songs, far more likely to be profane than sacred in character; and his well-worn music book, painfully but neatly produced by his own pen, gave substance to the boast of understanding more of music "than a hundred of men in this country."

Nor did he neglect the "exhibitions" of "the masters" who came his way. "I went to the concert to hear Thalberg on the piano and Vieuxtemps on the violin," he says. "Their execution was indeed wonderful, exceeding my expectations." But they were a bit beyond him, and their "flourishes to show off their wonderful skill," while admired, were not enjoyed. "I would have found more pleasure in hearing simple airs correctly and plainly played on a band or harmonized songs by a few good voices," was his confession, followed by the refreshing but caustic observation that "with the great majority of the crowded audience, even though most of them would affect to be pleased, the thing was worse than with me. One half of those who were present would have enjoyed hearing an ordinary fiddle playing common reels and Yankee Doodle, to the performance of this night. It is as strange as it is amazing to persons, who, like myself, love good music, but without much knowledge, that good musicians will confine their performances to pieces which not one in fifty of their hearers can appreciate. . . . I would by no means have them pander to bad taste and ignorance by playing . . . bad music, because popular. But there are thousands of beautiful and simple airs and simple parts of other music, which would give pleasure to the least cultivated taste and by hearing which, natural music taste would be gradually taught to understand and appreciate the compositions which at first are like Greek to the multitude." [14]

He was moved to similar comment on hearing Miss Richings in the opera "The Enchantress." He believed "her trills and cadences" were "introduced merely to show her wonderful power and command of voice" and chanced the guess that had she "introduced the most perfect imitation of the mewing of a cat, or the braying of an ass," the audience would have "applauded as much—provided they had been only assured that these imitations had been applauded by all preceding audiences and persons of musical taste." He was, of course, a bit cynical, but that was a gentleman's right when he was observing the masses. It was also a gentleman's privilege to speak the truth in the Old South, and gentlemen were forever exercising their privileges.

In much the same spirit, but without pretense to "artistic taste," Ruffin insisted on his right to pass judgment upon works of art. When the equestrian statue of Washington was unveiled in the capitol grounds at Richmond, he judged it "in very bad taste." In fact, it was "absurd." With this pronouncement he proceeded to offer sound reasons against "all equestrian statues of men," declaring that "if a horse alone were represented, noble and beautiful in appearance as nature made him, . . . nothing else would be more" pleasing. "But a horse under bridle and saddle and rider, is comparatively degraded by subjection and defamed by artificial equipment. And yet, the horse will be considered by all as the principal and great object, even though the rider is Washington. An equestrian figure is truly the statue of a horse, with a man attached." [15] Few could refuse the privilege of criticism to one capable of such comment. It manifests a taste for the appropriate which, when combined with a sense of line and proportion, explains the urge to beauty in house and garden that characterized this man and his section. It explains why, in the South, it was not enough just to be protected from the weather.

The early Ruffin home at Coggin's Point seems to have been a modest structure. Whether built by the family or acquired by purchase we do not know. In any case, it did not satisfy the needs of the young proprietor, for as soon as finances permitted, he replaced it with the "Beechwood Mansion," set in a favored spot to take advantage of certain great trees he had always loved and to make the most of the magnificent view a river frontage afforded. It was not a pretentious dwelling as James River houses went, but it upheld the Southern tradition of careful planning and spacious quarters for a growing family, meriting the term "big house" by comparison with the negro quarters and other buildings that clustered near.[16]

An early shifting of interests to publishing, which took him to Petersburg, and a permanent removal to Hanover County on the resumption of a strictly agricultural life prevented the fullest development of "Beechwood" under Ruffin's control and made "Marlbourne," in the valley of the Pamunkey, his real "seating." Here, in a region which offered unusual opportunities for intelligent farming and the restoration of worn-out soils, he acquired nearly a thousand acres of choice land with appropriate farm buildings. He described the dwelling house as "large and valuable," the kitchen, dairy, meat house, ice houses, laundry, stables, carriage house, overseer's house, and slave quarters as "all very good," though some were "unfinished." It was an estate complete from mansion to quarters, with even the family graveyard soon making its appearance on the ridge off to the right where the pines gave somber aspect and the morning sun first touched.[17]

The mansion stood on the brink of a hill which rose sharply from the bottom lands, enjoying, in Ruffin's words, "a prospect of rare beauty," which, with improvements to be made, would be "inferior to no view which does not embrace either water or mountains." It was a two-story, rectangular house of a type common in the region, with its high ceilings, its great hall cutting the center from a white-pillared double balcony in the front to a like one in the rear, its well-proportioned stairway to the bedrooms above, and on either side its commodious living room and dining room from which other rooms "rambled off" in both directions to care for family and relations and even "old friends" who became a permanent part of the household. A well-kept lawn in front and rear, shaded by great trees of oak and pine (ever the glory of the South), with gardens to the left where flowers were as essential as vegetables, blended on the outer edge into fields which swept off to purple horizons.

Back from the mansion were the negro quarters, where the faithful Jem Sykes, as foreman, dominated his fellow slaves by virtue of "the Master's" confidence; and near by was the overseer's house, where occupants came and went at intervals for a time and then ceased altogether, to the great relief of the owner. There were thirty negroes to begin with at "Marlbourne," the force at "Beechwood" having been divided, half remaining with the eldest son who took charge there and half being brought along to the new home. Others were added at once, so that by the end of the year there were on the plantation books the names of forty-one slaves. Contrary to the usual custom, families seem to have been separated in building this force, for during the next few years, at the end of harvest, at Christmas, and at other slack periods of labor some six or eight men were allowed to go back to Prince George County "where they have wives."

For service the slaves were divided into field hands and domestics, with a man set apart as gardener and carriage driver and a woman as dairy girl. The negro children had their tasks in herding cattle and hogs, cleaning up the trash about the yard and fields, or carrying water to the men and women at their work. The field hands were both men and women, some of the latter being reckoned as expert binders and valued only a trifle lower than their brothers of equal age. Four women cooked and cared for the mansion and its occupants, adding to their duties in periods of stress the preparation of food for the workers in the fields. Extra help was hired at harvest time, as many as eleven workers being gathered from the neighborhood to meet the needs that could not be cared for by the regular force.

At first a white overseer was employed, but Ruffin, like his friend James H. Hammond, found overseers inefficient, taking "pleasure in nothing else but thwarting their employer and abusing his negroes." "Being too wise to learn or to obey" was the great fault Ruffin found with them as a class. He soon decided, therefore, that personal direction by the owner was essential to good farming and that a negro foreman, with such qualities as Jem Sykes possessed, could work under the master's orders for greater efficiency. In the end he gave Jem "charge of the keys" and trusted him with everything, remarking that "If this trust be abused and my people make use of their opportunities for an unusual amount of pilfering, I shall continue to prefer, as now, having no overseer." Ruffin or one of his sons took charge of the farm thereafter, directing the slaves at their tasks and planning the course of development.

Under such a system there was bound to be enough of efficiency to render slavery more exacting of labor than was usual, but, on the other hand, there was a closer knowledge of, and interest in, the personal welfare of the negroes than was possible under the average overseer. Ruffin gave careful attention to the health of his slaves, furnishing medical aid as needed and paying bills which sometimes ran from twenty to forty dollars a year for services to a single negro. But he found, especially with infants, that "pains taken" did not prevent losses so great as almost to make him "eschew doctors & physic." From 1813 to 1829, of forty-six infants born at "Beechwood," twenty-one died, while from 1839 to 1847, of thirty-nine born, eighteen were lost. Perhaps it was this that accounts for the entry in his farm book for 1850 of an item of twenty dollars paid to a physician "for an unnecessary call for a common case of child birth."

Real affection developed between the whites and blacks at "Marlbourne." Jem Sykes was held in highest esteem by all the household, and words of praise for patient negro toilers sprinkle the hard, economic pages of its farm journals. When Ruffin withdrew from the active management of his plantation, there was real grief among the negroes. A restlessness soon developed under the less efficient control of his son-in-law, who then took charge, and it was necessary for Ruffin to restrict his visits to the old home because of the tendency of the slaves to look to him for sympathy and to consider him still the master. They loved him, and he returned their affection with good-natured tolerance. In historic old Blandford Cemetery at Petersburg, where sleep many of Virginia's illustrious dead, is an humble stone inscribed with the words: "In remembrance of Lucy Lockett, a slave, yet not less the friend of her master's family, by whom is offered this testimonial of their esteem for her excellent virtues and true piety, gratitude for her affectionate and faithful services, and grief for her death. Born, February 15, 1774. Died, January 29, 1836." This was Edmund Ruffin's tribute to a faithful negro mammy. For care and even "religious impulses" he gave her affection in life and a place among his children in death.

Ruffin always permitted preaching to his slaves, recording on one occasion the christening of young children by an

Episcopalian minister at the quarters, observing at the same time that most of those among his people professing religion were Baptists, "immersed on profession." He strove to respect their family relations, declaring that anything that caused the "partial or final separation of near members of the same family" caused him "as much regret" as it caused pain to the families thus separated. In fact, he granted to them every favor that he thought was for their betterment. To him the negro was an inferior being, incapable of self-directed effort and unfit for much responsibility. Without the white man to control and direct, he would not labor; without the protection of the superior intellect of the master, the slave would sink back into African chaos. He was surprised that even Jem Sykes, whom he declared to be "faithful and intelligent," should be able to associate the early application of marl to lands with their later fertility. He thought of his slaves as children, kept at tasks for their own good and made happy by freedom from responsibilities in caring for themselves amid the complexities of modern life. Slavery was not only a good but an essential for both whites and blacks. Although an expensive kind of labor, it was best for the South and necessary for the negro. Hence, he accepted the responsibility for the care and training of his charges, ever considering their well-being a matter of as great importance as the rearing of his children. Paternalism never had greater justification.

Family life at "Marlbourne" was serious and yet attractive. In the years between 1811, when Susan Travis, a mere girl of sixteen, became the wife of Edmund Ruffin, and 1846, when death came, she bore him eleven children. Three of these died in infancy; only three survived the father. Disease, childbirth, and war took their toll, making sickness and death a normal part of household affairs, while family graves, ever close at hand, kept the seriousness and uncertainty of life always in the foreground. Rural worlds have been wont to bury an appalling number of their folk, but have compensated in the closer binding of family ties. Such was the case with this group. An air of genuineness characterized their relations at all times. Childhood letters and those of mature years evidence intimacy and show real affection; family loyalty never weakened. The home was the center of their lives. There was in this South little restraint on pleasure, no tradition to asustere conduct, and spirited discussion, song and dance, or quiet with books from the well-stocked library drew and held the family to its own fireside. Visitors, who came far and stayed long enough to justify the trip, often filled the house, necessitating "a return of the compliment" and giving excuse for travel to distant corners of the Southland. When this excuse failed, there was always reason for a trip to "The Springs", where the gentlefolk of the section congregated by thousands. Courtships and marriages, tending, sometimes, to become family rather than private affairs, swelled a growing list of places that must be visited and an increasing stream of "relatives" who "came visiting."

As might be expected, the father dominated all family situations, demanding and receiving from his children strict obedience and deference. He knew what was best in conduct and taste. He believed in the things that experience had taught to elders. But, if exacting in his demands, he was equally generous with those who conformed, paying strictest personal attention to their training and granting them every pleasure his wealth permitted. He took the education of his sons, Edmund, Jr., and Julian, into his own hands, developing what he thought were superior ways of teaching the various subjects, and then sent them on to the best schools to be found in the nation.[18] Edmund, Jr., went to Dr. Dwight's Gymnasium at New Haven, Connecticut, and then to the University of Virginia. His letters from New England, wishing "that Virginia was as well cultivated and the manners of its inhabitants as polished as the inhabitants of Connecticut," though tempered by the information that "Yankees sometimes cheat if they can," may account for the fact that the younger son, Julian, did not go North for his early training but remained in Virginia. Both grew up into serious lads whose love for their father was always tinged with something of submission yet whose sterling worth evidenced the effectiveness of their training.

The youngest son, Charles, came too late to receive his share of personal attention and grew to manhood feeling discipline untempered by favors. He drifted wide of the pattern set by the father but achieved the love of his fellows, in good-natured violation of accepted codes, in compensation for threats of being cut off from home and denied his patrimony. Nor could sons-in-law, who had been denied the benefits of such training, ever be quite satisfactory. The ties between married daughters and father were, therefore, often under such strain that in one case at least they snapped never to be rejoined. Bitterness thus mingled with satisfaction in the heart of the stern old father, who, certain of his position in all cases, only increased the love he felt for those who remained to balance his losses.

Meanwhile, material prosperity had come, with better agricultural practices, to Ruffin and his fellow planters in Virginia. He purchased more land, as much to choose his neighbors as to increase his holdings, and added to his laboring force. As wealth went in the region, he was soon "well fixed." When he decided to retire, in 1855, from active control of his plantation, he reckoned his fortune at well over a hundred and fifty thousand dollars. He could set his children on a sound financial basis and retain for his own use a sufficient amount to insure comfort and independence to the end of his days. He had fulfilled his economic duties as a gentleman. He could retire to rest and travel and public affairs!

*   *   *

Such in personal aspects was the man Edmund Ruffin who was to live the everyday life of a Southern gentleman in the trying period when the planters struggled against the ruin which an exploitative agricultural system had long wrought and which the very opportunities in cotton threatened to perpetuate; when a section was becoming conscious of its interests as in conflict with another "civilization" rising to power in the North and West; when a "peculiar order" based on negro slavery was beginning to wince under the moral attacks of its opponents and to meet open restraint in its passage into western territory. It was to be a period of turmoil and strife, when bitter lines would run between men and groups and sections and when the fate of the Republic would hang in the balance.

And Ruffin felt, as a gentleman should feel, the obligation to service in his section's cause. Intelligence and practical experience fitted him to lead in the rebuilding of its agricultural life, opening to him the way to the public approval he so much desired. But it also created painful realization of the fact that politics held higher place in the average Southern mind than farming, and brought close home the knowledge of favors granted by a common government to the industrial interests of a rival section.

The road of service was thus to be filled, as had been the path of childhood, with impediments and disappointments. Would the old struggle that had raged within a young man's heart now fix the gentleman's attitudes on sectional and national issues? Would Yankees, far removed but very real as symbols of private and public restraint, gather to themselves the hatred he felt for all who interfered? If so, the guns at Sumter that April morning thundered forth a Southerner's answer to more than the Northland.

CHAPTER II

A GENTLEMAN'S RELIGION AND POLITICS

THERE was an old saying in the South to the effect that there were many roads to Heaven but that a gentleman would travel only the Episcopalian way. From early colonial times the Church of England had claimed the allegiance of those whose surplus of rice or tobacco permitted an approximation to the ways of English country gentlemen and had kept a precarious hold amid frontier conditions for which its organization was so ill fitted. In time it established itself as part of that Old World heritage which, under a mellow clime, came to be thought of as the essence of things Southern. Yet it was, in so far as the wilderness permitted, a part of old England transplanted to the colonies. To its pulpits came clergymen ordained abroad, who mingled, in good-natured tolerance, with their flocks at the race course or around the flowing bowl and who on Sunday mornings conducted their services in good Old World fashion to a nodding congregation. The Society for the Propagation of the Gospel sent its agents to seek out remote corners, and the commissaries saw to the erection of "chapels of ease" where those who wandered into the interior in search of fresher soils might still worship in acceptable forms. Even after independence it was taken for granted in certain quarters that those who stood high in social and political place should support, in spirit if not in truth, this symbol of things "established." [1]

As might have been expected, there early grew up among

gentlemen who read widely and held comfortable places in temporal affairs a tendency to independent thinking in religious matters, a following of the liberal, rational notions of the intellectuals of the Old World, who at the end of the eighteenth century were known as "Deists." Unundustanding neighbors called them "atheists," but gentlemen who were wont to employ logic on all occasions were as dependent on forms and phrases as their fearing brethren were on priests, and the worst that may be urged against them is that they cast aside old doctrines and forged new ones better fitted to their changed intellectual and material world.

But even here there was, in most cases, a continued observance of old forms, lest those whose minds were not strong enough to stand alone might also wander afar, to the destruction of existing authorities. Regardless of beliefs, gentlemen still attended services, paid church dues, and laid strong hands on those below who manifested tendencies toward irregularity. The Church was a social prop, and orthodoxy was essential for lesser folk, however unbecoming to gentlemen.

Early conditions changed sharply with the pouring of great floods of immigrants out of Pennsylvania down the "back country" of the South. Plain folk swarmed from Old World hives, steeped in evangelical faith that fitted well the willful forest about them, their individualism already productive of numerous sects, created a new world which stretched from Maryland to Georgia, pushing ever out irresistibly toward the setting sun. They added religious cleavage to the forces that already divided the East from the West, and they pressed the question of religious toleration until it became a reality in those days when political independence opened the way to a wider freedom all along the line. Growth in numbers, together with new political influence, lifted Methodist, Baptist, Presbyterian, and Quaker to new importance, and evangelical revivals sweeping these groups checked "unbelief" and drowned the voice of reason with showers of faith.[2]

In this turning the Episcopal church lost heavily in relative importance but kept its hold on those whose lines ran deep into the past and who reverenced quality as a thing which only age could give. It yielded ground, but not position. In the days when Edmund Ruffin grew to manhood it could still consider itself a bit superior to other churches, and its members, at least, assumed that quality was on their side.

Of Ruffin's early religious attitudes we know nothing. As a young man he was, of course, by family bent, an attendant at the Episcopal church of his community, regular in his contributions and quite satisfied that the dignity of its services and doctrines attracted those of the better sort. He reared his family in strict accord with accepted practices, encouraging them to conformity but insisting that they wait until they had reached maturity before becoming "members" of the Church, thus avoiding "childish enthusiasm." But outer conformity did not indicate the full acceptance of established doctrines. When his son Julian wrote to inform him that Edmund, Jr., had recently "joined the church" following "a series of meetings," the youth went on to say that he "earnestly hoped that this example" would weigh with the father. "May you deem it a special act of Providence calling you to acknowledge the Lord Jesus Christ to be the Son of God & Savior of the World," he wrote, adding by way of explanation: "I do not think I am mistaken in supposing you to be a Unitarian in opinion. I know that you do not forget to exercise the duties of prayer, gratitude to God, almsgiving, etc., but I fully believe that those things . . . will not avail, without a humble reliance in the mediation & atonement of Jesus Christ." It was evidently in such "reliance" that the father was noticeably short. Even his children had detected as much!

The parent's answer to this letter might well have come from the pen of Thomas Jefferson. He confessed deep gratification at the son's profession of religion, asserting that "such profession, made considerately, deliberately and sincerely and afterwards conformed to as nearly as possible in conduct," could not fail "to improve the morals of every one and [his] happiness even in this world." He explained the failure to discuss his own religious opinions with his children by a reluctance to "intimate a thought or tittle of belief different" from others, knowing that their beliefs ("or those of any other true Christian") were "good enough, if the obedience & conduct be as nearly conformable as may be." Then he added: "Heartily do I wish that I had to the fullest extent the same creed. I . . . would not, on any account, designedly intimate dissent to the faith of any one . . . [or] cause even the remotest risk of unsettling the faith of any of my family, by intimating my objections. . . . I have the most intense confidence that either extreme, or any middle ground, of such creeds, if the conduct of the believer be at all conformable, is enough for salvation." As to his own beliefs he would only urge that they were drawn "from the reading of the gospel itself" and that "belief, or the want of it . . . is not a voluntary action of the mind. There are many received opinions in regard to the invisible world, or spiritual beings which I doubt, or reject. There are but

few such that bring to my mind the convictions of mathe-
matical reasoning & proof. But among the latter, which I
embrace with full faith, without the shadow of a doubt,
are the doctrines of the infinite power, wisdom & goodness
of the creator & preserver of the universe." [3] Jefferson would
have subscribed to this confession.

The desire to preserve complete outer conformity for the
sake of others and a realization of the necessity of a good
example in such matters made him a regular communicant
to the end of his days. Only when physical weakness began
to thwart his intentions did he relax. With age and growing
deafness he found he could not remain awake during a
service which exercised only his will and not his mind; so
he resolved, out of respect for the minister and an unwilling-
ness to render himself "ridiculous to observers" to remain
away from services. Attendance did him no good and only
amused others for whom he had "heretofore aimed in this
respect to set a good example." But habit was strong, and
association with others, even at church, welcome to a rural
citizen; so succeeding Sundays found him in his place, alter-
nating slumber with remaking resolutions hereafter to stay
at home.

Furthermore, he found it exceedingly difficult always to
hold his tongue on matters of belief. He loved to argue,
and here was a field rich in opportunity. So many bub-
bles to be pricked! So many irrational positions to be
exposed! The "tolerant and patient" Mrs. Campbell, whose
prolonged visits made her almost a part of the household,
afforded in her attachment to the Presbyterian Church a
target he could not resist. John Calvin and a Southern
gentleman looked at things so differently! In spite of
earnest efforts at restraint he was often "seduced" to con-

troversy, "uttering . . . opinions of the construction of various portions of the Bible, differing from and in some cases entirely opposed to the received opinions among those called orthodox Christians." But how could this be avoided by one who presumed "to judge for himself of the true meaning of the Bible instead of receiving the interpretation of theologians, and sects and their preachers?" He was only exercising the Protestant's right to private judgment—a right which most Protestants "no more dared to exercise . . . (except on pain of excommunication from every sect and shade of Christians) than did the . . . papist." He was fighting theology, not true religion. And theology, he concluded, "is the science of misconstruction—to teach as the meaning of the scriptures, or of numerous important passages thereof, what no unprejudiced reader, with mind previously unoccupied, would ever have inferred, and often what is entirely opposed to the plain and obvious sense." Reasoning on passages of Scripture and making "deductions therefrom" could never make him "believe that the all-beneficent and benevolent and merciful Creator of mankind should have doomed the greater number . . . because of the first offense and fall of Adam, and irrespective of the acts in life, to misery and torture from which the most cruel monsters among mankind would have shrunk from inflicting . . . on their worst and most hated enemies." And if Calvinists pretended to love such a creature, he was certain that there was "nothing in Satan that would forbid his receiving all the amount of love and veneration professed to be given to God." [4]

Nor could he find anything in Matthew, "the fullest and earliest gospel, about the later absurd dogmas of the trinity, of the identity or equality of divinity and power of God the

Son, with God the Father, or of the Holy Ghost being God in any sense whatever." He questioned "the divine verbal inspiration of all the received or canonical books of scripture which have been acknowledged by the respective churches." He found other writings that had been rejected by "the rather ignorant men at Nice" to be as worthy as those accepted for the Scriptures. Purely on merit he rejected as lacking divine inspiration the Book of Judges, which had "as little connection with religion and morals . . . as the old British legend of the Knights of the Round Table, or the story of Jack the Giant Killer, as especially the counterpart of Samson." He insisted that the Book of Esther was "a mere Eastern and Jewish tale, without pretension to any religious tendency"; that the songs of Solomon were "not either moral or religious"; and that the story of King David, robbed of its assumed "inspiration," was only the tale of an Eastern despot, "a villain of deep dye." [5]

Such were the opinions that he confided to his diary and that at times, under "the ardor of controversy," were openly proclaimed to the consternation of family and friends. For they knew, as he so often asserted, that to question even non-essentials led to the charge of being an enemy of all Christianity, perhaps even a social disturber. To most folk within their circle orthodoxy and morality were one and the same thing. Little wonder then that the children trembled when the bishop came to dine and that they gave the father careful instructions beforehand that "he must not utter . . . opinions" on the questions of "colonization or Foreign missionary operations" or "express any other . . . views which he might deem heterodox." The good name of the family must be preserved. Clerical gentlemen must not be disturbed by intellectual agitations. One can but imagine the relief felt by all when the rumble of the good bishop's carriage died in the distance and the father was safely tucked into his bed, all danger points passed in safety.

And yet, with all his independence and all his insistence on the right of private judgment, Edmund Ruffin was fundamentally religious. His list of doubts was long, but his positive beliefs were far more significant. Late in life he declared:

> My belief is firm in the existence and superintending government and care of our God—the sole Creator and preserver of the Universe. . . . All wise, all powerful, and (especially in regard to mankind) all-just, all-merciful, and all-benevolent. . . . I utterly disbelieve that the God of justice will punish . . . any person for believing an erroneous religious creed, whether in accepting as true doctrines which are false, or rejecting as false, others which are true. Belief . . . is . . . dependent upon the evidence of the subject, or more generally and strongly upon the previous circumstances of the person, and the influences of education and prejudice. God's punishment for sin, in which I do believe . . . will be directed against vicious and sinful acts of mankind, and according to the motives for these acts, and never against creeds.

Character and conduct were Ruffin's means to salvation, not some mysterious plan in which "an inferior being," thwarting God's purposes, caused all humanity to be cursed so that they could be saved only by the human birth and violent death of God's only son. Such a "plan" was beyond his "power of comprehension." Neither reason nor faith could make it "Godlike." [6]

Strangely enough, he found no conflict between "the doctrines of geology"—a field in which he was well versed—

and "the Mosaical account of Creation." If there had been disagreement, he was frank to admit that "geology would certainly stand firm and the Bible, or rather the ignorant or bigoted priests and unfair reasoners who assume to be its only supporters, would have to give way." Assuming that the six days of creation were "but geological periods," he perceived the scriptural and geological orders of creation to be the same, and hence he found it difficult to believe that the account in Genesis, even if it were fabulous and a work of mere imagination, could have been dictated altogether by chance.[7]

And even more strange was his rejection of the idea that the curse on Ham was responsible for the degraded condition of the negro. He could find no evidence in the Bible that the negro was descended from Ham, nor could he believe that "the just and merciful God would sanction and consummate the curse of Noah, by which for an act of unfilial conduct, which . . . was not worse than almost every parent has to bear from some child, not the truly guilty son but his innocent posterity, through all subsequent time . . . were doomed to live in degradation and misery."

When we remember that Edmund Ruffin never doubted the inferiority of the negro and that he gathered and weighed every scrap of evidence to prove the justice of holding the race in bondage, our respect for the honesty of his mental processes increases. Science, not the Bible, must prove the institution just. Religious sanction might give greater force, but honest thinking was more than mere convenient "proofs."

Such were the expressions of this man's religious life—a strange mingling of reason and faith which produced a cold, calculating individual who retired to his wife's grave on frequent occasions for prayer and meditation, a stern rationalist who filled the pages of his diary with supplications to an "All-Merciful God." Again he was the individualist who in his own way followed his Creator, never able to surmount all that a rural order imposed on its members, never able to escape the social responsibilities that his station laid on him, conforming before his simple world, wandering alone with the feeble candle of human intelligence in the great secret expanse of his own inner self, winning there the right to peace and confidence and the respect of others who unknowingly sensed a hidden power and reserve. A gentleman's religion!

*　　*　　*

In the South, if duty to God constituted the essence of religion, then duty to man found largest expression in politics. Perhaps it was the old English notion of the importance of county officials who directly represented the king in their localities that, transplanted to Virginia, gave gentlemen to political office and political office to gentlemen. Perhaps it was merely the exigencies and opportunities of frontier living that developed a leadership which became exclusive under the favoritism of royal governors. At any rate, the county court, in which those with widest acres sat as justices of the peace, became the means by which "the few" dominated local affairs and stepped on into the choice offices about the governor. In time they constituted "a ruling element" which kept "King Numbers" in check and which accepted in full the responsibility for good government as comprehended in honest administration and a watchful eye for the rights of property. Among gentlemen politics became a profession for which sons were carefully

[35]

trained, and those who once entered the lower rounds of office-holding were, if they proved efficient, practically assured of a lifelong course of public service. The South early learned the wisdom of keeping her best ever at her call. She seldom repudiated a real leader.

A high degree of ability in politics in the early days of national life lifted the calling to new heights. Southern leaders took high rank in the young nation's councils and soon merited the charge of exercising an influence far out of proportion to their numbers. They were keen students of political theory; they possessed, to an unusual degree, personal charm; and they could speak in public with a force which carried conviction or excited hostility. Back home they became the heroes of the section and of the nation, while their profession became the highest medium to fame and service. Every man who aspired to fullest stature in the South must in time take his fling at politics.

It is not surprising, therefore, that Edmund Ruffin, by reason of his station, should early step from rural isolation into the wider public arena. It was his right; it was his duty. In the autumn of 1823 he stood for and was elected, for a term of four years, to the Senate of Virginia to represent the district composed of the counties of Sussex, Surry, Southampton, Isle of Wight, Prince George, and Greenville. He was twenty-nine years of age, already recognized as one of the most progressive planters of the state. He was ambitious to play a larger part in the affairs of his day, and the accepted way was through politics. This was to be but a beginning.

And there was much just then to exercise the well-thought-out political philosophy of a gentleman. The eighteen-twenties were perilous days for planters in tidewater Virginia. The agricultural life of the region suffered heavily from burdens which were in part of their own making but in part also thrust upon them in the form of protective tariffs which a common government had granted to the rising industrial interests centering in the North. The shadow of despair fell across the land as the roofs of rambling houses sagged and sedge and pine crept through the fields. Moreover, class and regional interests within the state were in bitter conflict. Asserting the rights of the majority, the "lesser folk" of the western part of the state demanded a wider franchise, better schools, internal improvements, and a more equitable system of taxation which might fall upon property in slaves as well as upon western farms. The planter thus found his station as well as his section threatened and turned with growing zeal to his store of political doctrines from which to forge those defenses best fitted to the protection of minorities and their interests. It was seemingly a splendid time to begin a political career.[8]

The Journals of the Senate of the Commonwealth of Virginia for the years 1823 to 1826, when Edmund Ruffin was a member, are not very illuminating volumes. In form so brief that all individual activities are lost, we catch there only glimpses of a staid body, strikingly like that in any rural state regardless of time and locality, struggling over the election of a United States senator or a state printer; pondering "an act divorcing Louis Bourne from his wife Dorotha" or others granting rewards for killing wolves or "restoring to the Executive . . . the power to grant respite from solitary confinement and full pardon to convicts in the Penitentury house;" or, perchance, on another day resolving "That the editors of newspapers in the city of Richmond be admitted to seats within this House for the purpose of taking notes of the debates and proceedings therein," and hastening on to incorporate "the Trustees of the Hickory Neck School Society in the County of James City."

Now and then the flavor was localized by "a bill concerning Patty, the wife, and Lucy, the daughter, of Samuel Johnson, a free man of colour," or others "authorizing the purchase and emancipation of Lucy, a slave, the property of Ptolmey Powell," and "allowing Jack, alias John Booker, a man of colour, to remain in the Commonwealth." But for the most part the pressing issues of the day, which centered around banks and internal improvements, held the floor. Toll bridges were authorized and roads laid out in various parts of the state, while the James River Company and the Chesapeake and Ohio Company received grudging assistance and the Farmers' Bank of Virginia barely obtained an extension of its charter.

The sectional conflict between the eastern and western parts of the state appeared in the proposal, sharply rejected, to submit the question of calling a Constitutional Convention to the people, and in the various bills offered for forming new counties from parts of older ones. But the friction that these issues and others engendered is hidden in the records by a brevity which has nothing to do with wit. There were, it seems, certain bursts of oratory that carried the day, revealing the Southern legislator at his best; there were bargains struck behind the scenes and open clashes in which quick thinking and ready repartee gained advantage. But details are lacking.[9]

As to the part that Edmund Ruffin played in these sessions we must be content with knowing that he was a faithful member, always present save when granted "a leave of absence from this House"; that he served on numerous committees, especially that on internal improvements; and that he did not shine as an orator or clever manipulator of conflicting interests. He was a bit out of place where plain, straightforward words and actions independently offered did not have their deserved influence. Too honest for intrigue, too stubborn to be manipulated, too sensitive to rebuff, he was not a success as a politician. With chagrin and disappointment he suddenly resigned his seat before his term had expired and returned to his plantation. Criticism from constituents and a realization of failure to achieve leadership mingled to make him desire to be rid of it all—to drop from a station in which he appeared to be less than he knew himself to be. His own explanation, given years later, may be taken at nearly face value: [10]

> I reached this position [in the Senate] almost without seeking either public favor or any of its rewards and certainly without my using any electioneering arts, which I always despised, and had not the tact to exercise, even if willing to be so aided. My chief and perhaps only merit as a legislator and representative was in zealously and diligently attending to the duties of the office, and aiming to decide correctly and vote honestly on all questions. But I soon found that my views of duty were very different from those usually acted upon by other representatives, and that for conforming to mine, I should be like to have no reward, save the approbation of my own conscience. In all matters for private legislation or appointments to office, or to place of emolument, every legislator is expected to promote the personal and private interests of his friends, his constituents or his political supporters, even at more or less sacrifice of the public interest. When such favors were expected of me, I was not always firm enough to withstand all such personal

influences. But it was very rare that I was so entangled and never to gain any selfish object. In nearly all cases, I firmly adhered to my rule of serving the best interests of my country, and of my constituents, according to right and justice, and to decide on the claims of individuals according to their merits, and of candidates for office by the measure of their fitness for the post sought.

Such a program, he found, could not be followed if he were to make a successful politician. His constituents found no fault with his votes on the great questions of the day, but they resented his failure to support their selfish interests, thus adding "straws" to the already heavy load of disappointment at failure to lead in oratory and debate, causing him to become "tired and disgusted with being a servant of the people." And anyway, being a servant of any kind was a trifle hard on a gentleman!

This failure in the one great accepted avenue to public service was of supreme importance in the life of Edmund Ruffin. It closed to him the way that would have given greatest outlet to energies and ambitions and sent him along other lines with the feeling that he had been denied the rights that mind and station merited. With intense energy he turned to agricultural reform and set his pen to gain what his tongue had not procured. He was to achieve what some called a greater success. But his own deep, inner reactions were revealed when ex-President John Tyler, in 1857, commended him by saying: [11]

> You, like me and most all Virginia boys, first turned your attention to politics. But you soon gave up the pursuit, and devoted your attention to agriculture, and in that pursuit you have done more good to the country than all our political great men put together. . . . How

much better was it for you to have seen at first, and refused to pursue the empty rewards of political life.

Ruffin answered:

I perceive that you, like many other friends, who have known me more intimately, have mistaken me in this respect. It was not because I was devoid of ambition, or of the desire to wield political power, that I have not sought political stations. On the contrary, few persons would have been more gratified by being so placed, and very few young men read more, or felt more interest, on the subjects of government and political economy. But, in the first place, I felt sour that I had no talent for oratory, or to influence popular assemblies, and I was too proud to be willing to be deemed below any station in which I might be placed. Next and mainly, if I could have obtained popular favor (which I never procured, or sought to gain) and political eminence as its reward, I never knew the time that I would have been willing to purchase the honor at the cost of paying the necessary price for popularity.

Here was his true attitude. Desire thwarted and ambitions unrealized! Enough to set a man in rebellion searching for ways to vindicate himself and to punish offending impediments! Whatever else he might do, whatever the success he might win, there yet remained the great service to his class and section that constituted achievement. Would the opportunity ever come to do and to be acclaimed?

From this time forward the independent who would not bow even to constituents set his course, free from group allegiance, as a more or less gleeful "party outlaw." His general political principles, already largely fixed by the fact that he was a gentleman, now stiffened to do service against any foe at home or from the outside. Two fundamental principles lay at the bottom of his political thinking—the old Federalist belief in the superiority of "the few" and the necessity for their control, and the new-old doctrine of states' rights. Hamilton and Jefferson reconciled!

These principles placed him, as a rule, in company with the great slave-holding planters and with the more extreme Southern sectionalists, but he developed his own expression of these attitudes and generally stood well in advance of those who plodded along with their party companions, shifting groups only as the larger interests required. He saw clearly that there were among his fellows certain attitudes that were sharply out of line with the facts and interests of his class and section. He was enough of a realist, in that day of opportunists, to know that democracy and slaves and "swollen acres" and superior gentlemen did not go together. He had that deadly, hated quality of being right first.

Thomas Jefferson had long been the patron saint of good Southerners. Just what his teachings implied beyond the lifting of agricultural interests above those of commerce and industry, men who thought less than Ruffin did not know. It was enough that he had resisted the unwarranted extension of powers by the central government, and had held slaves, and had builded a great house which all aspiring planters took for their model. Lip service, at least, might be given to his phrases so long as practice should take whatever course the accumulation and protection of property required. Virginians were like most folks, before and since, in their way with Jefferson. It was a bit more than mere discrepancy between preaching and practice: it was a way of following ideals and at the same time being comfortable in a world of realities.

Furthermore, without comprehending the changes taking place, Southern leaders had adhered to the "democratic dogma" as it swung wide under Jackson from the pure Jeffersonian form to the new emphasis on greater political participation and enjoyment by the masses. Nor were they clearly aware of any conflict between a social-economic system that sent gangs of slaves to agricultural planting and gathering and the teachings of the Declaration of Independence which the parties up to 1840 ever incorporated into their platforms. In the rising West, where necessity gave a high degree of social equality and economic opportunity for equality, emphasis might be largely on political rights for the masses, but even there tribute was paid to those who lifted themselves to place and property, as men of real "worth" and superior "service." Jefferson and his Declaration did not necessarily conflict with the existing order—in fact, with emphasis shifted to the rights of local units as against the central power, his teachings offered the great defense against attacks.

But Ruffin knew better. In the minds of idealists, such as he himself had once been, or even with "down-trodden simple folk," these teachings implied a social, even an economic, status where happiness was more to be desired than property. They set the many above the few, urged the capacity of even the most humble for improvement, and glimpsed that day when all men might be well-born and have that chance for equality which a free education and a restraining government might afford.

Instinctively Ruffin disliked Jefferson. He sensed the fact that the first great "Commoner" was an "abolitionist, covertly and cunningly," and wondered why he had not matured in his thinking on this subject. He saw the harm that the words of the Declaration of Independence were doing in the mouths of "anti-slavery fanatics" and boldly proclaimed that the assertion that "all men are born free and equal" was "both false and foolish." No man had ever been born free, and no two men ever born equal.

Moreover, from Jefferson had come those "corrupting and poisonous" political theories "of democratic perfection" which had "caused more evil and done more to destroy free and sound institutions and to upset all that was stable and valuable in our government than all . . . the real and avowed opposers of popular rights could have effected if their power had equalled their wishes, or than all . . . demagogues could have effected in practice, if they had not been given strength and power by constitutions founded on universal suffrage and equality of the people in theory, but truly the supremacy of the lowest and basest class led and directed by baser and mercenary demagogues, seeking exclusively their own selfish benefits." Ruffin hated it all so much that he could not even use short sentences in describing it! Belief in such doctrines might be "pardonable in boys at school," but it was "inconceivable" in men of "knowledge and wisdom . . . and . . . long political experience." For "there is no greater fallacy than the supposition . . . that men will generally be directed in their choice of representatives . . . by consideration of superior competency and trust-worthyness [*sic*] of the persons voted for." Universal suffrage was a snare and a delusion. Only those "with property to guard, and much more of education, ability and virtue than the general mass" could vote intelligently. A government based on universal suffrage "will be a government of and by the *worst* of the people." [12]

He later reached the conclusion that an hereditary ruler

was better than one elected by the people. Writing in 1864, he said:

> Practice has shown us fully and in the short space of seventy years "that the possession of the highest order of talent rather operates to exclude citizens from this high honor and position [the presidency]. Hereditary right of succession, so far from offering a continuation of virtuous and wise rulers, rarely presents one fit to be a ruler. . . . The born king is rarely either virtuous or wise and is much more frequently a fool or a villain. Yet the conferring the station by election . . . operates to place in regal power fools and villains and that at the cost of incalculable expenditures of wealth, of the establishment of widespread corruption, and rapid decay of public morals. This is the price paid for the election and choice of a President. . . . Much worse is to follow the inauguration of a new President, when he must reward by public office or otherwise out of the Nation's treasury, the services of every prominent partisan and supporter, who has striven for his election. . . . Rather than to submit to be ruled by such a government and without hope of reform of its constitution, I would gladly accept instead a limited monarchy . . . with parliamentary checks and indirect appointment and removal of ministers as existing in Great Britain." [13]

Alexander Hamilton would have subscribed to *this* confession.

When the western men in Ruffin's own state demanded constitutional changes to give numbers control, he declared that the South Carolina system of "a compound basis of representation," according "to taxation in one house and to population in the other," would offer "some security and refuge" to property, and he openly advocated the adoption of the system in Virginia. If such security were denied and "democracy introduced," he would welcome a "separation of the state, taking the Allegheny ridge as the line." Anything was better than the tyranny of numbers!

His second fundamental principle, states' rights, largely determined his attitudes on national candidates and issues. He would not accept the presidential candidacy of Crawford, Clay, or Calhoun in 1823 because they had "lost sight of the Constitution" in supporting the tariff, the United States Bank, and internal improvements by the Federal Government. Nor could he accept Adams, "an apostate federalist, who deserted his party at precisely the most convenient time for his own private interest," or Jackson, who had "so recently trampled on the Constitution." It would be preferable to vote for John Marshall, who "throughout his long public life" had "ably, honestly and consistently" advocated principles which Ruffin "abhorred," than to support one who advocated such principles and still claimed "the name Republican." He showed his strong bent toward irregularity by proposing that Virginia should support Nathaniel Macon, who had no chance of being elected, and thus be in an independent position to stand guard over the new president in defense of the true and limited powers of the central government. It was the growing fear of protective tariffs that had begun to pound a sectionalist into shape.[14]

From the very first Edmund Ruffin had opposed the tariff as unconstitutional and unfair. He had taken a leading part in the first moves of the planter class against this aggression on agricultural interests. He had penned "An Address to the United Agricultural Societies and a Petition to Congress from the United Agricultural Societies of Virginia" in 1820, opposing "exhaustive practices and abandonment of land for western migration" and protesting against taxing agriculture to support industry "by means of protective tariffs." "In plain English," his petition ran, "the hardy, independent sons of our forests and fields are called on to consent to be starved into weavers and button makers." It was a "monstrous anomaly in free government" which rendered "our boasted freedom and anticipated greatness but an empty name." It strained the whole frame of the Constitution; it completely prostrated the commercial and agricultural prosperity of the nation.[15]

Ruffin soon accepted the South Carolina doctrine of state interposition in behalf of interests and rights, developing a feeling of kinship with the more radical element in that state which was to play a peculiar part in his future career. He went on to opposition in the Whig Party against Jackson and Van Buren, voting for Harrison in 1840, though without "confidence in either his principles or ability" and publicly expressing gratification on hearing the news of his death. He was quite certain that "dying then was the only important service he had ever rendered to his country in all his long career of public life." All of which makes it quite apparent that Ruffin had become a Whig with considerable reservation of free-lance privileges. When Tyler assumed office, he turned quickly to him, declaring that he expected much "in maintaining state-rights principles and the checks of the Constitution," urging him in private correspondence to stand by such doctrines, "even if you should stand alone," and holding out the certainty of a second term in 1844 through the votes of all states'-rights men and all "who believe in republican principles."[16]

Such were the political attitudes and practices of Edmund Ruffin when the sectional conflict over slavery in the territories began to sharpen the lines between men of the South and men of the North. Independent though he was, in spite of himself he had followed, in the main, the same course as that taken by the more positive men of his class. He had swung from the Republican-Democrat Party at the end of the Era of Good Feeling to take that uncertain position which local class conflicts and sectional issues forced upon the property holders, going over to the new Whig group for a period and then drifting steadily back toward a definite denial of democracy within the Democratic Party as the first step to becoming an avowed Southern nationalist. It was the course of a gentleman planter—a process by which the Southern man would reach the conclusion that the gentleman's mind and ways were so exclusively sectional as to constitute a civilization there unique and worth dying to preserve; a development by which class rights were becoming sectional rights, by which personal attitudes were being transformed into social patterns and national purposes. Edmund Ruffin, Southerner, was about to emerge.

*   *   *

Here was a gentleman's religion, and a gentleman's politics! Station had contributed the elements of genteel conservatism, mind and privilege to elements of radicalism. Out of the South, steeped in rural individualism, had come a type which had preserved enough of its Old World heritage to be able to tangle emotion and reason, persons and property, and still avoid the charge of inconsistency.

CHAPTER III

A GENTLEMAN FARMER

O F grain and pulse they provide commonly no more than they reckon that their families will require, for there are no towns as markets where they can sell them. . . . The one thing of which they make as much as they can is tobacco, there being always a vent for that at one time or another of the year."[1]

Thus wrote an Old World observer of Virginia agricultural practices at the end of the seventeenth century. Unwittingly he had placed his finger on the central fact in the colonial history of the Old Dominion. Beginning in a wilderness, the early settlers had faced the possibility of a rapid degeneration to a grinding simplicity wherein every man and every group fashioned, from the materials the immediate environment afforded, the sum total of their consumption. Only the fortunate development of a profitable surplus of tobacco prevented a rapid lowering of standards and enabled them to procure, by exchange with the Old World, the comforts and luxuries of a mature and complex life and to reproduce in the forest a bit of "merry England" itself, "transported across the Atlantic . . . more merry, light and joyous than England had ever thought of being."

But it led, also, to the elevation of the first of those despotic Southern kings who brought so much of misery to their subjects. To base upon one staple alone, the whole of a standard of living centuries too old for its environment meant the establishment of a single-crop type of agriculture

[49]

in which the sole object was immediate great yields regardless of future consequences. Such a system, under frontier scarcity of capital and labor, threw the burdens of abnormal production squarely upon the land, in a region where sod formation was poor, rainfall heavy and concentrated, and the harmful microörganisms unusually active. There could be but one result. Tobacco-growing meant soil exploitation, unit expansion, and ultimate abandonment of once fertile fields.

Just what was implied is revealed in the comment of a second observer, three-quarters of a century later. "The Virginians of the lower country are very easy and negligent husbandmen," he wrote. "New land is taken up, the best to be had, tobacco is grown on it for three or four years and then Indian corn as long as any will come. And in the end, if the soil is thoroughly impoverished, they begin again with a new piece and go through the rotation." [2] He pictured a world of widening fields and retreating forests; white servants, come to toil, giving way to negro slaves under pressure for economy; acres growing weary, falling from cultivation, and returning again to forest; in time, planters frayed a bit at the cuffs, out at the elbows, down at the heels, bitter and complaining, as farmers are wont to be, of returns that did not pay the cost of production. And then, while some held on, shifting crops and yielding standards, others, more easily discouraged or more quick to accept the inevitable, according to the point of view, turned west, leaving the bones of their ancestors to keep watch in old familiar neighborhoods while they began over again where lands were fresh and cheap and debts were no disgrace.

Such a system, of necessity, ran its course in the older regions well before the American Revolution. Many planters turned farmer, dividing their lands and labor forces into smaller units, shifting production to wheat and corn, and seeking markets that lay outside the grip of the British merchant and his much despised Scotch agents. But the Revolution interrupted adjustments, adding its ruin to an already bad situation, which did not greatly improve for the masses until the French Revolution and its spread gave to the American farmers the profitable task of furnishing food to those whose efforts were absorbed by war. A few great planters, such as Washington, Jefferson, and Madison, led the way to changes for the better conservation of the soil, while such specialists as John Binns and John Taylor of Caroline preached a new gospel of fertilizers and crop rotation which would have altered fundamentally the whole agricultural procedure. But uncertain profits checked wide change, and the Peace of Ghent threw the whole old tobacco world back in ruins, sighing "for another Napoleon to restore to us by his wars the feeding of Europe." [3]

Thus, when Edmund Ruffin, just turned nineteen, took over the responsibilities of a planter on weary lands, the situation represented the accumulations of two centuries of bad methods. Plows and plowing were poor. Iron moldboards were just coming into use, but the great majority, suspicious of anything new, preferred to go on with their old implements, cutting shallow furrows up and down the hillsides to become veritable watercourses of destruction in time of rains. Furthermore, the rotation of crops, though followed by a few, met serious difficulties in the failure of clover or other legumes to grow on poor lands, which cut the supply of livestock and manure and precluded the profits that would have made possible the purchase of artificial fertilizers. Slaves multiplied out of proportion to agricultural needs, becoming a burden on masters and fields until the strong paternal sense which characterized the institution in this region weakened to permit the sale of the human surplus into the spreading cotton fields of the "Lower South." Tattered and briary, the lands lapsed back to become the haunts of deer and wild turkey, while stolid men and patient women plodded on with a persistence too mechanical to have been born of courage. Agriculture was steadily yielding ground in both a real and a figurative sense.

Travelers and natives alike in this period (1815-1830) agree on the impression that an "angel of desolation had cursed the land," many tracts presenting scenes of ruin "that baffle description—farm after farm . . . worn out, washed and gullied, so that scarcely an acre could be found in a place fit for cultivation;" "dreary and uncultivated wastes, a barren and exhausted soil, half clothed negroes, lean and hungry stock, a puny race of horses, a scarcity of provender, houses falling to decay, and fences wind shaken and dilapidated."

Meanwhile "an emigrating contagion resembling an epidemic disease" had seized the people. "Thousands . . . in the hopelessness of bettering their condition in their native land" abandoned "the beloved homes of their nativity." The rate of population growth in Virginia fell from thirty-seven and a half per cent in 1820 to thirteen and a half per cent in 1830 and then to only a trifle over two per cent in the next decade. Many counties lost population, and there were over 388,000 Virginians in other states in 1850. Ruffin himself later declared: "There was scarcely a proprietor in my neighborhood . . . who did not desire to sell his land, and who was prevented only by the impossibility of finding a purchaser, unless at half of the then very low estimated value. All wished to sell, none to buy." And what was true of lower Virginia applied with equal force to the older portions of Maryland and the Carolinas. The prospects for a young planter were, indeed, gloomy.[4]

With an enthusiasm born of youth and theories developed from childhood reading Ruffin assumed his task. His lands at Coggin's Point were extremely poor, "the larger part not averaging more than ten bushels of corn per acre, no more than six bushels of wheat, on the better half." From experiment to experiment he moved, failure dogging his steps. He drained his better swamp lands only to find their yields, after three years of good crops, so reduced as to necessitate abandonment. He turned to John Taylor's much discussed system of "enclosing," receiving "as sound and true every opinion and precept," but ended in "utter disappointment." The manure he applied "produced little of the expected effect on the first course of crops and was scarcely to be perceived on the second." Clover would not grow for him, and "the plowing on hilly land . . . into ridges, caused the most destructive washing away of soil by heavy rains." After four or five years of trial Taylor's methods "proved either profitless, entirely useless or absolutely and in some cases greatly injurious." He was forced to admit that no part of his "poor land was more productive than when . . . [his] labors commenced and that on much of it, a tenfold increase had been made of the previously large space of galled and gullied hillsides and slopes."

Old residents, grown weary in the struggle, had long since concluded that lands in this part of the state could not hold manure or be enriched. They smiled in tolerance as the young theorist continued to reject this "monstrous agricultural heresy" but did not withhold the "I told you so" when at last he too "was compelled, most reluctantly, to concur in this opinion." He had failed. He would seek "the rich western wilderness" where his "whole income and more" would not be required for the most economical support of his "small but fast growing family." Not the lure of verdant fields in Kentucky or Alabama stirred him, but benumbing pressure weighing heavily on one who thought of the future in terms of children and even slaves who must have the things that a gentleman gives to his dependents.[5]

In such a frame of mind Ruffin chanced upon a copy of Davy's *Agricultural Chemistry*. Though completely ignorant of chemical science or even of its terminology, he was struck by a statement to the effect that sterile soils containing "the salt of iron, or any acid matter . . . may be ameliorated by the application of quick-lime." The gentleman in him stirred. "Could it be possible that the sulphate of iron . . . which Davy found in this soil, and which he evidently spoke of as a rare example of peculiar constitution, could exist in nineteen-twentieths of all the lands of lower Virginia?" Should he migrate from paternal acres without one further trial? With rekindled enthusiasm he set about a clumsy testing. Early efforts failed to reveal the presence of any mineral acid, but the suggestion fell in with long observation that sorrel and pine abounded on poor lands and that calcareous earths were absent, leading him to the independent conclusion, reached well in advance of any then published confirmation, that "vegetable acids" were to blame for sterile soils and that the common fossil shells (marl) so abundant in the neighborhood would correct the evil. He would leave authorities behind and seek his own proofs. He would assume that his lands were inherently fertile if only the impediment of acidity could be removed. At least, it was a new theory worthy of a trial.

On a February morning in 1818 his carts began to haul the marl that puzzled negro hands dug from pits hastily opened on his lower lands. They spread some two hundred bushels over a few acres of newly-cleared, but poor, ridge land, and in the spring he planted the entire field to corn as a testing crop. Eagerly he waited. As the season advanced, he found reason for joy. From the very start the plants on marled ground showed marked superiority, and at harvest time they yielded an advantage of fully forty per cent. The carts went back to the pits. Fields took on fresh life. A new era in the agricultural history of the region had dawned.

With all the ardor of a discoverer Ruffin immediately set about to widen his knowledge by extended experiments and to spread the information which offered so much to his fellow planters and to his section. In October of that year he presented to the agricultural society of his own county the first of what was to be a long list of valuable papers offered to the cause of agriculture. Stating his theories as "to the nature of soils and the action of calcareous manures" on them, he adduced the slender sum of his experience to support what was, in fact, a revolutionary approach to the whole problem that vexed the farmers of the New World. While the great rural hosts, facing westward, moved steadily forward to the exploitation of a continent's virgin fertility in the name of progress, he offered a new program of restoration which had as its purpose an "about face" induced by the creation of opportunity in the lands of the older regions. He would save the Old South. He would commit that greatest of all agricultural crimes—he would rely on theory and books!

Three years later this paper, revised and enlarged, was published in the *American Farmer,* the new agricultural journal that John Skinner had started in Baltimore.[6] The editor hailed it as "the first systematic attempt . . . wherein a plain, practical, unpretending farmer has undertaken to examine into the real composition of the soils which he possesses and has to cultivate." So fundamental did he consider the contribution that an extra edition of this issue was printed to be distributed gratuitously to the farmers of the country. Eleven years later, grown into a volume of 242 pages, it appeared again under the title, *An Essay on Calcareous Manures,* to run through five editions and to be called at the end of the nineteenth century by a government expert, writing in the *Year Book of the United States Department of Agriculture,* the most thorough piece of work on a special agricultural subject ever published in the English language.[7] Contemporary writers, who had been lifting their jeremiads amid the agricultural ruins and "the draining off of our most independent citizens to the West," hailed him as a deliverer, taking rank at once with the great John Taylor of Caroline whose *Arator* had been the first cry in the wilderness. Even the doors of politics swung open to him, and in time a president of the United States would declare that his *Essay* "in its valuable consequences" would "be worth more to the country than all the state papers that have been the most celebrated in our time." Over John Tyler's mantel Edmund Ruffin's portrait would hang as a companion piece to that of Daniel Webster—the greatest American agriculturist and the greatest American statesman!

Ruffin's new agricultural gospel, stated briefly in his first paper and enlarged, but not substantially changed, in his later writings, was that naturally poor soils differed essentially in their power of retaining putrescent manures from those naturally rich but reduced by cultivation, and that the capacity for improvement in any soil was in direct proportion to the degree of natural fertility. This fertility, in turn, was primarily dependent upon the presence of a proper proportion of calcareous earth, which neutralized vegetable acids and gave the power of combination with manures for productivity. In the soils of lower Virginia this element was lacking, and it was useless to attempt to enrich lands by the use of animal and vegetable manures, as all were doing, until they had first received a supply of calcareous matter to correct the defect in their constitution. When this had been done by the addition of marl, then all the refinements of good farming would bring returns, giving "more productiveness" and yielding "more profits" than men had yet dreamed possible. It was a first step, to be followed by the wider production and use of barnyard manures, the rotation of crops, the building of covered drains, the growing of clover and cowpeas, better plowing, and even a more intelligent adjustment of slave labor in numbers and direction to agricultural effort.[8]

It is interesting also to notice that with respect to the decline of fertility under the planting of the same crop on the same land over a period of years, Ruffin was early acquainted with the theory of the removal of plant foods and also with that of harmful excrement by plant roots. Rejecting the first, on the ground that the application of organic matter containing few minerals or a change to crops that required many of the same foods restored fertility, he suspended judgment as to the soundness of the second, with the practical suggestion that rotation of crops destroyed insects that fed on a single type of plant and kept down the growth of bothersome weeds. Theory in this case could not stand in the face of experience that showed the necessity for such practices. He was, after all, fundamentally "a practical farmer." [9]

All of this has about it a modernness that turns our simple planter into a prophet. He was a half-century or more ahead of his time. And yet, in truth, the combination of gentleman and farmer forbids the assertion. We must leave him in his own day and place. The truly puzzling thing, after all, is the scientific approach which this untrained man had taken in this field. "Most farmers are determined *not* to understand anything, however simple it may be, which relates to chemistry," was his own statement when he undertook to explain his methods of soil testing. The traditions in agriculture were all against the theorist or scientist. For one to break from accepted ideas and practices, especially if he were youthful, was to make himself a subject of ridicule. Yet here was a young farmer who had so neglected his studies at college as to be suspended, who had only the gentleman's turn for reading, suddenly adopting a scientific approach, and beginning to conduct chemical soil tests "with such attention to detail and with such a truly scientific method of preparation and planning that we may look on his work as some of the best done in this country." That is the testimony of an agricultural expert writing in 1895.

There is something both pathetic and inspiring about this youth, amid the jeers of his neighbors, patiently acquiring scientific books from abroad, painfully building his apparatus, carefully running his tests over and over again, first to perfect his method and then to reach conclusions so sound that "doubting Thomases" would be convinced against their wills. Davy, Darwin, Dickson, Morveau, Grisenthwaite, and Dundonald he searched and pondered. He gathered soil samples from "the top of the bluff at Coggin's Point," from his "dry land . . . surrounded by the river and tide marsh," then levied on Eppes' Island and the farms of his neighbors, and even sent to far-off Huntsville in Alabama to obtain the varieties he thought necessary for conclusive findings. Each new move was whispered from farmer to farmer, to be laughed over wherever two or three were gathered together.

His own statement of the laboratory methods employed is more eloquent in revealing care and intelligence than any description possible. After discussing the method of measuring the proportion of carbonate of lime in a soil and the possible error because of the fact that magnesia on the application of acids reacted similarly and appeared in the result as lime, he goes on to say:

> There is another slight source of error; a small quantity of carbonate of lime, varying between half a grain & three grains, will always be lost to the result, either by the condensation or absorption of a part of the gas, or from the acid not reaching every particle of soil. This was ascertained, by frequently submitting to examination, known quantities of pure chalk, either alone, or mixed with other earth. Whether much or little was tried, the loss was always as above stated, except that when chalk was used alone, the loss never amounted to one grain. To diminish as much as possible even this small error in the results, large quantities of soil were used, and to each, a small known quantity of pure chalk was previously added, and as much deducted from the result. This served not only to shew a proportion too small to be otherwise indicated, but also, when no other carbonate

of lime was present, it proved in every experiment
whether the apparatus was in good order, and the result
perfectly correct. . . .

The soils were frequently subjected to two other
processes, for purpose of comparing results.

Crude as the process might be, here was a true scientist at
work—or shall we simply say a gentleman farmer? [10]
One further fact gives Ruffin modern standing. His con-
ception of soil fertility as a dynamic and not a static condition is in keeping with the more recent trends. Whereas
the advanced thought of his own day accepted the idea of
soils as composed of various elements mechanically thrown
together to be extracted separately and completely by the
growth of plants, Ruffin caught the notion of chemical
combination, organic condition, and lasting fertility. He
believed that soils that had once been fertile, though now
reduced, could be brought back to productiveness if hinder-
ing factors were removed and organic materials supplied.
If he erred in a too restricted definition of "calcareous
manures" and in a too broad notion of "acidity," it was
more from the zeal of an innovator than from any basic
fault in his way of thinking. Edmund Ruffin has good
claim to be called the father of soil chemistry in America.

*   *   *

Like all pioneers, Ruffin found his teachings, though acclaimed by leaders, at first largely ignored in general practice. Those about him, in true neighborly style, seemed
actually to prefer their own continued destruction to seeing
a new departure succeed. Two only gave marl a trial and
both quickly abandoned it, one of them always referring to
the pit from which the first shells came as "Ruffin's Folly."

With the publication and distribution of his paper by the *American Farmer,* however, interest was created great enough to produce the thorough trials necessary to enthusiastic adoption and hearty recommendation, indicating that the time was ripe for an agricultural revival of real import. The great need was for leadership and guidance along sound lines.

It was to fill this need that Ruffin now decided to launch an agricultural periodical. Accordingly, in June, 1833, the *Farmers' Register,* as he called his paper, made its appearance from his plantation, designated as "Shellbanks." It was the second such attempt to be made in Virginia, the *Virginia Farmer,* which now drooped "like the harebell before the sun," having been started at Scottsville a few years earlier. The venture was undertaken without sufficient advance subscriptions to ensure its success, but the editor was certain that the patriotism of the Old Dominion and the awakened interest in the possibility of improvement would be sufficient to bring all substantial gentlemen to his aid. He was not mistaken. By the end of the first year, when he moved his plant to Petersburg, he had, in spite of the high subscription rate of five dollars a year, 1118 subscribers from eighty-five counties and towns in Virginia and 197 more from fifteen other states and the District of Columbia.[11]

According to the advance prospectus, the *Register* was to appear monthly, to consist of sixty-four pages of solid reading matter (for all advertisements were to be excluded), and to contain information gathered from the best available sources, especially articles from the pens of practical farmers themselves if the editor could "command those fountains, and forbid their waters to stagnate in morasses, or be dried up in the sands." A picturesque way of describing the process of making farmers into writers! The subject of politics was to be entirely banned. It was asking too much of farmers to shape their political thinking according to their own interests, thus manifesting enough of unity to allow editorial or individual discussion of such issues. Safety and harmony could be maintained among rural individualists only through a discreet silence on all "matters of state."

From the very first issue the quality of the *Register* was high. The *Richmond Enquirer* hailed it as opening a new era in the life of the state, while John Skinner, first editor of the *American Farmer,* declared it to be the "best publication on agriculture which this country or Europe has ever produced." For ten years it held to this standard and increased its following, easily excelling any other farm publication of the country, sending its files down to us to-day to invite favorable comparison with the best in any period in any country. Although the farmers did not with one accord sit down to pour out the wisdom of experience, enough of them "took pen in hand" to make the pages of the *Register* a reliable barometer of agricultural changes. The editor, forced to write nearly half of the material he printed, set a high standard of excellence, supplementing his own work with intelligent gleanings from the agricultural writers of two continents. He reprinted, as numbers of his journal, John Taylor's *Arator,* then out of print, the *Westover Manuscripts,* Davy's *Elements of Agricultural Chemistry,* and the third edition of his own *Essay on Calcareous Manures,* to the benefit of his own day and the profit of modern collectors of rare imprints. No other force played so great a part in producing what the modern historian must rank as one of the great agricultural revolutions in American history.

The period from 1820 to 1845 was, indeed, a notable one in the development of the Old South. When it opened, as we have seen, despair and abandonment held complete sway. Early efforts at agricultural reform had failed, and early reformers had been discredited. By 1834 a visitor to "Mount Vernon," where the great Washington had struggled for better methods, declared that "a more wide-spread and perfect agricultural ruin could not be imagined." Jefferson at "Monticello" was closing his days in poverty as his fields and markets failed him; everywhere the agricultural societies dwindled for lack of support as farmers lost heart; and even John Binns and his gypsum yielded ground. With the use of marl, however, and the spread of information on scientific farming to which its discoverer had dedicated himself, the whole scene was altered. Aided by slowly opening markets and the opportunity for profits, the better farmers attacked their task in earnest. "Where marl is introduced," wrote one of them, "we hear no more of turning out land or of emigration to the West." Soon former residents of the region who had left a land of "poverty-stricken fields" and "fleeing emigrants" returned to find that "luxuriant corn" had taken the place of "scanty hen's-grass" and that the people were everywhere manifesting a "new spirit of industry." The tide had turned, emigration had lessened, crops increased, and hope had found new footing. From 1838 to 1850 the land values of tidewater Virginia increased by over seventeen millions of dollars, and one estimate placed the total increase from the application of marl, after 1820, at over thirty millions. One writer, evidently carried away by his own eloquence, declared that "Mother earth has changed her face, and . . . her constitution under the healing influence of this salutary medicament, and now presents an appearance as different from her former self, as the healthy and robust man from the lingering and hectic victim of consumption." "Verdant fields," "luxuriant clover," and "abundant harvests" had taken the place of "broomstraw and poverty grass," while a poor, thin, and stunted vegetation had "disappeared." [12]

With all due allowance for overstatement by enthusiasts we must admit that a new economic order had begun to rise on the foundations laid by this humble teacher. The letters and journals of plain farmers show that many had doubled their crops, a few had even quadrupled the yields of corn and wheat per acre, and most of those who had given the new methods an honest trial had been benefited enough to change their whole attitude toward the calling. Other improvements and other improvers caught the upward swing thus started and shared in the rejuvenation which by 1850 had caused this region to forget its lean days to the point where men could talk freely about them. Better markets, rising profits, sent this first "new South" confidently forward to its own destruction on the presumption that farmers are superior to those who toil in industry, that those who toil by force and necessity are as well off in slavery of one kind as of another. The region took its place beside the Kingdom of Cotton in 1861 on foundations less spectacular but more enduring and more sustaining than those afforded by the fleecy tyrant.

Without much self-deception Edmund Ruffin, if he had chosen, might have believed those who were saying that "his monument is more truly lasting than brass, for it is the soil of this state. . . . His memory will be cherished with gratitude, when those who occupy so much of the public attention, and who are ever parading before the popular gaze, shall cease to exist in the recollections of man." Perhaps, however, if we have understood the man, he would have preferred to do a bit of parading himself, to have exchanged a bit of the future glory for a few moments in the despised popular gaze.

Even the neighbors in Prince George, in 1843, looking about and seeing "with pleasure" their labors rewarded with heavy and abundant crops, were moved to enquire why their lands, "once so miserably poor as not to yield a competency for . . . [their] own consumption," should have been so changed. Were their ancestors less industrious? Surely not. Had the change resulted from favorable legislation? No. While "all other pursuits" were being "almost legislated to death," agriculture had marched "onward in the face of neglect." They could only "return thanks to Divine Providence" and to a native son who had "devoted his time, talents, money and industry, in endeavoring to convince us by practice, as well as by his luminous productions on calcareous manure, how we might use marl, [and] reclaim the barren fields with which our county abounds." They admitted that "single and alone, he had buffeted popular prejudice" and "by his untiring industry . . . enabled . . . [them] to make two ears of corn or two blades of grass to grow upon a spot of earth where only one grew here before." And then, perhaps suddenly remembering that they had not rewarded this benefactor in the approved way which had been within their gift, they added by way of consolation that "in the words of Dean Swift," such a good genius was "deserving more at our hands than the whole race of politicians put together." [13]

* * *

But, in spite of occasional fine words, trouble and neglect are the usual lot of those who seek to serve rural folk. And both were now falling to the *Farmers' Register* and its virile editor. The delicate question of just where agricultural topics ended and the forbidden political ones began was one well calculated to tax the judgment of any reforming enthusiast. The battle against the protective tariff had earlier found its chief cohorts among the Southern farmers, their agricultural societies constantly pouring out protests and petitions to the consternation of side-stepping politicians. Ruffin's signature appeared often, in that period, at the bottom of such diatribes, disclosing a keen interest in public questions and a sharp pen in their discussion. It was part of the farmer's fight for existence—the section's fight as well. It was, therefore, more than could be expected of human frailty that the question of bank reform produced by the suspension of specie payment after the panic of 1837 should not appeal to him as a matter of direct interest to agriculture and demand the columns of his paper in its service.

The issue involved was primarily whether or not banks issuing notes should be forced to restrict their loans and to redeem their paper in specie on demand. Under the system of chartering in vogue it was an issue localized in each state to its own banks and consequently involving purely local interests in the persons of bank officials and stockholders and those accommodated by loans. The evils complained of were those of depreciation and fluctuation, the floating of unsound issues in distant regions, excessive loans on insufficient security, and, indirectly, the creation of a powerful interest which controlled legislation and prevented reforms that would benefit the great masses as represented by the farming element.

From boyhood, if we may accept his word, Ruffin had been opposed to unsound banking. He now turned his pen, dipped in passion, against all banking evils, real and possible, declaring their removal to be a basic agricultural reform. "Fully aware of the danger, the certain injury, to be incurred by daring to oppose and in any manner expose the frauds and abuses of the banking interests," whose "submissive slaves" had already made him feel their disapproval, he determined "at all hazards" to "proceed in this course and endeavor, if possible, to awaken the members of the agricultural interest of Virginia, and of the whole Confederacy, to a sense of the enormous evils . . . suffered, and the system of pillage . . . still pursued by the banking system of this country." He was resolved to use no "holiday terms" in his attack, seeing no reason why "lying, fraud and swindling" should not be spoken of as such. It was language calculated to awaken a number of other people also!

At first Ruffin was content to discuss the whole subject of banking, good and bad, in articles of moderate length and tone printed in the *Farmers' Register*. They were clear-cut and sane, though sprinkled here and there with hard words that revealed a suppressed emotion which now and then broke through. They grew in fervor as opposition developed, as readers canceled subscriptions or newspapers launched attacks, giving the ardent editor the feeling of martyr and crusader in the cause of the oppressed. Strange spectacle, of the Federalist pleading the cause of a downtrodden majority, appealing to common folk against the privileged few who dominated even the government in their own interest! But consistency is not a virtue among gentlemen.[14]

Then came, with gathering ardor, the launching of a new periodical, the *Bank Reformer,* flaunting the motto, *"Nil Utile Quod Non Honestum."* It was a sheet to delight the propagandist of any period, with the Latin phrase to give it respectability in any Southern neighborhood. It was issued monthly, for the avowed purpose of "furnishing and diffusing information" on the correct principles of legitimate banking and the "actual wrong-doing and fraudulent practices and injurious effects, and worse tendencies of the existing banking system of this country." Copies were supplied gratuitously "to known & zealous friends of the cause," while those so inclined and able could purchase quantities for distribution, at five dollars the two hundred copies. Numbers were sent to postmasters in various communities with instructions to deliver to any one paying the postage. The object was widest appeal even though the editor paid the bills.

It is not necessary to follow in detail the fight waged in this journal against the evils already mentioned. Sufficient to note that Ruffin found himself sharply arrayed against an interest of strength great enough to bring the frown of respectability and substantial position upon himself, this result arousing his deepest resentments and loosing his adequate supply of invectives. Attacks by the formerly friendly Petersburg editors now became "charges . . . calculated to defame my character, injure my reputation," and their newspapers became "receptacles of scurrility, and servile banks tool [s]." The banks themselves were "plundering and prodigal," engaged in "fraud and tyranny," their officials often neither respectable [n]or honest," while those who supported them in the press or the legislature used methods resorted to only by "knaves" and "deluded fools." The

Bank Reformer aimed to make "higher-ups" wince. The editor confessed it to be a sort of "amusing" sport.[15]

Nor did Ruffin's campaigning fervor and genius for propaganda end here. Over the signatures of ancient Romans whose names had been connected with the struggles of the masses against tyranny he slipped his telling arguments into the columns of friendly newspapers. He organized the Association for Promoting Currency and Banking Reform—constitutions, officers, dues, and all, which enabled those with a passion for "joining" to function and which poured petitions of his own framing upon the legislature. He climaxed his efforts with the clever device of printing on the backs of his envelopes and of all bank notes, by way of endorsement, terse statements in condemnation of the existing system, and then he distributed, free of charge to all comers, sheets of such statements ready to be pasted to notes, so that each might "instruct by its back as many persons as it cheats by its face." He printed, free of charge, statements on all notes brought to his establishment, declaring that if all friends of reform would follow his example, the banks would be so exposed as to be shamed out of existence before another year should pass.

The following samples of endorsements appearing on his letters and notes witness a skill in pressing a cause that accounts for some of the hatred he now enjoyed:

> The promise on the face of this note is FALSE; and the issue of such notes is both a banking and a government FRAUD, committed on the right and interest of labor and honestly acquired capital.

> The paper banking system is essentially and necessarily fraudulent. . . . The object, as well as the effect, of the paper-money system is to enable those who have earned

or accumulated nothing by labor, to exchange this *nothing* for the *something,* and often the *everything* earned by the labor of others.

He hoped that "by so labeling a lying bank note with a truth-telling endorsement, and putting it into circulation in the country, every such note . . . [would be made] an itinerant declaimer, operating widely and effectively against the frauds and evils of the present banking system." It might seem "a petty and impotent" mode of attack, but Ruffin testified that "the banking gentry . . . [were] more annoyed by these small shot than by the heaviest artillery." If the degree of hostility aroused was evidence of effectiveness, then he was demonstrating how capable a gentleman thrown out of course into the work of agitation might be. He had developed into a skilled propagandist. Such talent, backed by approval, under the guise of patriotic endeavor, might yet play a part in the affairs of a wider world.[16]

But without such approval, running amuck from staid, substantial patterns could not be tolerated in the land of vested interests. Political arrangements could not be upset; after all, it was not well to talk about social good and individual justice in a region where property in lands and persons and even paper money constituted the balance to established ways. Charges poured in that the *Farmers' Register* and its editor had broken the pledge to abstain from politics. Gentlemen requested that: "You will . . . oblige me by placing my account in the October number of the *Register,* and withdrawing my name from your subscription list." Pecuniary losses followed. It was an amusing sport, but it was also an expensive one. The editor soon found it impossible to continue either of his publications, and so brought them to a close, leaving the field clear to a rival agricultural journal which had been launched by more conservative hands to care for the now established and accepted "new agriculture."

Another disappointment crowded fast upon the first. In 1841 a State Board of Agriculture, a thing for which Ruffin had so long labored, had been created to give leadership and stability to the rural interests which had been reëstablished in economic, and consequently political, importance in the last two decades. Ruffin, of course, was made a member and, at its first meeting, elected corresponding secretary. Seizing the opportunity, he drew up and presented a plan of procedure which had long been in his mind, calling for a careful gathering and diffusion of information, the conducting of experiments by selected groups, and the division of the state into eight districts with a Board member assigned to each for most effective supervision of all activities. It was a dream come true—the agricultural leader recognized and official aid given to the cause.[17]

But political troubles, some of them connected with the bank fight, stirred personal enmities, bringing "niggardly support & contemptuous treatment" and in the end a "speedy extinction," causing Ruffin to resign with the feeling that all he had striven for had been lost. Bitter and disillusioned, he turned back to his farm, concluding that "the public of Virginia was wearied of him and his writing" and resolved to "withdraw entirely from all connexion with the public." Somehow he was not made for public service. Virginia did not appreciate him; he would turn back to his own interests and seek the rewards of work well done in the satisfaction of doing it. And then, as if to confirm his feelings, the farmers of South Carolina called for his services. The old kinship of nullification days asserted itself again,

[71]

to allow him more gracefully to retire from the scene of his failure.

Thus another period in his life closed. He had succeeded as a progressive farmer and had lifted his section from the "Nadir of agricultural depression" to an "abundant prosperity" on which the future would build. He had become a figure of some importance, not only in his own state, but all over the South where the first process of exploitation had come to an end and men faced the choice of flight or reform. He had been tempted by his success and influence to enter again the course of public affairs, only to be forcibly reminded that he did not fit. His zeal burned too brightly, too steadily, for the clever ways of politics which often preferred darkness. Yet he had mastered the technique of propaganda and come close enough to the warm approval of his fellows as agricultural and bank reformer to make the bitterness of reaction even more sharp. For the present, however, all was dark.

* * *

The frail little man who turned the key in the old Petersburg office with so much bitterness in his heart felt that all was lost. He was, nevertheless, unknown to himself, now entering a wider field, where new allies were to be found and more suitable objects against which to vent his force awaited. His talents would yet find larger compensation, inadequate, but large for those who know peace only in conflict and action.

CHAPTER IV

CHARLESTON AND "MARLBOURNE"

WHEN the outsider thinks of the ante-bellum South, he is liable, unconsciously, to have South Carolina in mind. And if he is not careful, he will be thinking of Charleston as constituting South Carolina. Romance has done more for this spot than any other in America, making her charm the symbol of a section, her qualities those of a widely varied people. The sand hills, the uplands, the mountains, the poor whites, and the yeomen, these enter the picture only as shadows. The real South—a coast land where wide rivers idle in mirror to the sea; great trees, hung with moss, canopy roadways or crowd down through swamps; and birds and flowers and air heavy with sweet odors give background to stately houses and splendid gardens wherein genteel folk, who always do and say the proper thing, dwell with their strange-speaking negro slaves!

First in almost everything that makes life more than existence, Charleston's colonial efforts had soon swung wide of furs and deerskins to center on rice and indigo plantations, whose harvests her own merchants carried out to the world to make art and music and theaters possible for her while most others dwelt in homespun simplicity.

Thrown well off by herself over against the hostile Spaniards, Charleston had learned to care for her own interests, developing the spirit of a city-state and the capacity in her people for independent action. The great arms of sand that the continent had thrown out as if to cover its face against the long roll of the Atlantic, with their inner sounds and swamps, cut her off from her northern neighbor, Virginia, humble North Carolinians scattering in between, and tied her interests up with those of the West Indies and Europe rather than with the continent of which she was a part.

A rich hinterland, divided sharply by the fall line and sand hills, became tributary by Revolutionary days to the great market center whose magnificent harbor lay quiet behind sheltering islands and protecting bars—joint entrance to the sea of two rivers, making it the flowering point of all that grew for a hundred miles or more around. Planters built town houses and came with their families for the races and "the season," their chaises and high-swung coaches, emblazoned with coats of arms, crowding the streets on their way to St. Cecelia or in answer to the bells of St. Michael's or St. Philip's. To have been born outside the favored society was an offense not easily overlooked.

But this was not all of South Carolina. Well back of fall line and sand hills another world was in process of formation. Crowding across the Virginia piedmont and the red hills of North Carolina, the Scotch-Irish, Germans, Welsh, and other simple peoples had early come to carve out of the forests homes for their broods and to live a plain, self-sufficing life which tended to fall back to the Indian level on the one side and to achieve "near respectability" on the other. Presbyterians, Baptists, Quakers, or German Pietists they might be, holding fast to their sects to the extent to which the shepherds of souls had followed them, but reaching a common level in the emotional starvation that made all religious expressions strikingly alike. A people notable here only because of the sharper contrasts

they presented to the splendors of Charleston, they made
in national days the conflict between coast and interior more
bitter and long drawn out than the usual southern struggle.
Poor folk, without labor other than that of their own hands,
so poor that they did not even realize it! [1]

Hard times had fallen on Charleston and her vicinage
in the days of the Revolution and after. Indigo planting
failed with the ending of British bounties, rice markets
weakened, and slaves fell in price; business languished and
merchants closed their shops. In September, 1785, the
governor's message called attention to the "calamitous state
of affairs" in which a scarcity of money prevented the payment of debts to a degree that produced demands on the
part of radicals for paper money and stay laws. Many
planters saved themselves in the period by hiring out their
slaves to work on the Santee Canal, while others facing
ruin migrated to more favored spots. [2]

Such conditions held until the cotton gin made its appearance in the early nineties, sending the short-staple
cotton plants out over the coastal plain, on the first stretch
of their triumphant journey westward. The price of slaves
recovered as the call for black hands to gather snowy harvests came swelling down from the once hostile upcountry,
and the wharves of Charleston grew busy again when cotton
bales poured in to find their way out to the new machines
that the Industrial Revolution had set going abroad.

But it was a short-lived recovery. The true realm of
cotton lay farther west in the Lower South, whose river
highways carried the crops out through other ports, leaving
Charleston to draw on a limited territory of now old and
worn soils. Neither the planters nor the city could bear the
competition. The lure of fresh lands and the seemingly

insatiable demand for cotton laid too heavy a toll on the region. A steady stream of emigration set in toward the West—single families, great planters and their slaves, or younger sons with a parcel of field hands easily spared from the working force at home, and all added, from new seats, their share to the flood of cotton which had already stricken the first home of the staple nigh to its death. In the 1820's and 1830's South Carolina suffered even more than Virginia. Robert Y. Hayne spoke of the "mournful evidence of premature decay" in the city of Charleston, of "merchants bankrupt or driven away," "shipyards broken up," "the very grass growing in our streets and houses falling into ruins." He pictured the rural scene as one of "fields abandoned, agriculture drooping, . . . slaves, like their masters, working harder, and faring worse, the planter striving with unavailing efforts to avert the ruin which is before him." [3]

On such economic foundations the tariff controversy that ended in nullification developed. A few saw the fundamental economic shift that had assigned a new rôle to the older regions, but the majority found it easier to lay all the blame on the half-guilty central government, creating thereby the situation in which South Carolina took her place as the champion of states' rights—Charleston leading the way.

Moreover, the rapid expansion followed by a sharp decline greatly affected the relations between the two sections of the state. The coming of cotton to the upcountry softened feelings against negro slavery, and necessity and profits soon made it acceptable. Farms widened into plantations, in certain neighborhoods, and evangelical folk crowded into places of power to check the liberal thinking of lowland gentlemen or. at least, to lessen their influence in the educational institutions where upland sons now sought the good things of the spirit. In time the capital was moved to Columbia, at the fall line, and a few reluctant but inadequate concessions were made in the direction of democracy. But cotton changed back-country people more than they could change old practices. Demands soon weakened, and the minority still ruled. South Carolina was to be gentlemen's territory down to the War between the States.

But, most important, bad conditions stirred a proud people to thought and action. Not only did some, for the future protection of the state, spin into a political philosophy the practices by which the coast had long checked the rule of the majority, but others, of a more practical turn of mind, urged the impossibility of competition with the fresh lands of the West and advocated the diversification of economic effort by the establishment of manufactories, the building of internal improvements, and the altering of agricultural practices and production. The use of logic has never been excelled. Extreme thinkers had their inning as nowhere else in the South. Charleston and South Carolina assumed a place of advanced leadership, sometimes more advanced than leading, which turned the eyes of the more radical in other states toward her and her statesmen. From this time forward this was the Southern South.

Of those who had taken a leading part in the nullification controversy and who had urged and practiced agricultural reforms as a means of saving the glory that was Charleston's, few were more important than James Henry Hammond. He had bitterly opposed the tariff on constitutional grounds, and his editoral efforts in the *Southern Times* had won warm commendation from Hayne, Hamilton, and Calhoun. He had gone to Congress in 1835, there to proclaim slavery "the greatest of all the great blessings which a kind Providence has bestowed upon our glorious region" and to suggest that the natural differences between North and South, if widened by abolition agitators, would "inevitably separate us into two nations." As a planter, believing that his kind were "essentially what the nobility are in other countries," he had taken personal charge of his estate, "Silver Bluff," struggling to rebuild "the poverty of his thin acres" and keeping in touch with the best practices advocated at home or abroad. He had watched Edmund Ruffin's work in Virginia with interest. It fell in with his own purposes.[4]

In November, 1841, in an anniversary oration delivered before the State Agricultural Society which he had helped to organize two years before, Hammond insisted that cotton must be replaced in South Carolina by general farming with diverse crops, and that manufacturing, even with negro slavery, must become a part of the future economic effort of the state. He envisaged the older regions as no longer hopeless rivals of the new Cotton Kingdom, but forming, with the adoption of general farming, manufacturing, and commerce, an essential part in the economic life of the whole South. He would have them supply those things now purchased from northern rivals—a proposal which marks the beginning of a rift between those who followed theory, as best expounded by Barnwell Rhett in his drive for independent state action against the central government, and the more practical Charleston group who now moved gradually over to what came to be called the coöperationist or Southern Nationalist position.[5]

In 1842 Hammond became governor. His administration, though notable for a sharp attack on the Bank of South

Carolina and for the expulsion of Samuel Hoar, who had come to protect the interests of Massachusetts negroes entering Charleston harbor, was far more significant as a turning point in the federal and Southern relations of the state. In the so-called Bluffton Movement, urging extreme action against the tariff and the abolitionists who dared to oppose the annexation of Texas, the division between those who desired separate state action and those who would delay for the united action of the whole South was for the first time sharply manifest. Hammond's attitude, though softened by his official position, was temporarily that of the coöperationist who believed the break-up of the Union in the end inevitable. The wise policy was, as he saw it, to delay and draw nearer in economic relations to the other Southern states, binding their sympathies and interests to South Carolina until the proper time for united action or until resistance by a single state seemed necessary.[6] In this spirit he sought first the economic reordering of the life of the state, turning to Virginia to secure the leadership for rebuilding the agricultural foundations on which all else must rise. He invited Edmund Ruffin to become agricultural surveyor of South Carolina.

To the eager reformer, "soured" on the conservative and unappreciative Virginians, no approach could have been more welcome. Here was a congenial governor, fighting banks and tariffs, upholding slavery, and taking a radical position, with evident public approval. South Carolina, the home of gentlemen, was calling him, at the very moment of repudiation at home. Too bad he had not been born among those whom he might have served with most profit.

Ruffin had seen Charleston for the first time only two

years before. But it had been a case of love at first sight. His description of the city, published in the *Farmers' Register,* revealed unusual enthusiasm and regard for her many virtues: [7]

> Without touching on other matters, the buildings and general appearance of this city are more pleasing to me than of the more populous and splendid cities of the north. In the usual style of this one, there appears to be an unpretending dignity and beauty, and in some cases even grandeur, combined with simplicity. In this respect, Charleston may be likened to a gentleman born and bred, simply but perfectly well dressed, compared to a mustachioed dandy and exquisite. Indeed, it seemed to me that the population contained a larger proportion of those who appeared to be gentlemen than I had ever seen in any other city; and, for some time, I believed that not a pair of *moustaches* disgraced the city; but I was compelled to learn otherwise, by seeing before my departure several specimens of these ape-imitating "lords of creation."

To be honored now by such a city made Virginia's slights even greater. His pleasure deepened the bitterness already felt for his native state, and this bitterness, in turn, magnified the qualities of his new benefactor. From that day forward, South Carolina and Charleston in South Carolina became to Edmund Ruffin the incarnation of the highest Southern good. Kindred spirits there to be found; honor for prophets; action that freed the forces within without creating bitterness! Fate had taken a hand to shape events that would move in unbroken course to culminate one April morning at Sumter in Charleston harbor.

The official task that Ruffin now assumed was, in its real import, the same as that he had so successfully performed in Virginia in the capacity of a private citizen. Worn lands in competition with fresh western soils needed allies. Good farming, as comprehended in the term "general farming," must replace single-crop production. Soils worn and washed must again hold their people in comfort against the tug of the West. To Ruffin it meant, in practical terms, the "investigation of the extensive but heretofore neglected beds of marl and of limestone, and other rich resources of calcareous manure." That was again the first step in rebuilding a ruined agricultural life. Upon marl South Carolina could follow Virginia back to prosperity. Perhaps even a whole South could be restored to equal power in the councils of government or prepared for a glorious independence.

Lest he expect too much of her farmers, in spite of the fact that they were Carolinians, Hammond warned Ruffin: [8]

> They will *receive* you cordially everywhere, but I cannot promise that many of them will go far to *meet* you. You are sufficiently acquainted with human nature in general & the traits of agriculturists in particular, to have made up your mind, I am sure, to make the best of things, as you find them & not to expect to see them as they *ought* to be. You must have expected in the performance of your task to meet with much obstinacy & some opposition. It will not be your least difficult part to keep your temper & press forward over all these obstacles with unabating perseverance and resolutely to do good in spite of those for whom you do it.

Ruffin's experience, however, did not justify the warning. His reputation had preceded him, resulting in a year of labor which stood out, in satisfaction returned, above any other of his life to that time. Hammond was sympathetic and understanding; other public leaders and the press of the state treated him with marked deference. The record he kept of his services, full to the point of weariness, shows him following the river courses in quest of marl beds, searching the swamps with an eye to possible draining, visiting the plantations of progressive planters in all corners of the state with evident enthusiasm and pleasure. Labor was a joy when recognition was forthcoming.

The reports he made to the governor pointed out the location of marl beds and reënforced the five hundred copies of his *Essay on Calcareous Manures* that had been distributed gratuitously over the state to explain the benefits of their use. The information he gathered on agricultural practices in the period alone justified his employment, and the interest he awakened in better farming, though not revolutionary in results, was the beginning of a better day in the eastern cotton belt.[9]

But intensive labor, however gratifying, that carried him into the swamps and entailed severe exposure at all times was too much for a frail constitution. Before his period of service was ended, ill health forced withdrawal, with regrets this time on the side of the public. But friendships formed continued. Three years later Hammond, then in retirement, assured him that in South Carolina the "universal feeling towards you is one of the highest respect in every way." He congratulated Ruffin as "one of the few benefactors of mankind whose services have been appreciated by the world, while still living." Ruffin in turn warmed to the state and her citizens. Favored land where leaders were appreciated!

More resentful than ever, the prophet with his honors returned to his native state. He had determined to remain silent and inactive in public matters. Virginia did not wish his words or his services. It was even best to seek new neighbors, new fields to till.

*   *   *

When the Autumn of 1843 came around and the bountiful harvests in Prince George had been gathered, the farmers of the community took notice of the fact that the proprietor at Coggin's Point was preparing to move. One is a bit puzzled to know whether it was from a sense of duty or from a love of "resolving," serving on committees, or engineering a public affair that the neighbors considered "the propriety of tendering to Mr. Edmund Ruffin, Sr. a Farmer's Dinner." They said it was the former. In consequence, on December 28, with the kind words and extravagant praise that might have been acceptable if scattered over a longer period of time, and with the gift of a silver plate appropriately engraved, they paid tribute to the one who had lifted them and their farms from poverty to plenty. The recipient, confining his true thoughts to his diary, accepted the proffers with remarkably good grace—and moved to Hanover County.

The new home, "Marlbourne," on the Pamunkey, has already been described. A "seating" befitting a gentleman; lands poor enough to challenge the most confirmed agricultural reformer; but also a place "distant" and "almost unknown," where a gentleman might sulk a bit over slights and find new neighbors whose weaknesses were yet to be discovered.

Ruffin described his lands as "highly susceptible of improvement and greatly in want of it." But he was certain that " a few years of marling" would "put a new face on the fields." It is interesting to notice that certainty had taken the place of hope. He was, in fact, now entering into the rewards of his earlier agricultural services. The developments on this farm in the next few years may be taken as illustrative of the "new agriculture" that came to the Old South in the decade and a half before the storm of war broke upon its people—a period of diversified and specialized farming, of profits that gave comforts and confidence, and even of a trickle of immigrants coming from New York and Pennsylvania to find opportunities here greater than were to be found in the West. Building on the work already done, this man and his section were to know a prosperity greater than any that had come since earliest colonial days, to frame a life nearer akin to that of their northern neighbors than to that in the Cotton Kingdom —and yet with gentlemen and slaves and great estates. Where would interest lead such a region in the stormy days ahead? [10]

It has been said that an angry woman turns out a clean wash. In like manner a sulking gentleman turned out a magnificent farm from worn lands. With its owner resolved to ignore the public and to concentrate his interest and his efforts upon his own soils, "Marlbourne" at once began to manifest the effects of knowledge, energy, and experience A few days after the arrival of the "negroes with the mules, wagons and etc." Ruffin had arranged with his neighbor, Carter Braxton, to obtain marl from the beds on Braxton's farm and had set about spreading it over "800 acres or more" in preparation for clover, keeping a careful record of the different kinds and quantities used on different parcels of land. His farm journal for the next two years is so filled with the details of marling that one gets the impression that his force, when not engaged in the absolutely

[84]

necessary work of planting and harvesting, were always hauling and spreading marl. Tradition has it that when on one occasion, due to this devotion, he had neglected to fill his ice house and the neighbors had sent their teams during a sudden cold snap to assist him, he could not resist the temptation to set the whole force to hauling marl for the fields.

But he was doing more. He tried greensands, the value of which he doubted, but with the declaration, *"I shall rejoice to find myself mistaken;"* he gave the most careful attention to the preservation and use of barnyard manure; and he persisted in the face of failures with his trials of clover until it grew too rank for his machines to cut. Cowpeas of different kinds were grown under every condition he could devise, and when he had found the type and method best fitted to his needs, he made them a regular part of his cropping. "I am now riding a pea hobby," was his way of describing the move to his friend Hammond. Barren lands would "smile" under such treatment.

The next step in his program was the development of a well-planned system of drainage. Open ditches in sandy loam were satisfactory only where the natural lay of the land made them arterial carriers to the river; the topography of "Marlbourne" necessitated covered drains over most of his fields. These he constructed by laying at the bottom of a trench two fence rails parallel and two or three inches apart, covering them over with boards and straw to prevent the earth above from falling through when it was replaced and treaded down. He worked constantly to improve his system, later finding that one rail served as well as two, until, after a few years, he had perfected a drainage plant which he considered as essential to the fertility of his lands as marl itself. To a region of heavy rainfall and much swampy land this pioneer effort was of greatest importance. "Marlbourne" became a model from which others far and wide took pattern. His writings on drainage took rank with his work on soils.[11]

The crops grown at "Marlbourne," in spite of the facts that its acres had increased to over fifteen hundred and that it depended on negro slaves for labor, were those of the average farmer in Pennsylvania or New York. Wheat, corn, oats, potatoes, fruit, and melons, together with hogs, sheep, and cattle, constituted the surplus that went out to market at Baltimore, Richmond, or Norfolk. Pork, eggs, and dairy products sufficient for the needs of mansion and cabins alike were produced at home. Improved implements, from four-horse McCormick or Watt plows to McCormick reapers and Haw threshing machines, were in use.

This variety of effort allowed the most advanced rotation of crops to be adopted. The first tried ran: corn, wheat, clover, wheat, and pasture; but this soon gave way to a six-field system in which corn, with peas broadcast and plowed under, opened a series which included wheat, clover mowed, clover grazed and plowed under, wheat, and pasture. Variations were introduced as experience dictated, but the principle of a system in which each crop prepared for the one that was to follow and which gave a maximum production of wheat as the cash crop was always followed.

The negro slave, in such a system, proved just as efficient in applying marl, spreading manure, mowing clover, binding wheat, cultivating corn, or butchering hogs as he had once been in the wholesale destroying of land with his crude hoe in tobacco fields. Slaves fed and cared for the mules and oxen in the morning before the Master left the mansion; for periods as long as two months at a time they kept the affairs of the farm going when the Master was absent and his son could visit them only once in two weeks; they worked with the most complicated machinery of the day with seemingly no more accidents to themselves and the machines than an equal number of white men would have had. Ruffin confessed these complicated and varied tasks "well done." In spite of rising prices of field hands he found slave labor profitable when reduced to a suitable quantity and given proper supervision. He was no nearer to replacing it with free white labor than was the most optimistic planter of cotton in Alabama or Mississippi. Those who have so enthusiastically declared that slavery would have passed when expansion ceased will do well to consider the institution in this oldest of slavery regions. Those who have called the whole ante-bellum South "The Cotton Kingdom" might with profit remember that the Capital of the Confederacy, whose cornerstone was slavery, lay in a region where wheat was king.[12]

The results of scientific farming were early manifest at "Marlbourne." In 1845 from 134 acres Ruffin harvested only 1,977 bushels of wheat, and from 112 acres only 1,600 bushels of corn. In 1848 the wheat crop rose to 5,127 bushels from 254 acres and the corn crop to 3,080 bushels from 106 acres, his profits on wheat alone being nearly $6,000. From that time forward his lands became more and more fertile, and his profits, now spread over corn, oats, hogs, wool, etc., as well as wheat, rose with European wars and South American demands for flour. It was a far cry from the early days at Coggin's Point. There was little here to justify the notion, too long current, of a backward, tumble-down South looking with jealous eyes toward the prosperous North. The general farmers in this region were too busy to be jealous.

Meanwhile, important things were happening in the personal life of the prosperous planter. In the early years he kept to himself, harboring resentments against all men because of the slights of the few. Only South Carolinians were exempt. When, in February, 1845, a new Virginia State Agricultural Society was formed and he, though not in attendance, was chosen its first president, he rather curtly refused the honor, explaining to his friend Hammond that this was in accord with his "previous determination to have no further or renewed connexion with the public." "My business as well as my pleasure keeps me at home," he declared, "and I rarely leave it for more than a day, and only to visit my children." "Any compliments and honors offered" now came *"too late."* [13]

But for one so filled with ideas it was a hard course. Before long he was admitting that he had "departed somewhat" from his "entire" separation from the public and had agreed to perform at his "discretion or caprice . . . something like the sub-editorial duties for an agricultural column or two in each No. of the Richmond *Enquirer.*"

Then followed a series of valuable papers on practical farming subjects—the proper use of manure on clover, the value of field peas, etc., breaking the silence and gradually renewing the service he thought he had so firmly forsaken. Although he kept quiet on the banking question, he sent a printing press to Hammond with samples of the most telling statements that he had been using on the backs of his envelopes, and he rejoiced when that dignitary informed him that he was writing the "Atty. Gener. of the US. and shall to the Gov. of Va. and the Atty. Gen. of Va. [and] all will receive such enveloped letters."

In the next few years the *American Farmer* also requested and received articles from his pen, resulting, to his satisfaction, in the increase of subscribers for the paper in Virginia. The spell of silence was entirely broken in 1850, when the sectional conflict resulting in the Compromise of that year sent him into South Carolina to have his say on the issues involved, and when the Agricultural Society of the Eastern Shore of Maryland enticed him across the Chesapeake to make the principal address at their meeting. How far he had yielded is shown by the fact that in this latter address he took occasion to chide the Virginia Agricultural Society, which until now he had ignored, for its "still-born" condition—the first public protest on any matter he had offered in eight years. A new epoch was beginning for the South. His keen mind sensed the fact that the past was rapidly sinking out of sight and understood that it was a poor time for a man with opinions to be keeping it in memory.

Shortly afterwards a significant event occurred. *DeBow's Review,* which was becoming something of a Southern oracle, presenting to its readers in a "Gallery of Industry and Enterprise" the most important benefactors and leaders of the section, wrote asking for Ruffin's picture and for a sketch of his life and services. The article, written by a Mr. Baulwane from materials furnished by the subject, was widely noticed by the people and press of Virginia and afforded the occasion for a burst of rather extravagant, if long delayed, praise of the great agricultural reformer.[14] The Richmond *Whig* was "happy to see that the well-merited fame of this enterprising, learned and able agriculturist was so widely diffused and so justly appreciated." It spoke of the thousands who were now "indebted to him for the large measure of prosperity which they are enjoying" and recalled the days when emigration, now ended, threatened the whole tidewater region. The Fredericksburg *News* declared that Edmund Ruffin "has done more for Virginia than any man living—indeed we doubt whether the man has ever lived who has been in fact a greater benefactor to this State." Roger A. Pryor, in the *Southside Democrat* of Petersburg, referred to him as "this ornament and benefactor of the State" and asserted that the monuments of his genius, energy and worth, to "be seen in the once barren and wasted but now teeming and verdure-covered fields," were "more to be envied than 'storied urn or animated bust'."

The next year the "Committee on Honorary" of the Virginia Agricultural Society, after giving Ruffin credit for the agricultural revival that had come to the state, proclaimed him "Not Edmund Ruffin of Prince George, of Petersburg, of Hanover, but Edmund Ruffin of Virginia. He now belongs to us all, and him we hail as the field marshal of the army of fathers and planters of the Old Dominion." The United States Agricultural Society made him an honorary member because he had ended the age of agricultural barbarism and by his "generous example and distinguished services" driven the "garb of barrenness and desolation" from the land.

It was too much for the grim old planter. He accepted the presidency of the Agricultural Society that he had already helped to revive and became in the next two years the most important factor in its activities. He attended every meeting of the Executive Committee, wrote most of its important papers, and delivered most of its addresses. At its fair held in Richmond in 1853 he modestly admitted that, from his own observations and those of his children and friends, he "was the chief object of interest & the 'observed of all observers' "—an honor he tried to ignore and to bear "meekly." Winfield Scott, ex-President Tyler, William C. Rives, and others of the stamp were also present.[15]

The whole outlook changed. Assuring himself that the notice now given was to a "person in private & almost recluse life, never seeking such favors & having no rewards to give," he concluded that it must, therefore, be the evidence of "the prevalent opinion of the intelligent portion of the community." In a new strain he wrote to his friend Hammond: [16]

> You may remember some of my former letters, in which my wrongs and resentful feelings were strongly though concisely referred to. My consequent entire seclusion you then opposed—especially in regard to my declining . . . the first returning mark of public approval, when I was elected to the presidency of the first Va. Agl. Soc. . . . And I was wrong, . . . in construing the hostility or ingratitude of *many* to be the like feelings of *all*. This difference I did not allow myself opportunity to discover. . . . I know now that when I was most separated from my fellows, fancying that I was slighted, if not even disliked by all, that I retained numerous approvers and friends . . . ! Envy loves a shining mark! Envy, hatred, and Calumny are the only tributes that many men can pay to worth—& for my own part, I have learned to esteem such tributes as compliments to superior merit. . . . The occurrences of the last few years . . . have shown me that . . . with the better and larger portion of my countrymen, I hold a place in their esteem, regard, and gratitude, more exalted than my own

[91]

self-love had ever designated as my deserved rank and portion.

By 1854 Ruffin was so completely back into the life of his state that he was willing to accept the position of commissioner for the Agricultural Society to collect funds and secure members. Even the old reforming zeal returned. Within a short time he had "moved and carried" changes which "checked abuses" and which he thought saved the Society fifteen hundred dollars a year. Calls to speak before groups of farmers came from all parts of Virginia and from other states as well, giving opportunity to air his views on the problems of the day, which he did not always confine to strictly agricultural topics. His appearance before the Institute of South Carolina brought "the most cordial welcome and respectful attention," and his address, "On Opposite Results of Exhausting and Fertilizing Systems of Agriculture," struck a new note in presenting his program of changes as a means of increasing the strength of the South "against the plundering and oppressions of tariffs to protect Northern interests, compromises (so-called) to swell Northern power, pensions and bounty laws for the same purpose." He was broadening his appeal.[17]

This was also a period prolific in writing. His more recent farm experiments were described, the practices at "Marlbourne" written up, and in 1855 a series of fourteen essays were brought together in a volume under the title, *Essays and Notes on Agriculture*. Once again political articles began to go out to the newspapers, first to those in Charleston, later to those in Richmond. At first they appeared over some assumed name, with great pains taken to keep the writer's identity a profound secret. Then gradually the writer's own initials were used, and before long his name stalked forth boldly to reënforce his statements. He was under full sail again—rocks ahead!

Two events of the most personal kind belong to this period. In 1846 his wife died—the first of a series of sudden and tragic deaths in the household which were to hasten the day of retirement from active control of his estate. The second event, for the present seemingly of little importance, nevertheless left an impression which, under grief and age, was one day to rise to dominance. In February, 1840, a lifelong friend, Thomas Cocke, took his own life. A recluse, weakened by an apoplectic attack, and saddened by the trouble he thus imposed on others, he had deliberately and carefully planned his own destruction. His purpose had been accomplished through a rather ingenious deception of the family and the servants and with a daring which was in keeping with the cold reasoning with which he penned his defense in a note left behind. Ruffin had visited his friend only a few days before his death and was present a few hours afterward. So profoundly was he affected by the occurrence that he wrote a minute description of the whole affair and filed it with his papers. He ended it with these words: [17]

> I venture no comment upon this awful deed. It is not for men to judge, but for God—and God judges it in mercy! But while I cannot attempt to justify & will not try even to offer excuses in mitigation of the last & greatest offense of his life, neither will I in any manner join in the universal cry of condemnation, which in all such cases proceed not only from the moral & pious & from those who hold in reverence the laws of God, but also from those whose opinions & acts are altogether different & opposed to those of a virtuous life. When death calls me from this world, may my dread account

of sins over-balancing virtues, be not greater than that
of my self-slaughtered friend!

Years later, when the grief of self and of a broken nation
lay on his own heart, this picture in all its gruesome details
was again to take possession of his mind. Strange impressions, long hidden, would rise to become more potent in
action than the realities of the day.

But for the present, on the public side at least, Edmund
Ruffin had come to better days. He was back again in the
current of affairs which were widening out from local into
sectional and national scope. It promised him a broader
activity and renown. Yet it could only mean ultimate failure and grief. The "new agriculture," which he had helped
to build and of which "Marlbourne" was a part, had thrown
Virginia into new relationships with neighbors north and
south. It had helped to fix slavery even more firmly in
the economic structure of the region, but had shifted crops
and markets to those of the Northern farmers who were
now becoming abolitionists. It was a situation suited to the
opportunist, not one that promised much for the radical.

Furthermore, he had linked his name and interests with
the group who were striving to diversify the economic
efforts of Virginia and South Carolina for closer unity with
the whole South at the very time when his temperament
and attitudes threw him to the side of those who would
step forward *alone,* if necessary, for the preservation of the
rights of the states.

It was a strange situation. He could not lead or know
comfort in his own state; he could not, for the present at
least, expect to find those of the more extreme position
in control in South Carolina—his entry to sectional influence. His friend Hammond was in retirement, still hold-

ing his coöperationist position, but by his positive belief in the certainty of disunion in reality closer to Barnwell Rhett than to B. F. Perry or Waddy Thompson. Fate was playing strange tricks. Ruffin was being pressed forward to action with assurance of grief and disappointment because of the very conditions that his own efforts had played so large a part in creating. The course ahead might be a wider one, but it was certain to be more stormy.

*　　*　　*

So another period closed, scenes shifted, outlooks changed. Twice in Edmund Ruffin's life he grew sentimental and wrote descriptions that glow with fervor and beauty. Once, when he came down the harbor towards Charleston, the thrill of the city, with its noble spires and its river setting, moved him to poetic words. On another occasion, when as an old man he stood and looked across the fields at "Marlbourne," heavy with harvest, his words warmed and colors of rich and delicate hue glorified his description. Charleston and "Marlbourne"!

CHAPTER V

THE BIRTH OF A SOUTHERN NATIONALIST

I THINK anybody who prefers pumpkin pie to sweet potato pie suffers from a derangement of the intellect. I never take maple sirup if I can get New Orleans molasses. I maintain that a cook who deliberately puts sugar in corn bread is a menace to our national civilization. A man who would crush the mint in his mint toddy would put scorpions in a baby's bed. Sir, I am no dam' Yankee."

In these words a character in one of Irvin S. Cobb's delightful stories declared his whole-hearted allegiance to the South in the face of the fact that he had fought for four long, bitter years in the armies of the Union from 1861 to 1865. He was ignoring trifles; he was dealing with fundamentals. And, in so doing, he was not only revealing the flimsy substance from which provincialism, whether sectional or national, is made, but also making a much-needed distinction between the *Southerner,* as such, and the *Southern nationalist.*[1]

It is always difficult, in spite of the constant assumption to the contrary, to think of a land as varied as that which sweeps southward from Mason and Dixon's Line to the Gulf as ever presenting unity in either the qualities or the actions of its people. Between the Virginia capes, where settlers to a new world first came, and the wind-swept plains of far-off Texas, to which the most recent pioneer painfully pressed his way, there lay in 1850 a region as varied as the patch quilts that covered Southern beds. A land of tide-

water gentry, upland farmers and planters, mountain cabin-
eers, blue-grass herdsmen, Louisiana bayou and Mississippi
river folk—every race that contributed its blood to the colonies and every religious sect, divided from each other by
social barriers as high and as wide as the mountains and
plains that cut the physical region! Tennessee and New
Orleans; Arkansas and Charleston! Yet it was called "the
South." And in 1861 it struck for independence.

Most of the so-called "Southern characteristics" are pure
fiction. The weather, ever a willful thing in the South,
did add force to the "drawl and drag," excusing delay and
allowing a pause for conversation when there was nothing
to quarrel about; it did, perhaps, lead to a more graceful
bowing to fate, but it never destroyed the capacity for sudden or sustained action or lessened the desire for physical
well-being. Always more important than weather in giving
character to the region, moreover, was the fact that its
people were nearly all planters and farmers, living in a
rural world. If they were backward in roads and schools
and other social accumulations and if the home held a
larger place in their lives, the reason lay in a scattered population and dependence on a few great crops; if the people
were individualistic, emotional, orthodox, and conservative,
it was from the same reason, and their fellow farmers in the
Northwest were fundamentally like them.

Only two factors seem to have contributed to the making
of anything distinctly Southern—an Old World country-
gentleman ideal and the presence of negroes in large numbers. The first of these turned the talents of the South to
farming and gave the landholder position and privilege.
The country "seating" and the amusements and airs of a
gentleman which went with it, even the reverence for

women and the liking for military display, belonged to a people whose traditions were borrowed from abroad and who were struggling to reproduce an old order, not to build a new one. The second factor was more characteristically Southern. The negro as a laborer checked the inflow of other workers from Europe, keeping the original stocks pure save as they mingled in rural simplicity to form a typically American human product. He brought with him the necessity for the institution of slavery, by which a comparatively few families were surrounded by dependents, yet by which a whole region was ever threatened by a race problem of serious proportions. Perhaps, also, the negro gave to his white folks something from association, especially in a certain poise he fostered by his attitudes, but more certainly by adding to their leisure for books and association with their children and by enhancing the value of white skins regardless of the merits of their wearers.

If these things made the South and the Southerner, then they worked with enormous inequality on those who lived in the region, and their influence, at best, was vague and uncertain. It is well to speak warily of "the South" before 1850, to be quite general when referring to "Southerners." Irvin S. Cobb's old Union soldier based his claims to "belonging" on quite substantial grounds.[2]

On the other hand, *Southern nationalism* was a very real thing. The *belief* in being different from other Americans was far more important than the realities in the case, leading to jealousy, haterd, and finally to war. It was an emotion, produced by an assumption on the part of outsiders of a unity there which did not exist, by propaganda within which emphasized likenesses rather than differences and created a unity of fear where none other existed. It was the product of slow growth, brought to completion when attacks from the outside seemed to threaten those few interests common to the whole people, driving them almost against their wills into a working agreement.

The high protective tariff, endangering all rural-agricultural people, brought the first consciousness of "being different" from the dominant elements in the North and sent the first thrill of "oneness" through the South. It was an attack on all who lived by farming. Up to that time men of the great, disjointed South had been engaged in the most bitter internal conflicts—the old American struggle between older sections and newer ones that dwelt under a common government, testing whether property should rule or majorities control. "Our property imperiously demands that kind of protection which flows from the possession of power," thundered Judge Upshur in the Virginia Constitutional Convention of 1829-30; "King Numbers . . . is the legitimate sovereign of all this country," echoed back the leaders from the western part of the state. This was a conflict which knew no sectional boundaries. In it every interest that was later to be considered "Southern" was attacked by men who represented the majority of those who lived in the South. In it every weapon later used to protect a section was fashioned for service against neighbors. If the protective tariff had not struck at an interest common to a wide region, a general reaction, faint as it was in the 1820's, would not have come. Even as it was, the old enmities were plainly apparent in the struggle, and the iron and sugar interests ran counter to the popular course.[3]

The more important step in the creation of "the South" was the demand of the abolitionist for the immediate destruction of slavery. Hostility to the institution was not new, nor was it a thing foreign to the South. Some Southern men had always opposed it, and most of them had looked forward to the day when it would pass from the land. But slavery solved the perplexing race problem that the presence of so many ignorant negroes created. It made near-savages economically profitable and gave order and security even where the blacks greatly outnumbered the whites. How was it possible to free the slave without creating an intolerable race situation? How could the South get out of the frying pan without jumping into the fire? No one had been able to answer. Colonization had stirred hopes without giving satisfactory results; and then the spread of cotton had lessened the pressure by the old call for raw labor to push out the frontier. Yet up to 1820 men still talked of freedom for the slave, and few rose to defend the institution in the abstract.

But freedom for the negroes in the dim future when all dangers had been removed, granted by willing masters to their own slaves, was quite a different thing from the harsh program of a Garrison launched from a hostile industrial center. The false assumption of the capacity of the negro for immediate place in Southern society and the harsh words used on masters, implying the wish to see the racial pyramid turned from its base, brought white men of the South, high and low, shoulder to shoulder in the determination to keep the land of their fathers "a white man's country." To defend slavery was to protect the home, defend a civilization, preserve a superior race. The abolitionist had touched the second great bond that tied the straggling Southland together.[4]

But these forces, powerful as they were and assisted by differences in points of view as to the ways of life—even the comparative merits of pumpkin and sweet-potato pie, would have been insufficient if they had not become tools in the hands of politicians who did battle "in the halls of debate"; the dangers in tariff and abolition were not real enough. But the politician, North and South, sparring for advantage of person, party, or region, coined phrases and erected symbols, to the destruction of realities, which shifted the struggle from the values actually involved to one of words which stirred emotions by implying danger to "rights," to "honor," and even to "God's purposes." Southern men were soon led to think of "the North" as a single hostile force composed of "Yankees" who would destroy Southern farmers and lift the negro to social equality and ultimate control. Northerners saw the South in equal distortion. Ignorant negroes thus made to carry forward political programs on which united action was otherwise impossible! It is a way which even perfectly sincere politicians have.

In the 1840's the contest for power in the political realm centered about the old American destiny to expansion. Democrats, North and South, united for the annexation of Texas with boundaries to the Rio Grande and for the occupation of Oregon to the line 54° 40'. A more youthful element, representing the western states, crowded out the old leaders, made James K. Polk president, and ushered in a buoyant new era of widening horizons. Mexico was conquered and Texas "reannexed"; John Bull was "looked straight in the eye"—but a compromise line was drawn across Oregon. The Northwest was furious. New England, already ringing with charges of a great pro-slavery scheme in the whole expansion movement, joined them in urging the Wilmot Proviso to prohibit the extension of slavery into any lands obtained from Mexico. The politician was loose.

Slavery and expansion were to be hopelessly tangled. A fateful struggle had begun.

In all this movement, normal interests would have dictated to the older Southern regions and to those nearest the border strict opposition to the annexation of Texas. Expansion could mean only new competition in labor and crops. But outside opposition and passionate leadership at home, especially after the slavery issue was introduced, swung the South into line, save where Whig party allegiance interfered, and men who knew better "believed" that the white man's supremacy was being threatened. A right denied made an evil into a good; the use of false and irrelevant charges by a "hostile section" made necessary the arousing of the deepest fears a people were capable of knowing.

To what extent the Wilmot Proviso, at its inception, was actuated by genuine opposition to slavery is a disputed question. The men back of it, such as Hannegan of Indiana, Wentworth of Illinois, Brickerhoff of Ohio, etc., spoke openly of a "breach of faith" on the part of Southern politicians in not carrying out "the bargain of 1844" as it concerned Oregon. One of them declared that if the whole West did not go together, "there was a class of politicians who would make a deal of capital out of it," and a prominent New Yorker referred to the Wilmot group as "politico philanthropists who really have as little regard for the negro as they have for republican institutions or the constitution of the United States," which was, by inference, none at all. President Polk in those troubled days spoke of "Northern Senators . . . excited and in bad temper," "lashed into a passion" over the "bad faith of the South." A newspaper correspondent insisted that there were "few whose real aim is to guard against the extension of slavery." [5]

Yet there can be little question as to the antagonism to the extension of slavery that resulted from the raising of the issue in that form, of the genuineness of the support that plain people of the North, close to the soil and the evangelical church, gave to the cause under a leadership which made use of interests in lands and industry as well as of fear of slavery. Vague sentiments rose to the dignity of firm convictions; differences became hostilities; thousands who had been indifferent became staunch partisans.[6]

On the other hand, it is quite as difficult to discover the real attitudes of Southern leaders. One South Carolina congressman declared that he would not support Calhoun's "Address from the Southern Delegates in Congress" because the "slave question is agitated alone for party purposes, party effect." He agreed with Alexander Stephens, who referred to the whole affair as the "excitement the 'Free-Soilers' and the factionists of the South have been able to get up about the 'Niggers'," and with Joseph Lumpkin, who called it a "false issue" and insisted that his "mind was never more at ease than at present upon this subject." Robert Toombs viewed the movement as a "bold strike to disorganize the Southern Whigs." He was perhaps speaking as a partisan, but the same cannot be said of John H. Lumpkin, a staunch Democrat, who brushed aside the whole slavery issue and declared that the real differences between the factions in his party were over the tariff and the appropriations for rivers and harbors, which Polk had checked. Calhoun meanwhile was insisting that the Wilmot Proviso meant the "prostration of the white race" and the lifting of "the blacks . . . above the whites of the South in the political and social scale."[7]

The problem is again one of disentangling political motives from genuine attitudes and of tracing the interesting psychological processes by which defense mechanisms became real convictions. It is hard to say just when any large number of Southern men honestly believed that Northerners were so bad that it was impossible to live longer under the same government with them; but it is certain that in the period from 1844 to 1851 many turned Southern nationalist and accepted the notion that the farmers who owned slaves were bound for independence. Some had at first only convicted the New Englanders of gross crimes, believing with James H. Thornwell that "Abolition is a humbug. . . . Take out the Yankees and the overwhelming force of public opinion is with the South." But after 1851, when the politician had finished, a large number of honest men agreed with H. L. Benning that "it is . . . manifest that the whole North is becoming ultra Anti-Slavery." They accepted at face value J. H. Hammond's declaration that "if we do not act now, we deliberately consign our children, not our posterity, *our children* to the flames." They saw safety for the white man and his South only under a separate government.[8]

*   *   *

Of those who took extreme ground in this period no man was more certain of his position than Edmund Ruffin. He was, in spite of wide intellectual contacts, somewhat provincial. He had not traveled widely, and his type of mind easily assumed the superiority of those things with which he was familiar. With an outlook almost entirely agricultural, he had early conceived of the farmer as the guardian of all virtue and looked upon the industrial sections as hostile lands. It was, therefore, easy for him, in spite of a general lack of faith in the breed, to accept the politician's charges against the North. He was of the stuff from which the Southern nationalists were made.

Ruffin had probably been in the North but once. In 1828 he took his eldest son to New Haven to enter the school of one Dr. Dwight. The youth's description of the trip may explain why the father did not go oftener:

> We started from City Point about half past ten o'clock in the Potomac Steam Boat and in the evening a little after dark met another boat in Hampton Rhodes, which we got on board of. We arrived the next evening in Baltimore, where we did not stay half an hour. We then took another boat and went to a little town called Frenchtown where we took a stage about twelve o'clock at night and crossed over to New Castle where we arrived a little before day. This is a beautiful little village situated upon the Delaware River. We went up the river then until we reached Philadelphia, where we passed from one boat to another and kept on our Journey. After we had gone up the river some distance we took the stage a second time and rode 25 miles. We took the boat again and arrived in New York the same evening. . . . Do you not call that fast travelling? Going from City Point to New York, a distance of 500 miles in 58 hours?

Beyond the fact that the father lost his luggage in New York by leaving it in a cab in the hurry to reach a theater in the evening, we know nothing of his experiences. If he ever ventured farther north than Baltimore on any future occasion, he has left no record of his travels. "New England" and "the North" were largely names of places indistinct enough in detail to become carriers of any notions of them he might find it necessary or convenient to form.

Just when he began to shape a definite picture of the region and to contrast it with his own we cannot say. The passage of tariff legislation stirred him as an agriculturist to sharp complaints, with inferences regarding the selfish attitudes of industrial groups but with no general condemnation of the "Yankee" as such. That he early recognized differences between his own general outlook on life and that of those who dwelt to the North we cannot doubt. His son's letters from New Haven told him often of boyish struggles between students from the two parts of the country, over ways of speech, the observance of the Sabbath, and even codes of honor. When praising Connecticut the youth seemingly recognized some violation of propriety and expressed a fear that his father might be offended, but nowhere indicated any knowledge of open hostility. It seems quite clear that Ruffin's early attitudes merely reflected the provincialism of a rural man.

Certainly, not until the abolitionist attacked slavery did such differences as had been earlier recognized begin to indicate superiority or inferiority. Charges of criminal intent and practice in holding slaves, followed by agitation which threatened masters and their families with destruction, first brought "knowledge" of the "ignorance and dishonesty" of Northerners. In 1836 Ruffin wrote of the abolition agitation: [9]

> There will be no lack of such effort . . . as long as the most selfish and base interests are to be best subserved by words and acts which go forth in the guise of pure morality, religion, and distorted love for the human race. They who rob and murder, professedly in the name of virtue and religion, and for the glory of God, are an hundredfold more dangerous than ordinary villains who pretend no better motives than the love of gain. . . . From our slaves of themselves, and from any

political effects of the institution of slavery, as it exists in the South, we have *nothing* to fear . . . ,—but the South, *and the Union,* have everything to fear, (and danger far greater than from servile insurrections) from the restless, mad, and *sustained* action of Northern abolitionists.

By the early forties he was writing of a Northern chemist as being "able, but a true trading Yankee withal. . . . I do not suspect him of reporting his actual analysis falsely, to bring other customers, but I do suspect him of being willing to select and test unfair specimens of peculiar character." In September, 1845, he declared: "We shall have to defend our rights, by the strong hand, against the Northern abolitionists, and perhaps against the tariffites. I certainly hope it will be done, if necessary." A few years later, when attending a United States Agricultural Society meeting in Washington, he was introduced to three gentlemen from Massachusetts who welcomed him "so cordially and in so complimentary a manner" that he felt "a little conscience struck" because of his "general dislike of all Yankees." The transformation was complete. There was a North and there was a South, and they were hostile lands! [10]

The process by which this change had come was a gradual one, moving along with events in his own state. In the early period Virginia had her share of those who disliked slavery, but as time passed most men had accepted it as a necessary evil, while a few even rose to resist attacks. The Nat Turner Insurrection, however, made the issue acute, and the discussion it produced revealed a sharp difference of opinion between the eastern and western parts of the state, the one defending the institution, the other seizing the occasion to urge its extinction. Argument, as usual, only served to clarify the ideas of each and to fix both parties more firmly in their original positions. The defenders of the institution envisaged with fear the negro problem involved in any scheme of emancipation and drew together in the declaration of its positive good; the opponents, busied only with a slave problem, lacked the emotional force of their neighbors and were unable to make headway against them. Soon the opponents lost numbers by emigration to the West and suffered from the extreme positions and actions of the radical Northern abolitionists. The pro-slavery group thus gained in solidarity and influence, weaving slavery and states' rights together and bringing Virginia into closer unity with a wider South. Yet real division remained, and party allegiance, more often than not, proved more powerful than social or sectional interests. Only the more extreme thinkers comprehended the larger forces at work in the nation's life.

Edmund Ruffin followed this general course with only his usual personal variations. As a young idealist he had considered slavery an evil to be eliminated in good time. Only gradually did he rise to its defense. The *Farmers' Register* in all its ten volumes contains little on the subject, and that little is sane and moderate. Not until he made his South Carolina connections after 1840 did he begin to take what might in any way be considered a radical stand. True, he had absorbed Professor Dew's great defense of slavery when it appeared in 1832, but he had published alongside of his review of the work in the first issue of his journal a review of Harrison's unfriendly *Review of the Slave Question,* insisting that it was a duty to consider both sides of such a vital problem. In the next few years a more positive note appeared. In 1836 was published, with editorial comment, James Madison's description of the failure of Richard Randolph's negroes, when freed, to maintain or propagate themselves, and in reprinting an article on the results of emancipation in the West Indies Ruffin went out of his way to denounce the abolitionists although admitting their sincerity. He was moving forward with his section to more extreme attitudes.[11]

Yet, even then, banks and banking evils were paramount. Local interests and personalities were the real disturbers, exciting most of his emotional outbursts and attracting most of his thrusts. Moreover, the revival of the tariff controversy in 1842, combined with the slavery conflict rising out of Texas and expansion, touched him largely through South Carolina rather than his own state. Hammond in particular he followed, accepting the idea of disunion well in advance of most Virginians, but doing so rather as one not directly concerned save as a friend of South Carolina who was urging a principle in which every Southern gentleman should be interested. In 1845 he told Hammond that his trust was in South Carolina to resist both the tariff and the abolitionists, "for though part of our people would be as zealous and determined as yours, unfortunately we are divided on both points." But he was not greatly excited about conditions. In fact, they became a matter of personal responsibility only as he dropped the bitter feelings against his own neighbors, found himself mistaken about their hatred, and adjusted himself comfortably again to his own immediate surroundings. He seems then to have transferred his "feelings" to Yankees and found in them a substitute for enemies who had vanished at home. For the first time those who lived in another section became the foes who were set on thwarting all that he held dear.

Extreme Southern ground was fully reached only with

the Wilmot Proviso. The politician, playing his game, there presented to the radical, ever sincere and deadly in earnest, the distorted clash and overdrawn arguments which in new hands were to become "the irrepressible conflict" and "eternal principles." They had stirred deep economic and social apprehensions in order to produce political unity for the clash with fellow politicians. They expected to fight out the issues in political maneuvers with opponents who had done the same. There justice would be secured. But they had gone too far. Ruffin had taken them at their word. The sections were fundamental enemies. A crusade was in order. In this spirit his keen mind set to work to reduce the elements in the struggle to an acceptable pattern, to reason out the steps by which forces ever hostile had followed a course in which "the North" had constantly checked and cheated "the South" and made necessary either a righteous revolt or an humble yielding. Years later he boasted that he "was the first, and for some years the only man in Virginia who was both bold and disinterested enough to advocate the dissolution of the union between the northern and slave-holding states." [12]

Suddenly, out of a taciturnity which to now had yielded only agricultural wisdom, there appeared in the newspapers of Richmond and Charleston, a series of articles over the signature, "A Virginian," which indicated the radical at work, the propagandist set free. "Concessions to fanatics never satisfies fanaticism," was his text; the South on the defensive, the North in aggression, that the theme. [13]

"If Northern abolition action has goaded and driven us to be *also* fanatical," he declared, "our fanaticism has been, and is altogether, defensive; while that of the North has been throughout aggressive on our most vital interests, and actively hostile to our constitutional and just rights." This aggression, he thought, had begun with the exclusion of slavery by the Missouri Compromise—an "unjust and unconstitutional restriction" which should "have been resisted . . . to the last extremity" because it became a "precedent for . . . like restrictions . . . to cover the later acquired territory of Oregon" and California. It was a concession to fanatics who now demanded the Wilmot Proviso for the prohibition of Southern expansion into any new corner of the territories. Fanaticism would never be satisfied until slavery was at an end. There was but one "defense or means of safety left"—"separation from, and independence of, the present Union." It was a step ultimately to be taken. How much better to have taken it in 1820 before "the hundreds of millions which have since been drawn from the South, by legislation to pamper the prosperity of the North" had weakened her. Delay only meant loss of more "wealth and strength."

"Through all the long course of Northern aggressions on the rights of the slaveholding states," he argued, "the latter have merely remonstrated and promised and threatened to resist." It was, after all, simply "repeated submission" until "the formerly small and despised party of avowed Abolitionists" had "so much increased, that it already wielded the political power [as to the question of slavery] of all the Northern States." No aspirant to popular favor there dared to oppose it. A condition had been reached in which for a measure of political strength there was no longer need of distinguishing between the majority of the public men and the abolition party *par excellence*. Regardless of differences in motives, their actions against Southern rights were now one and the same. The purpose of all was plain—to "confine slavery to its present limits, extinguish it in the District of Columbia," and destroy it in every place possible under a "lax construction of our constitutional guarantees."

In the end, under such a program, slavery would be restricted to such a degree that in most places in the South the negroes would outnumber the whites and turn the region into a Jamaica or a Haiti. The North, meanwhile, would grow until its power was great enough to change the constitution by the regular process of amendment, to the "utter prostration of the South" by the "speedy emancipation of all slaves and their advancement to equal political privileges with their former owners." It was the old appeal to the white man! The final argument to a race!

The remedy proposed was "TO SUBMIT NO LONGER." True men must refuse to be "continually insulted and derided by Northern politicians and Northern publications, as braggarts and boasters who will not dare to defend what we claim to be our rights." Dissolve the "existing Union" with the "so-called Northern brethren—actual enemies and depredators!" It was not a "mad-dog" proposal. "The movers and abettors of the abolition crusade" were "the true and only disunionists." They had always been the "acting and assailing party"; the South had always been "passive."

His program stated, Ruffin next considered the consequences of such action. He refused to believe that a war would follow the break-up of the Union. The South would not make war, and the greedy North would not "waste millions in dollars and men to gratify the abolitionists." But if it should come, the South would have little to fear. Slave labor would release all white men to fight. "In case of an invasion then in a few hours a body of men under arms amounting to half the number of all of military age could be gathered, half of them mounted on their own horses." And it would be an intelligent force, too! "This advantage," he added, "as well as many others, social, intellectual and moral, we owe to our institution of slavery." The confidence of the gentleman! The contempt of the gentleman for those in trading houses!

And the advantages of independence? The new nation would control the mouth and the lower course of the Mississippi River, along which the trade of the "Great Valley" must flow; would have a monopoly of cotton, the "basis of the prosperity of Europe and the North itself"; and would profit alone from the tobacco and rice and grain now forming with cotton a large proportion of the export of the United States. An Army of farmers, freed from paying tribute to Northern manufactories, would carry their own produce, buying and selling in markets of their own choosing—in fact, keeping for themselves the wealth that under the existing union had "gone to build New York, Boston," and the other great cities of the North. What a glorious future to be forced upon a people as the alternative to "degradation and final prostration . . . to glut the appetite for power and prey of the Northern political abolition party."

Then, to enforce good with evil, the spell of fear by the "last appeal" reiterated in enlarged forms. The Southern states under abolition rule and the certain freedom of the blacks were pictured as sinking first to the "condition of Jamaica, then as certainly [to] the still deeper degradation of Guadeloupe, and later (if indeed this shall not be induced earlier in the series), [to] the bloody horrors of St. Domingo, and then the extinction of the white race, and the brutal

[113]

barbarism of the black." These results were to be produced with "no difference of operation worth consideration, between the action of the rabid abolitionists of the Garrison and Giddings school and the great body of the Northern people and their representatives, who profess at least to respect the constitutional rights of the South, while their votes were working for their destruction." The whole North with a single purpose! All its people abolitionists and haters of the South!

On the practical question of the admission of California, Ruffin proposed the drawing of her southern boundary at the line 36° 30', permitting the formation of a free state of reduced size, but yielding not another inch to the "insatiable grasping disposition of the North." If the "political Judas, Seward," and his kind refused this settlement, it would prove their unfairness and drive California to independence, a settlement affording the South more than she could otherwise get. For the South stood to lose, whatever occurred. California's gold would only enrich Northern enemies; new states formed by later division of the territory would be free states. The true policy was simply to prevent gains by the North.

The reception that such doctrines met in Virginia in 1850 was not enthusiastic. Although ready to talk rather strongly of her rights, she yet moved on an economic foundation which was improving too rapidly to permit extreme action. She had, moreover, developed a political situation in which party division and an eastern-western conflict operated to check agreement. Some Whigs had followed Tyler in 1842 in his split with the party over its nationalistic attitudes, and some Democrats in the eastern part of the state had gathered under the lead of R. M. T. Hunter, well ahead of their party, in defense of states' rights and slavery. But Richmond, with a new economic outlook, was at the same time petitioning for protective tariffs, and the western part of the state, where the strength of the Democratic Party lay, was nationalistic as well as hostile to slavery as an economic system. The Democrats achieved temporary unity under the call of "Polk and Texas," even Thomas Ritchie following Calhoun; and in 1847 the election of Hunter and Mason to the Senate as Calhoun men seemed to indicate that Virginia was moving to closer relations with the South. "Old Virginia is now sounder than for twenty years on the great principles which you hold dear," wrote Robert G. Scott to Calhoun in April, 1845. "Texas and the Tariff have this Spring done the work." [14] But it was a harmony more apparent than real, as was shown by the narrow margin by which Cass carried the state in 1848, largely on the basis of family connections with western Virginia, and by the sharp western reaction against the positive resolutions of the legislature in condemnation of the Wilmot Proviso and the sending of delegates to the Nashville Convention. Whereas early in 1850 the Richmond *Enquirer* was declaring "that the two great political parties" had "ceased to exist in the southern states so far as the present slavery issue is concerned," and the legislature was shouting for "the preservation of the Union, if we can, the preservation of our own rights if we cannot," by the time the Compromise was offered all but the radicals were deeming "it a duty to tell South Carolina that the people were unwilling to take any step to destroy the integrity of the Union." Thus again Edmund Ruffin, consistent and logical and independent of parties, was laboring in a hopeless cause. For the present he was far in advance of his native state.

One further step marked the first public efforts of this Southern nationalist. In constant correspondence and contact with J. H. Hammond, he had followed closely the 1850 movement in South Carolina, finding in its advanced character his own desires expressed. The effort there in 1848 to start an independent Southern party had met with his approval, and resistance "at any and every hazard" to the Wilmot Proviso suited his own temper. Favoring the group who were urging separate state action, he had watched the two Nashville conventions at work and had given whole-hearted approval when South Carolina, holding the Compromise of 1850 unsatisfactory, had proceeded to call a state convention and to elect delegates to the stillborn Montgomery Convention. He prayed that the grand old Palmetto State would go out of the Union, alone if necessary. Yet when the coöperationists, Charleston leading, chose their own delegates to Montgomery and the state convention spent its radicalism in mere words, he saw what most outsiders then and most historians since have failed to see, that both parties in South Carolina were in fact secessionists, differing only as to the best method of procedure. He thereupon evolved a scheme to capitalize the situation and at the same time set himself to make the real facts in the case clear to his own state and the larger South.[15]

Writing as if from South Carolina to the Richmond papers and as if from Virginia to the Charleston papers, he launched his campaign.[16] On the Carolinians he urged the necessity of making clear the true meaning of their recent action, interpreted in the Northern abolition press and by all enemies of Southern rights as indicating submission to "the (so-called) Compromise measures." "I speak of the opinions of others," he said, "not of mine. I . . . do not need to be told that much the greater number of Co-operationists are true and strenuous sustainers of Southern rights, and as much in favor of secession as are the immediate Secessionists." He pleaded with the triumphant group to adopt some mode of reaching the ultimate great object of all: "The question of immediate secession was merely one of expediency. That question has been settled, and is no longer before us. The next question is what measure can be adopted instead which will come nearest to avoiding the dangers and evils imputed to immediate secession by its opposers, and which shall be nearest to securing the benefits which were expected by its friends." That measure, as he saw it, was one he had long ago conceived of as the best and which he now found embodied in an ordinance published under the title, "A Plan for State Action." It consisted of South Carolina withdrawing her representatives from Congress, taking no part in presidential elections, and having "no other voluntary participation in the Federal Government." Such a plan would lose the state nothing that was not already lost; would prevent the use of force by the central government, because all taxes would be paid and all Federal laws obeyed; and would "keep their flags flying" and resistance alive until others came to her support or the North did justice.

Such a move would do more. It would stir and enhearten "every anti-Compromiser out of South Carolina." "I, claiming to be one of the most ardent and earnest among them," he wrote, "deem the speedy and effective action of South Carolina in this respect to be all-important to maintain the existence and insure the increase of the supporters of Southern rights in other states. We look to South Carolina as our leader in this holy war of defense of all that is worth preserving to the South. So long as she shall contend with success, we, her allies, will fight for the same cause. If she submits or even appears to submit, her allies will lose all moral power and cannot longer continue a hopeless struggle."

In his articles to the Virginia press Ruffin attempted to make clear the fact that the parties in South Carolina were "the *immediate secessionists* and the *co-operation secessionists*." His mission was to hearten all true friends of the South, to check distorted reports and inferences drawn from the recent victory of the coöperationists, and to show the anti-Compromise group in Virginia that their leader was still true to the cause. He explained his "Plan of Action"— his "armed truce"—and declared that if "the good people of Christiana and Syracuse, and thousands like them in other parts of the North," continued their abolition efforts, they would "exhaust the remaining patience . . . of the acquiescing majorities of the Southern states" and bring them one after the other to the South Carolina position "for a virtual dissolution of the now existing Union."

But South Carolina did not adopt the plan. The Charleston interests (some said "the controlling interests of trade") swung around into line with Mississippi and Georgia, which had decided not to press their rights (if they had any) for the present. The conservatives, even though they represented every shade of opinion from intense love of the Union to mere suspended action on asserted rights, had triumphed, leaving the radical either to bide his time or to consider all lost. Ruffin was not certain which to do.

A few years later a Southern nationalist opened a letter in the handwriting of James H. Hammond and read:

> I am as sick of politics as you are. It has become everywhere, in South Carolina too, . . . a small game played by small men with the keenness of desperation. If you want something to relieve you—a treat such as you never had and can never have again—get Mr. Calhoun's book, and read it. I have just devoured it. Since Aristotle there has been nothing like it. I repeat . . . it will be the Text Book of coming ages, I know that it must be.

A short time later Ruffin made two entries in his diary. One of them was to the effect that "Old Ritchie" had accepted from Henry Clay a bribe of one hundred thousand dollars in government printing as the price of his support of the Compromise of 1850; the other was to the effect that New England's "vices and crimes have been eulogized as if virtues, and their actual merits have been magnified tenfold by the general system of Yankee self-laudation, built upon falsehood." He concluded that the region had been settled by "fanatics and bigots in religion," dominated by a hierocracy "more despotic and oppressive and unjust and cruel in its exercise of power than most of the modern and acknowledged arbitrary monarchies of Europe, and moved by selfish material interests even in the American Revolution." [17]

The process was complete. A Southerner had become a Southern nationalist.

CHAPTER VI

THE PRO-SLAVERY ARGUMENT

TWICE in the history of the South, slavery was a "positive good." In Virginia in the last half of the seventeenth century, when glutted tobacco markets and governmental restrictions brought the colonial planters to the verge of ruin, men gave up the expensive indentured servant and substituted the negro working under slavery. By expanding their farms into plantations and introducing division of labor for the simplification and specialization of tasks, they were able to secure the economies of large-scale production with inferior workers and to develop a laboring force of greater permanency than indenture had ever permitted.

Meanwhile, amid the swamps of the Carolinas, where white men sickened and died, the patient negro was finding a second home on the continent. There his labor laid the foundations for the coming of rice and indigo plantations and for the glory that was to be Charleston's. Before long even lesser men were making use of "a few hands" to round out the family's efforts; and in time the struggling settlements in far-off Georgia were demanding that the restrictions upon slavery set by pious founders should be repealed. The negro in turn prospered under the Southern sun, and white men and women learned to love him. Slavery rendered ignorant Africans economically profitable and solved the race problem that the presence of a dangerous foreign element created. It was apparently a happy solution of a pressing situation.

Throughout the early part of the eighteenth century the black flood thus started poured in. The Royal African Company, with great advantages over its rivals after 1713, eagerly gathered from the interior of the Dark Continent negroes who had been captured in wars or were already held in bondage and who had been carried by native traders in long coffles through the jungles to their trading stations on the coast. There were well-built Coromantee from the Gold Coast, proud and capable; Mandingoes from Senegambia with almost as much quality; Eboes, with yellow tinge in eyes and skins, from the Slave Coast; Whydahs and thick-lipped Gaboons from the middle and southern regions. Some traders attempted to keep the tribes separate, and some communities developed a special preference for certain groups, but the average Southern man, when they had become his slaves, failed to perceive differences and came to think of all as just "negroes" with the usual human variations.

From the stations on the coast of Africa, slave ships, crowded with decks too shallow to permit standing and jammed with a human cargo bound into mass by chains, sought the trade-wind course to the west for speed that might lessen the suffering and death that cheapened their precious freight. Gaunt ships with bare board decks cleansed with vinegar; stifling tropical heat; filth and stench; agony and death to men bound fast to the unafflicted; contagion and brutality until those of spirit courted death if chance permitted—a long, steady stream out of African misery, the slaves came toward the great unknown land of toil which lay somewhere ahead. A people were beginning emotional experiences deep and fundamental enough to give to the new continent, along with the first rugged pioneers who battled the wilderness, song and story and tradition alone worthy in lasting human values.

It was the means of saving the kingdom of tobacco and making that of rice, of establishing the colonial South on firm foundations. It was more, for the North too found slavery good, and a raw continent, blessed with all save capital and labor, believed that God had sent these poor souls hither to help in building the great new land for His glory.

Again, a hundred and fifty years later (1820-30), when the cotton wave was rolling west and Northern factors and tariff-burdened supplies took the profits of planting, the call for negro slaves grew loud, and attacks on the institution of slavery by Northern abolitionists brought those who lived by its profits and under its racial shadow to the second declaration of its good.

The need for labor in the fresh interior was indeed great, and the promise in cotton was enough to set another black stream flowing west. The negro constituted a section's only labor supply. Expansion was dependent upon him. This time caravans of healthy, laughing men and women, most of them having been given the choice of remaining amid old surroundings or joining in the trek, wended their way overland with "the Master" and his family—some on foot, some in carriages, some in clumsy, canvas-covered wagons, all eager for adventure and a new life in a new land. Tents to sleep in; well-cooked food in abundance; paternal care for the sick; a century and a half of understanding between blacks and whites to ease the way!

Or again the slave trader and his coffle, not unlike the

first in Africa save in the quality of its human links, raised high by the cruel law of survival, apt to break forth in Christian song or Christian curses, plodded westward or crowded the ships that set out from Norfolk or Charleston toward Mobile or New Orleans.

Cheap labor in cotton fields was a necessity for building new commonwealths—a fact, not a theory. It needed to be justified only when questioned. The abolitionists of the North required an answer. And when it came, it was positive.

*　　*　　*

In between these periods, under waning profits and the growing talk of human rights which the Revolutionary struggle engendered, many prominent Southern leaders condemned the holding of men in bondage, joining with others to check the slave trade and the expansion of slavery into the Northwest Territory and speaking with confidence of the temporary character of its existence among them.

But here and there, persistent enough to indicate what would have happened under any real threat, came the positive assertion of the benefits of the institution and the quick defense against criticism. In fact, so clearly had the whole pro-slavery argument been stated before 1830 that we seem justified in saying that it would have been forthcoming in its most forceful form at any time it became necessary to repel really serious attacks. It is a false doctrine that holds that profits in cotton alone produced the defense of slavery; some men always believed it right in theory and in practice and needed only a serious threat to cause them to state their position for public consumption. It was the attacks on the institution that produced its defense, not its profits.

Reaction against Jefferson's doctrines of equality, objections to Quaker abolition petitions, and the frank discussion stirred by the Missouri Compromise all marked a steady drift away from Revolutionary attitudes and a tendency to revalue the facts in Southern life. Men like William Smith, Edwin Holland, Bernard Romans, Timothy Ford, and John Drayton had early come to the defense of slavery with arguments which forecast those of the later period. Smith defended the institution on the floor of Congress in 1820, and Holland issued in 1822 a pamphlet which touched upon every defense later to be offered by Southern men in "refutation" of "Northern calumnies." In 1825 Whitemarsh B. Seabrook openly proclaimed slavery a good, and a year later Dr. Richard Furman and Edward Brown called on both the Scriptures and history to prove its justice. Brown wrote: "Slavery has ever been the stepping ladder by which countries have passed from barbarism to civilization. . . . It appears, indeed, to be the only state capable of bringing the love of independence and of ease, inherent in man, to the discipline and shelter necessary to his physical wants. . . . Hence the division of mankind into grades, and the mutual dependence and relations which result from them constitute the very soul of civilization."

The same year Thomas Cooper wrote his defense, calling attention to the fact that the Bible did not forbid slavery and insisting that the slave's condition compared very favorably with that of the poorer classes in other countries. It was a much needed suggestion, for men then, as now, failed to think of the negro as constituting the lower element in Southern life, with social and economic returns to be measured as much by that fact as by his position in slavery. Three years later C. C. Pinkney wrote: "That slavery as it exists here is a greater and more universal evil than befalls the poor in general, we are not prepared to admit"; and Governor Stephen D. Miller declared to the legislature of South Carolina that "Slavery is not a national evil; on the contrary it is a national benefit. . . . Upon this subject it does not become us to speak in a whisper, betray fear, or feign philanthropy."[1]

Yet it was not until William Lloyd Garrison, proclaiming slavery a crime and slaveholders criminals, demanded the immediate emancipation of the slave, and Nat Turner's insurrection flared up in Virginia seemingly in reply, that the real attitude of the South on the institution began to find expression. It was then that Thomas R. Dew of William and Mary College, in his *Review of the Debate in the Virginia Legislature of 1831 and 1832,* penned the classic to which all others who would break a lance turned for power and inspiration.[2]

The good professor looked back into history to find "not a race of freemen, but of slaves," to see mankind toiling up the grooves of civilization on the backs of those in bondage. In fact, he had "no hesitation in affirming that Slavery" had been, "perhaps, the principal means of impelling forward" the human race. When captives in war were put to work instead of being slaughtered, or when the possession of property by the few or famine or crime gave some the power to compel others to toil, then progress to permanent abodes, freedom and respect for women, and leisure and dignifying responsibility for gentlemen developed to the advantage of all concerned. If the domestication of animals marked a stage in the evolution of human society, then how much greater the step when restless, idle, wandering man was tamed and rendered "fit for labor."

Furthermore, he could find nothing in either the Old

or the New Testament "to show that slavery when once introduced, ought, at all events, to be abrogated, or that the master [committed] . . . any offense in holding slaves." Nor could he accept the notion that slavery was in conflict with the republican spirit. Rather he found that, by assigning the menial tasks to an excluded class, it gave greater equality among those above—Greece and Rome proving the point.

And practical considerations reënforced theory and history. For no scheme of emancipation yet offered promised anything but ill for both masters and slaves. To free and deport the negro back to Africa would be but to invite his ruin in an environment for which long residence in America had completely unfitted him; to free him and leave him in the South would be as ruinous. He would not work, and if he would, he could not compete with the whites, condemned still to be a servant, "virtually a slave," without any of the benefits now enjoyed in his master's care. Moreover, to free him with compensation to the owners would bankrupt the government, and without payment would destroy the masters. Slavery, from any practical viewpoint, was the lesser of many, many evils.

Here were the foundations upon which others were to build. The origins of slavery had to be enlarged to include the curse of Canaan—even the "Fall in the Garden" with the negro in the rôle of the snake, and its benefits had to be widened in order fully to demonstrate the superiority of a stratified agricultural society over a free industrial order. But, in the main, later defenses were enlargements and variations of the theme as stated by the first great spokesman. John C. Calhoun, Chancellor Harper, George Fitzhugh, J. H. Hammond, Thornton Stringfellow, Josiah Nott, and others, following after Dew, rounded out the complete defense by which the South justified itself, at least to its own satisfaction, in continuing the institution of slavery and even in expanding it. They wove a web of logic which is hard to break. They turned it into a song of praise for the civilization wherein property ruled and "superior faculties and knowledge" received due recognition. It became the social philosophy of the Southern nationalist. It made slavery the cornerstone of the Southern Confederacy.[3]

*   *   *

Of course, Edmund Ruffin had opinions on slavery. And it goes without saying that his pen was early at its service. Rumors of negro uprisings flashed through his neighborhood, proving always to be false but leaving a keen sense of the horrors that the abolitionists were about to loose upon the heads of his people. At first he was uncertain. Then the sectional conflict of the 1840's closed his hitherto open mind. The desire to see both sides of the question vanished. A gentleman must strike back in defense of all that was Southern and declare it good. Two and three times he read over the writings of Dew and Fitzhugh, then turned to Bledsoe, Fletcher, Armstrong, Stringfellow, etc., gradually making the stock defenses of slavery from nature, history, and the Bible his own and strengthening and adding to them by his own thinking. As a result, when he began to give public expression to his opinions, his writings were in part a summary of the works of others and in part an original contribution to the defense of his section and her peculiar interests.

He began, like other Southerners, with the understanding that he was dealing with a practical social-economic situation, not an abstract theory. The negro was first of all and always a negro and secondly a laborer, constituting the common working element in a great rural section. His present and his future had to be considered from both of these angles. Was he, or was he not, better off under slavery both as a negro and as a laborer than his kind in Africa or in the North or in Europe? What was the status of the negro in his native jungles or in the wider world into which he had been transplanted and given the opportunities for development? Had he shown the capacity freely and independently to carry forward all that white men of the nineteenth century had evolved in complex social-economic-political organization? Was he as a slave worse off than those who occupied the lower rounds of life and toil in other societies? And if he were freed, what about the effects on the region of which he constitued so large an element? As Edward A. Pollard said later when freedom was a reality, "In the North, the question of Negro reconstruction . . . may be a dull and distant speculation. But the South is daily crucified upon it." [4]

In the second place, Ruffin understood slavery not as a relationship in which one man was given the power over another to the extent of being "absolute master of his life and fortune," but as one in which the owner had a right only to the slave's labor. It was a sort of contract in which one man owed his work and the other owed economic support and accepted the responsibility to society in part for the conduct of the other. He knew that the negro was protected in his larger personal rights as a human being by the same laws that protected white men and by the even more powerful forces of public opinion and personal affection which assured him, in almost all cases, of fair treatment in hours and person, as well as in food, shelter, and clothing. There were abuses, of course. Some men abused even their wives and children and took advantage of those who fell under their authority in any way. But no sane man would condemn all marriage and all employment on that score. As a going concern he knew slavery to be quite a different thing from what the abolitionists, who in most cases had never seen a slave or a master, imagined it to be on the mistaken assumption of the owner's complete power over the negro. He assumed, and it was probably true, that the negro's health, virtue, and life were as safe under this system of employment as they would have been under any other in which simple folk were thrown into close personal relations with those upon whom they were economically dependent. He pitied factory girls. He smiled at the stories of discontented slaves. Sometimes he honestly felt that the slave had all the best of the bargain with the white man, and then he warmed with the thought of himself in the rôle of philanthropist caring for his black children, who would suffer if he did not accept his responsibility. He thought ever of the race problem involved in the situation and of the more important question of how the human race was to be evolved to higher good as comprehended in the term, "a superior civilization."

His writings on the subject consist primarily, but not entirely, of four pamphlets enlarged and developed from articles published in such periodicals as *DeBow's Review, The South,* the *Weekly Day-Book,* and the *Southern Planter.* The first, "The Influence of Slavery, or of its Absence, on Manners, Morals, and Intellect," grew out of an address to the Virginia State Agricultural Society delivered in 1852; the second and most important, "The Political Economy of

[129]

Slavery," appeared early in 1858; the third, "African Colonization Unveiled," was completed the same year and reprinted by DeBow during the following spring and summer; the last, "Slavery and Free Labor Described and Compared," published in both the *Weekly Day-Book* in New York and the *Southern Planter* in Richmond, belongs to the year 1859.

All of these pamphlets were printed by the thousands, sometimes at the author's expense, sometimes with the aid of others, and scattered widely by use of the franking privileges of such men as J. H. Hammond, W. O. Goode, J. M. Mason, and Thomas Ruffin. They were placed on the desks of all senators and representatives in Washington and mailed out to governors and public men both of the North and of the South. Whether the recipients read them or not and what they thought of them we do not know, but the author modestly confessed, when he re-read them in 1864, to be "gratified and surprised at the ability shown in the discussion of these subjects." The reader of to-day will not quarrel greatly with his estimate of their quality or think him unduly prejudiced in his comment. They are worthy of a gentleman's mind.[5]

As to the origins of slavery, Ruffin followed Dew back into history to find it "existing as early . . . as historical records furnish any information" and "to have been born of the dread of work" inherent in the "reckless, wretched drones and cumberers of the earth" who predominate in all primitive societies, making "forced labor" the necessary concomitant to any improvement. Consequently, as soon as society outgrew the strictly family form, the strong put the weak to work as slaves, and war gave captives, and crime and debt provided outcasts who toiled under compulsion.

It was thus that progress was made toward higher levels, wealth accumulated, leisure afforded "to cultivate mental improvement and refinement of manners," lifting people originally barbarous to the heights attained by Egypt, Greece, and Rome. Without slavery, there could never have been enough work voluntarily given to have lifted a single primitive people above the level of the North American Indians, who remained at those stages fixed by the returns from spasmodic hunting and the more regular toil of their women folk in the fields.

But slavery not only made advancement possible, it sustained culture when once achieved. All civilization, even in its most advanced forms, rests upon some kind of exploitation of the many by the few. The necessity for compulsion to procure the labor essential to highest development does not pass. When personal pressure by the master upon the slave no longer suffices, then "want" appears to drive the worker on under the direction of those who control the capital in land and machinery by the use of which men must live. Always some were enjoying leisure and refinement by "consuming their fellows." Fitzhugh had labeled it "Cannibals All."

This latter condition is reached when there are more laborers than are needed. It is then no longer profitable to own the workers, for want drives them into competition for the jobs by which they can eke out an existence and the capitalist can secure them for less than the cost of maintaining his slaves, trusting to society to care for them in sickness and old age by charity. All "free society" tends toward this "pauper slavery." It is simply a condition in which "the master" in a new form obtains the greatest returns for himself and his class, and the laborer, under new compulsion, receives less than under personal slavery, where care and supplies are his, regardless of conditions, to the end of his days.

Such was the status of the English factory workers under the industrial régime, such the end toward which the factory hands of New England were moving. The final stages had been postponed in our North only by the abundance of free lands in the great West, which drew off the surplus workers and checked the power of the employers to reduce wages. But "whenever the valuable vacant lands shall have been all settled upon, and there will be no longer sufficient inducements for emigration; and when by the retaining and crowding of population, the supply of labor shall (as is inevitable) greatly exceed the demand, then in New England, as already has been effected in Old England, *slavery to want* will be established rigidly, and in the form most oppressive and destructive to the laborers, but the most profitable of all slavery to the employers, to capitalists." Here was the iron law of wages clearly stated. It was an indictment of free society under capitalism and competition which was enough to make the factory worker pause to think and the factory owner reach out a sympathetic hand toward the masters of the South.[6]

As Ruffin saw it, there were but two escapes from this course of development, socialism and negro slavery. The first advocated "the association of labor in some form or other" to check the tyranny of machines and the "evils of society arising from the starving competition for labor." It aimed to preserve the benefits of large-scale production and associated labor, but to put an end to "wage slavery" and the unfair distribution of returns by social control or ownership of the agencies of production. Its doctrines were correct.

Associated labor and mass production were more economical; the workers under competition did not receive their just share—in fact, not even enough to make them the most efficient laborers. Yet socialism had failed wherever tried because it destroyed the individual initiative so essential to any undertaking and lacked the efficiency which self-interest gave in private business.

The second escape, negro slavery, offered all the advantages of socialism in associated production, affording the laborer care in sickness and old age, as well as an abundant supply of the necessaries of life for himself and his family at all times. It lacked the injustice of the earlier systems of slavery because the negro was an inferior, benefited under white guidance as he could never be if left free—a menial filling the position for which nature had intended him. Moreover, it corrected "the great and fatal defect" of all socialistic plans in a single ruling power actuated by all the driving force possible under an individualistic society. Food, machinery, and other supplies purchased in quantity for economy; cooking, washing, care for the children or for the sick, community enterprises; division and supervision of labor—what more could be asked for efficiency? And yet labor freed from the worry and losses that encumber the free worker, and the master permitted the "leisure and opportunities for much social intercourse" for the maintenance of culture! In fact, as Ruffin phrased it, "In the institution of domestic slavery, and in that only, are most completely realized the dreams and sanguine hopes of the socialistic school of philanthropists." [7]

The emphasis placed on *negro* slavery implied, as has been said, some peculiar advantages that lifted Southern society to a superior place among civilizations. To begin with, the negro himself had profited there to an unusual degree by close association with the most cultured class on the continent. He had been Christianized to an extent never possible if he had remained in Africa. In 1855 there were in all the "heathen churches" of the world only 180,000 members. In the Methodist Church, South, alone there were 175,000 negro members, and in all the churches of the South nearly twice as many. Negro slavery was the world's greatest missionary movement.[8]

In the second place, the negro had been saved from a most cruel servitude in Africa. With all its horrors "the middle passage" could not match the brutality of the native masters or that of the captors in African warfare. The negro child born in the South looked forward to a degree of comfort and personal development never attainable by even the few in the old life. They were starting up a comparatively short ladder to civilization. They acquired habits of industry, learned better ways of living, and became useful members of a higher social order. Nor were they, in fact, especially degraded below their level by slavery. It was only biased thinking that made personal inequality any more to be resented than inequality in property or in station. The sailor, the soldier, or the "wage slave" was free and independent only in theory and was not debased only because realities were covered by high-sounding words. Slavery was only the recognition of the fact that some men were inferior and the ordering of society upon that basis to the highest advantages of all.

The inferiority of the negro race Ruffin accepted without question. The failure of the free negroes to achieve property or standing, save in rare instances, seemed to furnish ample proof. In the North and in the South he found them a despised class, "noted for ignorance, indolence, improvidence." Investigation of conditions in Liberia convinced him that the negroes carried there by the Colonization Society had constantly declined in every way and that they were, by 1858, well below their original condition before they had been brought to America. He concluded that the race, without the guidance of the superior white man, would ever "sink to the state of savage barbarism and heathen ignorance and vice." The real cause of the conditions in Liberia, as well as in San Domingo and Haiti, where the negro had failed so miserably to hold his own, was found in his "aversion . . . to regular and laborious toil" and in his inability even to care for himself when left alone. For instance, Liberia was a comparative healthy place, yet the mortality there was frightfully high—the deaths exceeding the births. The country was fertile and productive to a high degree, yet the "colonists" had been unable to live without help from the Society. It all proved "that the negro race is greatly inferior to the white in natural capacity, and is incapable of self-government and improvement to the extent of civilization except under the direction and control of a superior race." [9]

And if such evidence did not convince, then science had something to offer. Some had turned to the Scriptures to find authority for placing the negro in an inferior position, but Ruffin was too modern for that. He followed that fascinating but neglected movement in the South forwarded by Samuel Morton, Josiah Nott, Richard Colfax, and John Van Evrie to show that mankind was not a unity; that there was not a single creation from which the whole human family came, but that the negro was from the beginning an inferior, perhaps even a special creation. Some of them came close to the doctrine of evolution, all of them would have had the South follow science, not the Bible, to justify the holding of the negro in bondage. No wonder the clergy and their friends were stirred to action, that J. L. Cabell, S. D. Baldwin, Dr. John Bachman, and others rushed to the defense of the Scriptures, creating a situation in which the South had to decide between orthodoxy and science. She had to choose whether she would defend her favorite institution with the assistance of the clergy or with the aid of the scientific mind. She chose the former and thus linked herself with the past.[10]

But not so with Edmund Ruffin. He could interpret Genesis to suit himself, and if science offered him evidence of the thing he already believed, then he was willing to follow science, not pausing to see that it necessarily upset his notions of "the first book." He could at least chuckle when the pious abolitionists of the North were forced to adopt a most liberal interpretation of the words of the Bible in finding evidence against slavery. The situation was certainly amusing. Southern men defending slavery by a literal acceptance of Holy Writ; Northern men, who believed the Southerners almost Antichrist, reading the Bible in such a way as to cause Southern men to call them atheists! Well might a gentleman laugh!

So certain was Ruffin of the benefits of slavery to the negro that he seriously advocated the elimination of all free negroes from his state by a system requiring them to show at regular intervals evidence of industry and thrift. Where crime was found, punishment should be sale into slavery; where idleness, sale for a term of years according to the degree "of the habit." He was certain that if such a plan were adopted, most of this undesirable class would soon be back in that condition most beneficial to themselves and to others. Nor was he alone in that opinion, for John Tyler wrote him saying, "You have fallen upon the *juste melieu.*" [11]

With the inferiority of the negro settled and his advantages under the white man's control demonstrated, the next step was to show the superiority of that social-economic order in which he occupied his true position. Certain supposed weaknesses had to be explained away; certain features of Southern life had to be emphasized if true values were to be understood. To begin with, it had been said that slavery accounted for the fact that lands in the South in general were lower in value than in the North. The fact few could deny. The explanation, however, was greatly in error. The real reason for such difference as existed in cases like Massachusetts and Virginia was to be found in the completely opposite nature of their agricultural efforts, not alone in their labor systems. In the one case, the labor of the farmer, his sons, and his daughters was concentrated upon a small parcel of land. It was their one capital. It had to give the whole return for the maintenance of the family and the social institutions of the community. In the other case, the crops produced required about twice as much acreage to yield equal returns. Land was only part of the capital employed in production, and the methods of cultivation were extensive, not intensive. Abundance of land of equal fertility justified such a system and fixed the values in proportion.

In the second place, the unproductive character of the soils in Massachusetts forced a large proportion of the population into navigation, fishing, whaling, trade, and manufactures. These groups had all been favored by government bounties, protective tariffs, or other aids, wealth having been drawn from the slaveholding states in order to build up home markets for the farmers of New England. Such markets gave larger profits and increased the values of the lands so favored. If Virginia had a population engaged in as diversified endeavors offering markets close at hand, then her lands too would rise to an equal level. But the costs of such a life were more than Ruffin was willing to pay.

Others had said that the slaveholding states were far behind the free states in wealth and general well-being. The census figures for 1850, however, did not bear this out. A comparison of the New England states with "the five old and more southern states" showed that the South excelled in the number of churches erected and in use, in the number of dwellings, and in both the total value of property and the average amount for each white person. The Northern states excelled in the number of families, in the value of churches, and in the number of paupers, insane persons, criminals, and those who were blind and deaf. It was merely a matter of whether one chose the greater human benefits of an open rural world wherein a farmer might also be an individual of culture and refinement, or the questionable material gains of a more compact and diversified one with its sacrifice of quality in persons.[12]

This latter suggestion, when more fully developed, forms Ruffin's most interesting contribution to the pro-slavery argument. As an agriculturist he was most interested in the future effects of any social-economic system upon the farmers of the nation. In the rise of intensive farming, with small proprietors in competition with one another and with the new urban-industrial order, he saw the destruction of the farmer as an independent force in American life. In slavery alone he found salvation from peasantry. Under freedom

each rural family was forced to intensive and continual toil
to the neglect of social pleasures and the highest intellectual
improvement. Even the negro slaves enjoyed "more comfort and pleasure, than the wretched and hard-working
peasant-proprietors." The city tended to draw away the best
elements from the rural world and to hold a monopoly on
the intelligence and influence of the region. Soon, under
these forces, *gain* became the sole object of endeavor in farming—industry, economy, and frugality the great virtues. In
a few generations, under such conditions, the people who
remained in the country were "rude in manners and greatly
deficient in refinement of feeling and cultivation of mental
and social qualities."

Such was the condition of the farmers in France and
Britain, such the general trend in the North. Even in New
York and Pennsylvania the cities were already beginning to
contain "all the great intellectual power," and social and
political control was passing to industry. Ruffin prophesied
that if the Northwest tied itself to the industrial East, then
the farmers of that section also would in time lose political
influence and, with their best blood drawn away to the
cities, fall back into peasantry, their wives "domestic
drudges," their sons and daughters boors. He was talking
the way other men, yet unborn, would talk some seventy-
five years later.

How different the rural scene under slavery! "This institution, which by confining the drudgery and brutalizing
effects of continued toil, or menial service, to the inferior
race (and of which the subjection, notwithstanding, has
served greatly for its benefit and improvement), gives to the
superior race leisure and other means to improve the mind,
taste and manners." Here alone white men were truly free,

here farmers in their true station. "The most distinguished men, and especially statesmen of the South, were . . . often . . . natives and continued residents of the country." Even lesser men, with comparatively few acres, found time for "social and mental occupations," leisure for relaxation and for the improvement of mind and manners. The use of slave labor and extensive methods relaxed the constant attention to petty details and small economies that kept the spirit of gain ever in the mind of the Northern farmer and fostered an easy-going attitude which made for tolerance and larger human interests. Men were less materially minded; the family was a real institution; sons and daughters grew up "under the advantages and influence of social communication." No wonder the "intelligent" strangers admired and praised the "domestic manners and refinement of the Southern country population." The South was the one spot where a farmer was also a gentleman, and could remain so.[13]

With benefits to the negro and society affirmed, there remained but one further service to render. The alleged evils of slavery must be denied. There was no use doing a halfway job of it. These Ruffin grouped, for purposes of demolishing, under two headings: "First, the great injustice and wrong of subjecting human beings, our natural equals, to slavery, and of so holding them and their posterity; and second, the hardships and suffering of persons subjected to and held in slavery."

As to the first, it was "unjust and wrongful" in the same sense as the possession of "property, wealth and political rank and power, in almost every civilized and even free country," by a small number of persons, and justifiable on the same grounds, "the general and great benefit of the whole community, and of all mankind." Only the most rabid socialists or the followers of Proudhon had denounced "all hereditary magistrates and rulers as usurpers, and all property-holders as unjust and fraudulent possessors," and advocated depriving them of their acquisitions. Only the same group should, in reality, object to the institution of slavery on the same grounds.

The second objection was more real. Yet it was one common to all situations where some men have power over others. Its answer was the same in this case as in industry. Self-interest in both demanded that the employer give such treatment to the employees as would yield the greatest amount of continued, useful labor and service and would avoid the greatest amount of discontent and disobedience. Some men might be temporarily shortsighted enough to be oppressive, but in the long run fair play would work itself out in any mature society. It was proving thus in the South. With the supply of raw slaves cut off and with long association between native-born whites and blacks, cruelty had lessened and personal attachment increased. Harshness went only with early pioneer conditions and with expansion; fair treatment of workers, normal in all mature systems of labor, was the general rule under slavery in the older South. It furnished the greatest good to the greatest number! [14]

That Edmund Ruffin believed what he was saying there can be no doubt. His sincerity was beyond question. No abolitionist of the North ever strove more honestly to state harsh truth or to demand uncompromising justice. He did not wish to think or speak or write with moderation. He was in earnest. He would not equivocate. He would be heard. And mankind would be the better for listening. That which was his own had been attacked by those who were different, even hostile. They had not struck at reality;

they were largely substituting slavery and slaveholders, of which they knew little, for the forces about them that were doing damage to certain ideals of democracy and well-being to which the American was ever wont to lay claim as his right. Slavery was being distorted for their purposes into the great tyrant that was destroying liberty and equality; slaveholders were being fashioned into unbending aristocrats. To meet such approaches slavery had to become the great good; Southern society, the perfect order; Northerners, fanatics who would check the forward sweep of mankind.

And so Ruffin stood, a Puritan in reality, battling other Puritans with words. Both sides were seeking logical arguments rather than the exact truth. Both were hurrying on the day when stronger weapons would be necessary to settle the differences they were raising. Both had found a *mission*—and God pity humanity when serious souls find that!

CHAPTER VII

THE PERIOD OF TESTING

THE sectional struggle resulting in the Compromise of 1850 left the South divided and uncertain. Hostilities and apprehensions too deep to be easily allayed had been stirred, and the settlement reached was, after all, only a halfway measure for either party. The great majority of the people, no doubt, wanted peace and quiet and were willing to call the agreements "final" if for no other reason than the comfort derived from saying what they wished to be true. But others were as certain that nothing had been accomplished—that secession should have been resorted to instead of compromise; a few, including Ruffin, hoped that this was the case. The decade from 1850 to 1860 was to form a testing period to show which of these groups was correct. One of them, after a time, would be using that most devastating of human expressions, "I told you so!"

The real issue, stated in its simplest form, was merely whether the South could secure what she considered her constitutional rights within the Union, or whether the Northern people had become so extreme in their opposition to slavery and its expansion that they would find ways of circumventing the Constitution and, with a growing majority on their side, deny the South both security in her property rights and an equal share in the territories. The conservatives insisted that in the Compromise the North had "given practical evidence of its intention to stand, in good faith, by the Constitutional Union of the fathers—recognizing and enforcing all the rights guaranteed by that solemn compact to the brethren of the South." "As to the Rhetts, Yanceys and c.," they 'were certain that "the sooner and more effectively we get rid of them the better." [1]

Their opponents, however, declared that although "old associations, old pledges, old hopes, perhaps convictions . . . [might] keep a few old leaders of the Northern Democracy in their old position on the slavery question . . . the body and present leaders of the party . . . [were] gone, gone forever." As one of them wrote in 1852 to a staunch Unionist: [2]

> You know well that it has been my conviction for the last two or three years that nothing we could do, short of general emancipation, would satisfy the North. Your idea was that the measures of the Compromise would substantially affect that object, and you went for them for that reason chiefly, I think. Should it turn out that I am right and you are wrong it will not be long before it must be known. And it is therefore now time for you to be making up your mind for the new "crisis." Suppose the Whig party shall be beaten, and especially at the North, will not that disband it and send the elements of which it has been composed into union with this late Pittsburg free-soil anti-slavery concern? Manifestly. What then? That concern takes the North. The Democratic party there, in conjunction with pretty much the whole South, may be able to make one fight, say in 1856—a grand Union Rally—but then the thing will be out. Is it not so? You must have thought of all this. Have you made up your mind as to what is to be done?

Positive that nothing had been gained, the more radical members of this group turned at once to the task of preserving the Southern unity that had been born of the struggle. Jefferson Davis hurried home to take up the fight in Mississippi that John A. Quitman had abandoned, accepting the decision for Union but certain that the people of the state had not "approved the action of Congress on the subject of slavery and the territories." J. H. Hammond launched a movement "to cut every tie" between South Carolina and the Federal Government "without affording a pretext for collision" on the assumption that conditions were still such that other states would soon be forced to follow her lead. Rhett and Yancey went on urging secession, and even a Georgia editor arose amid the victorious shouts of the Unionists to declare that "the elements of that controversy are yet alive and they are destined . . . to outlive the government." "There is a feud between North and South," he said, "which may be smothered but never overcome." [3]

The immediate reactions of the people, however, were against such attitudes. Mississippi refused to consider Davis' interpretation of the issues and made Foote governor; the coöperationists carried the day in South Carolina; while Yancey lost his fight in Alabama to the more moderate Hilliard. The Union party swept Georgia with a thoroughness that could not be mistaken, and the Virginians refused to listen to Ruffin's appeals. The movement for Southern nationalism seemed to be but a flash in the pan—a step (to mix the metaphor) from which the people had suddenly drawn back in horror. Yet the forces that had produced the movement were genuine, and withdrawal was conditioned by a very definite understanding. Elwood Fisher put the whole matter in one sentence. "I learn to-day," he said, "that Toombs has written here that Georgia can be saved for the Compromise if the North can only behave itself, a thing the North won't do more and more every day." [4]

* * *

The origins of the abolition movement and the development of the attitudes of common men who lived north of Mason and Dixon's line toward slavery and the South have never been satisfactorily treated. The great unrest that stirred the Northeast when the factory came and when the rural regions offered up their sons and daughters to the West and to the rising towns had in it something more than a Puritan conscience. The shift from "harbor to fall-line" left old maritime centers like Salem, Beverly, and Newburyport to dwindle before the rising power of Lowell and Lawrence and Boston and put new wealth in greater quantity into new hands; ruinous competition from cheap and fertile western lands soon fell heavily upon an agricultural life which had just undergone a revolution in adjusting itself to new home markets; new banks and banking systems made the outlying regions tributary to "the hub centers," and foreign masses crowded the cities to the worry of the countryside whose own children were also seeking these new lands of opportunity.

A veritable social-economic revolution was in process in which industry was overshadowing agriculture and "the living of the many was passing into the hands of the few." What was to happen to the economy of the nation as a whole in the years after 1865 was already happening to the Northeast.

The intellectual ferment that accompanied these changes was a queer mixture of resentments, of rural folk against the towns, of the poor against the rich, and of dreams of a more perfect order, economic and social, which stirred those "capable of large and disinterested thinking." Evangelical sects swept the back country with emotion as the more rational Unitarians gained a foothold in the East, but both emphasized the necessity for social reform and added something of religious spirit to every movement; "embryo heavens," usually representing a return to a more simple and wholesome rural life, sprang up at Brook Farm, Hopedale, and Fruitlands; and men set about seeking the realities that transcend the material, offering peace to the earth, equality to women, comfort to criminals and the insane, and urging temperance in all things, perfection in character, and freedom for all humanity.

It was not a series of separate and distinct movements but one common urge to better the lot of mankind, which in the eighteen thirties and forties was particularly uncertain in New England. It was a struggle against the injustice and inequalities that were close at hand, a questioning of the whole foundation on which the existing order rested. The leaders in one movement were also leaders in others, and it was often difficult, as in the case of William Lloyd Garrison, to tell whether the larger interest was in peace, temperance, women's rights, or abolition.

In fact, it was not until the anti-slavery movement, as part of this general stirring, swept out into New York, Ohio, and Michigan, where the notion that heaven was to be reached through political action prevailed, that it took on the definite form of a great practical crusade worthy of the "respectable" man's attention. Even there it grew upon foundations already laid for securing a more perfect democracy by the anti-Masonic group, the labor demands for public education and free homesteads, and the Loco-Foco struggle against privilege which produced the clearest statement of pure Jeffersonian doctrine made in the period.

Just how the slavery issue rose to supremacy out of the general reform program and how it became tangled with canals, public lands, corporations, and tariffs is a difficult problem to solve. Sufficient to say that in the 1830's, slavery was directly connected, by the agitators, with the immediate troubles from which the North "suffered," and the notion of a "slave power," or "slavocracy," in control of the central government carrying out a program injurious to the section was then given currency. Southern extravagance was responsible for the panic of 1837, they charged; Southern control accounted for the failure of the government "to procure a market for the free products of the grain-growing Northwest," they insisted; that slaveholders were one with the privileged group at home against which they already battled for the well-being that America guaranteed to common men was the general conclusion. The remedy for both fundamental and immediate ills, therefore, lay in political action to secure "equal rights in all social relations" and to restore government to its original purposes. Southerners, liquor dealers, banking corporations, all subject to the will of the people! They had made slavery a political issue in a region where dreams were most extravagant, where interests were in intense conflict, and where politicians had reached a degree of mastery unequaled.[5]

Into such a situation came the struggle over slavery in California and New Mexico, fixing the slaveholder in men's minds as the great aristocrat and slavery as the great force diverting government from its true Christian-republican principles—equality and prosperity for common men. It rose above temperance, corporation control, and women's rights, which had also entered the political field, and relegated peace, prison reform, etc., to a more abstract realm. The Liberty and Free-Soil parties became the carriers of old Loco-Foco and labor teachings as well as participants in the bitter local personal-interest quarrels. The South began to do service for all the "knaves" who checked prosperity and principles. Slavery became the symbol of all oppression, proving to be an excellent political weapon regardless of the real issues involved.

It goes without saying that the Compromise of 1850 had been accepted by the radical group in the Northeast with serious reservations. John Brown thought its fugitive-slave provision would make more abolitionists than all the lectures of past years and talked of trusting God and keeping his powder dry. Garrison burned the act, and Theodore Parker declared that nothing could save slavery. But the majority, viewing it in much the same way as the Southerners did, were willing to abide by its terms until a people they had been taught to distrust showed signs of renewing their "aggressions." All depended upon "behavior."

But more important, after 1850, to both the anti-slavery cause and the national destiny was the rise to greater influence of the farther Northwest, with Illinois as its center. By that date the upland Southerner and the New Englander there had blended into a unity under common experiences, and the home market had broken sharply to indicate the closing of the first period of pioneer development. What has been called the "provincial stage" had ended, and the region was ready to take its place in the larger national pattern. New markets had to be found, internal improvements made, manufactures established, and free lands provided for those who, under economic pressure, now turned their faces westward in increasing numbers. It was a condition like that which Henry Clay had capitalized a generation earlier in the Ohio Valley. But the Whig Party was dying, and either a new party was needed to carry out the program or the

Democratic Party must, under western leadership, look after these interests. Lincoln and Douglas were to have their opportunities.

It was a section, furthermore, whose settlers from New York and Pennsylvania had borrowed heavily in social attitudes from their native states. Reform movements had taken firm hold, especially those dealing with war and intemperance, and the Liberty and Free Soil Parties had found adherents who opposed slavery on both practical and abstract grounds. Many had already lodged the blame for pioneer privations against the "slave-power" in control of the central government, and the period of expansion against Mexico, as we have seen, had produced open expressions of hostility.

This region looked upon the Compromise of 1850 in much the same spirit as the Lower South. It was anxious for prosperity and certain that peace was essential to the solution of its great problems. Yet there were basic considerations involved. Fundamentally democratic in spirit, the section was ever ready to respond again to the teachings of the Declaration of Independence as against the assertions of the superiority of a stratified society, and it could hardly be expected to accept personal responsibility for the return of fugitive slaves. A land of small farmers, swarming once more as home markets failed, it resented competition in the territories from the plantation system under negro slavery, and it was not inclined to yield new ground for the "peculiar institution." It needed liberal land laws and welcomed foreigners who added value to their property, so it felt itself oppressed when Southerners opposed homesteads and immigrants. Nationalistic by necessity of passing through other sections to market and because of needs in lands, transportation, and tariffs, it was in no mood to understand states' rights when urged by others.

The Northwest was thus ready to join hands with the Northeast as trade turned along the Great Lakes and bands of railroad iron began to bind them into the wider national life. Their politicians began to see new fields of activity—perhaps even presidential prospects. If the Compromise was "final" for them, it certainly did not imply a yielding of principles or a sacrifice of interests.[6]

*　　*　　*

With the stage thus set for a decade of testing, the men who were already certain of the outcome began to prepare for the "irrepressible conflict." The Northern radical went on with his fight, and his rival in the South, whom we must follow, marked out his program. To the Southern nationalist the first task was to reveal the true Northern attitudes and to show the impossibility of securing Southern rights within the Union. Every occasion must be seized to scatter propaganda; a people must be made ready for independence. Plans were set on foot to establish direct trade with Europe; drives launched to keep Southern sons at home for college training and to give to them Southern textbooks for study and Southern periodicals for reading; writers set to work to prove the superiority of Southern institutions and schemers to find new territory into which to carry them. The radicals would make a nation.

Edmund Ruffin, bitterly disappointed at the outcome, reluctantly joined these agitators. In 1855 he gave up the personal direction of his estate (it was irksome) and turned all his efforts to public affairs. Freed from the plow, he set his pen to work to defend slavery, to reveal Northern duplicity, and to raise a new nation into life. His very health seemed to improve; his energy grew boundless. He had found, at last, the great enemy who brought out all the drive in his nature and afforded full play to his talents. It was a course for which he had long been fitting.

The unfriendly atmosphere in Virginia in the first years after the Compromise kept the agitator more or less on the defensive. He made an effort to obtain a seat in the Constitutional Convention of 1850-51 in order to help check the demand for a wider franchise, but the politicians would not have him and his radical ways. Yet agricultural interest was high, and the services of the old master could not be entirely ignored in a period when large profits were possible. The call for addresses and surveys was insistent; the railroad companies, accepting him as a public benefactor, furnished free passes; and the Virginia State Agricultural Society pressed him again into its presidency (1855). And what was to prevent the leader who conceived of the great contest between the North and South in terms of a struggle between industrial and agricultural interests from bringing into the discussion of fertilizers, crop rotation, and drainage the now tabooed political issues? He "exulted" when the United States Government republished in its Patent Reports his harsh condemnation of its policy toward the South tucked away amid the praises of "fertilizing systems of agriculture" in his South Carolina speech of 1852. He made the benefits of slavery to the quality of a people the theme of his speech before the Virginia State Society in the same year, and he formed friendships with radicals on trips which were supposed to be solely for the purpose of farm inspection. He was preparing "against that day." [7]

The Kansas-Nebraska Act first brought home to the average man of the North and West what was involved in granting to the South all that its people considered their constitutional rights. When that became clear, great numbers stirred to check the extension of slavery into new territories where free men wished homes, and the radical element found the way open to renew its charges against the South. John Brown hastened to Kansas, convinced that the only arguments a Southerner could understand were embodied in a Sharpe rifle. The Republican Party sprang full grown into being to champion both democracy and the material prosperity of the common men of a section.

It was, however, the election of 1856 that served to break the illusions of the Southerner. To that time the moderate men had considered the great masses of the North to be perfectly sound on fundamental issues. Only in such places as Massachusetts, "where for a long time the right minded . . . men kept the raving agitators down," had "fanaticism triumphed . . . until the name of the once grand old commonwealth" had become "as much a synonym of reproach and disgrace as it erst was glory and renown." And even there conditions were not serious. The Yankees had to have "some hobby to ride or they would be exceedingly uncomfortable. The abolition hobby being most convenient and handy, they at once mounted it and . . . rode the poor thing to death." But if cotton were cut off from Massachusetts mills, "thirty days would not elapse before the old Commonwealth would turn with arguments to illustrate the righteousness, elevating tendencies, humanity, purity and indispensable necessity of the institution of domestic slavery in the South." [8]

The election of 1856, with the majority of Northern votes for "Col. John Fremont, the candidate for the presidency

of the free-soilers, abolitionists, haters of the South generally"
delivered "a stunning shock to the settled convictions of a
lifetime" in those who had formerly "never allowed a
thought to harbor . . . for a moment that, by any con-
tingent or remote chance, the Union of these states could be
brought into jeopardy." It raised grave doubt as to the
willingness of the North to abide by its agreements and
threw the finality of the great Compromise into question.
The radical could now begin to talk more freely.[9]

Ruffin, of course, had expected things to turn out this
way. He had long been certain that the North was determined to destroy slavery and to ruin the South. He had
said before the Democratic Convention of 1856 met that "no
truly capable, talented, and honest man" could ever "be again
chosen for the office of President"—meaning, of course, that
no Southerner could be elected. He voted for Buchanan
but accepted him as another Pierce, meanwhile secretly wishing that "the Black Republicans" would carry the country
and thus reveal the true situation.

When the autumn lull after harvest sent the second wave
of gentlemen farmers to the Springs for much needed rest
and more essential conversation, Ruffin joined the crowd.
He mingled with "numerous persons from all of Virginia
and other Southern States" and "used every available occasion to express . . . [his] opinion and the grounds
thereof, that the slave-holding states should speedily separate
from the others and form a separate confederacy, as the only
means of warding off the continued and increasing assaults
of the Northern people to impair and finally destroy . . .
[the] institution of slavery and thus ruin the Southern
States."

He was surprised to find how many concurred with him,

though few would "have dared to utter the opinions at first." The knowledge increased his zeal, and he "became desirous to treat the subject before the public," willing to incur "the odium of opinions so unpopular with the many" for the sake of the cause. He approached Roger Pryor of the *Enquirer* and obtained his promise to print such articles as he would write. He was at work within a few days, and four articles, under the title, "Consequences of Abolition Agitation," appeared in the *Enquirer* before the end of the year, to be reprinted later in *DeBow's Review* when it became the spokesman of the Southern cause.[10]

The approach was that of the realist. If the "enemies" had been united in the late election, they would have won. With the constant addition of foreign immigrants and the certain admission of new free states, they would win in the next election. No Southern man could ever again obtain Northern votes; the South was a minority now, and the North would soon have the necessary three-fourths votes to change the Constitution and brush aside such frail legal restraints as now protected the South. Delay was only to court disaster. Resistance should have come in 1820, when the South could have checked the whole movement led only by a few "sincere abolitionists" and a few "knaves" who sought political gain. But things had now reached the point where the only salvation was "another Declaration of Independence," another separation from "a despotic party whose wrongful oppression exceeds ten-fold that of England in Revolutionary Days."

Then came the old assurance that secession was possible without war, for even recognizing the hatred of the abolitionists, the interests of the North were against such a thing. And then the stirring of confidence in case the struggle should come—superior leadership, defensive warfare, and slaves to toil while masters fought. At the end, independence, with everything gained and nothing lost. The South already was denied a just share in the territories; slaves were now lost forever if they escaped to Northern soil; commercial relations with the North were worse already than they could ever be with any foreign nation. The South was only delaying her fullest development into a land of prosperity and diversified interests by refusing to take now the step that she must ultimately take under continued oppression. He was talking as he had not dared to talk since 1850.

Early in 1857 the desire for closer contact with the sectional strife carried Ruffin to Washington, where for a few days he gathered the political gossip and confirmed his bad impressions of the Northern leaders. He was much with Hunter, Goode, DeBow, Dudley Mann, and other radical Southern leaders who seemed to him restrained because of political ambitions. He talked with Toombs regarding the proposed taxing of Northern imports by the Southern states and asked assurance of its legality. He visited the House, then about to investigate charges of bribery made against some of its members, and concluded that "as a body, the Northern members of Congress are as corrupt and destitute of private integrity, as a majority of Southern members are the reverse." He left Washington convinced that Buchanan's "reign" could "bring him little of either pleasure or honor." There was little hope for the country governed by politicians—Southerners who wanted office and Northerners who wanted spoils.

Finding it best not to return to "Marlbourne" because the slaves insisted on bringing their complaints to him, Ruffin now turned to North Carolina and then to Charleston, where he sensed at once a more congenial atmosphere. He hunted up Russell and subscribed for his new magazine in order to encourage a movement which would furnish Southern reading for the South; he spent long hours in the office of the *Mercury* urging the secession of the Lower South as a unit, leaving the border states as a barrier to protect them from invasion or to join them in confederation if the North insisted on crossing their territory to get at the seceders. Barnwell Rhett called on him, and together they bemoaned the fact that ambition for high office had robbed their section of leadership and that "sullen despair" had caused others to abandon the struggle. They resolved anew to toil on, content in the knowledge that their cause was just.

Charleston and such contacts brought forth another public appeal. On May 13, 1857, the *Mercury* printed his startling declaration "that if Abolitionism sets its fatal seal upon Kansas, then the Union itself will be abolitionized." Kansas, he believed, indicated the course that all territories henceforth must take. Under the squatter-sovereignty doctrine every Northern emigrant would "become a potential abolitionist," free to speak and print incendiary doctrines until the mind of every slave carried into the region must be corrupted and slave-owners thereby effectively debarred. The territories must become all slave or all free! There was but one course open. The more southern states must seize "the period of truce presented by the late election" to withdraw from the Union, using the border states to protect them, and form a nucleus about which the other states might collect one by one. Gradual secession would thus avoid the clash that might follow a mass movement.

And so it went throughout the year and on into the next. When his friend Hammond took a seat in the Senate in

1858, there was strong incentive for Ruffin again to visit Washington where the struggle over Kansas offered new materials with which to wage his campaign. The figure of the fiery agent of disunion, now entering his sixty-fourth year, erect and distinguished by the long white hair which hung to his shoulders, became a familiar one about the national capital. By intimate associations with the more radical leaders he saw something of the bitter sectional struggle from the inside, and he comprehended the true situation in Kansas far more clearly than most of those who took a hand in the debates. He was certain that the anti-slavery party there was much stronger than its rival and that if a pro-slavery constitution were foisted upon the people, it would be a "victory to the South, but in a bad cause," to be undone by the people of Kansas within a year or two after it became a state. He felt that both parties were guilty of "rascality" and that the struggle was being prolonged in the hope of influencing the next presidential election. Why could the South not see the real facts in the situation? The expansion of slavery was ended. It was "simply a question of the relative increase of federal numbers in the two opposed sections of the Union," and the outcome was as plain as any "simple problem in arithmetic." Only by dividing Texas could the South gain new slave states—a useless procedure because the North might easily find twenty more free states if necessary by the same method. The North was becoming a political unity for the accomplishment of her purposes within the Union; the South must, as a hopeless minority, become a unity outside of it.

Ruffin entered into the moves for the economic independence of the South with enthusiasm. He early proposed "the adoption, by the Legislature of every Southern State of a system of heavy taxation, through the license laws, on the sale of products and supplies from the Northern States." By requiring a heavy license to sell such products home industry would be developed and home markets builded for the section. The legality of such a move might be questionable, but the principle was sound. The logic so recently employed to denounce cities and factories and intensive production was now turned about to prove the benefits of all these things and to denounce a government whose policy had bestowed them upon one section. They were now "good" because they best prepared "for the condition of independence" which was the "only remaining alternative to the extinction of . . . freedom and everything dear to freemen."

The establishment of direct trade with Europe was also an object much to be desired. If license taxes were laid upon goods from the outside, they should be refunded in cases of importation directly from abroad but maintained if entry were made through a Northern port. A refund might also be made on goods from the North that could not be produced in the South and a balance struck with the cotton that the Northern factory consumed. But Europe, as the great consumer of Southern produce, must furnish all that she could offer at lower rates, and Southern commerce be built to carry on the exchange. A further advantage of direct trade was revealed in his argument that "this general policy, if adopted . . . would operate to shut out three-fourths of all the present supplies from the Northern States," reducing them to ruin and bringing them to their senses so that they would "do all that both justice and policy required for observing and securing the rights and future safety of the South." [11]

A chance to render larger service to this cause came in

May, 1858, when he was elected as a delegate from his county to the Southern Convention to meet at Montgomery, Alabama (May 10). Twice before Ruffin had attended commercial conventions, and although uncertain of the benefits derived from previous meetings, he now saw the opportunity "to meet and exchange views with men of the South" and to forward "the Union of the Southern States" for secession. He had urged Hammond to go to Knoxville the year before to take the leadership in these gatherings from those who would lose "their profits, if not their bread, by the immediate and complete establishment of direct trade from the South with Europe." He now turned toward Montgomery resolved to act in that spirit.[12]

The delegation from Virginia included such men as Lewis E. Harvie, Roger Pryor, and William B. Preston, with whom Ruffin was well acquainted and with whom he found living quarters. They were soon joined by Barnwell Rhett of South Carolina, and their rooms became a center of radical interest. Dr. N. B. Cloud, of the *Cotton Planter,* William L. Yancey, the extreme Alabama leader, and Judge J. A. Jones of Georgia called early to discuss the larger affairs of the South and to lay plans for securing sectional advantages. Ruffin found himself almost "oppressed with invitations to various places" and was particularly gratified by the attention given him by many prominent leaders whom he had never met before in person. All referred "in most kind and flattering terms to their previous estimation" of his "labors and usefulness," and many took occasion to express "a strong feeling of disunion."

When the convention opened, Ruffin was chosen chairman of the Virginia delegation. He spoke but once, rising to repel the insinuation that Virginia's opposition to the

reopening of the slave trade was based on her desire to sell
surplus labor to the Lower South for higher prices. "He
declared that ninety-nine out of a hundred slaveholders in
Virginia desired to retain their slaves, and that few sold
them, except when compelled by necessity to do so. As for
himself, he wished that all the slaves that had been sold out
of Virginia for the last thirty years, with their posterity,
were back in the State again." His opposition to the proposal to open the slave trade, he insisted, was based on
practical grounds—presumably the strife it would produce
among the Southern states, and he rejoiced when the resolutions were laid on the table because "northern enemies"
would not learn of the division in Southern ranks.[13]

After this one speech he remained quiet, talking much
outside of sessions but an observer within. His comments
on individuals and affairs were keen and critical. He described Yancey as a very eloquent and powerful speaker but
so fluent he did "not know when to stop." "He is too wordy
and too long," was his statement after the gifted Alabamian
had spoken for some four hours; "he was under the influence
of strong drink and his speech suitable to his condition," was
his conclusion. He described the filibusterer Walker as
"reserved, retiring and modest," his famous gray eye not
gray at all but "light greenish blue"—enough to take the
romance out of any character. He was not certain when
the convention was over that it could show a single con-
structive measure to its credit.[14]

When adjournment came, agricultural friends insisted on
some inspection of Alabama agriculture by the great Virginia reformer. He traveled about, many persons seeking
his acquaintance and offering him attentions, testing soils
here and there and viewing the country, gratified by the

progress being made toward better farming. He returned to Montgomery on the 25th of May for a conference with Yancey in which he launched his great plan for future action.

Ruffin had been struck by the power that Yancey yielded over popular assemblies and had resolved to enlist his services in a movement by which Southern opinion might be given unity and direction. He would organize what he chose to call a "League of United Southerners" to operate "by discussion, publication and public speeches" on the public mind of the South. There was wanting "some suitable means for bringing together the minds and wills of all true and patriotic men for consultation, for concert and combined action." By such means "even a small minority of a people, though the great majority . . . be either opposed or indifferent . . . [might] exercise great and sometimes controlling influence." Southern men were too individualistic; they needed a rallying point, some one to direct them.

Ruffin desired that Yancey should launch the movement at a meeting arranged for the 4th of July, at which he should urge Southern independence, using the example of the "disunionists of 1776" and showing that they had far less cause for action than had the present South. There were to be local clubs composed of all citizens who would pledge themselves to defend and secure the constitutional rights and interests of the Southern states. Each local club should choose members according to its numbers to sit in a general council which was to direct the work of the whole organization, and funds were to be obtained from the local groups according to the seats they held in the council. All money thus collected was to be used for the purpose of procuring and publishing tracts and for "promoting knowledge in regard to the rights and interests of the Southern States." In other words, it was an organization to carry forward propaganda for secession.

Yancey printed the plan in the Montgomery *Advertizer and Gazette* and long before the day set had an organization in full swing. Ruffin brought it forward in the Charleston *Mercury* and sought support for it in Virginia and North Carolina. Yancey prefaced his statement by ascribing the movement to "that profound thinker, that practical farmer and statesman, that true and fearless patriot, Edmund Ruffin." The author, inspired by modesty or caution, kept his own name so successfully hidden in the older states that few knew of his connection with the plan, causing the historians of a later day often to give credit for its origin to Yancey himself.[15]

The League met with harsh criticism from the conservative element. They called it "mischievous," meaning, of course, that it threatened the "National Democratic party and the chance for retaining Northern votes to support Southern candidates." Most men were like Judge Thomas Ruffin of North Carolina, whose refusal to support the organization caused his more eager relative to say: "He is too cautious, perhaps too wise, to go with me. . . . He would adhere to the Union much longer, as a greater good than all to be gained by separation." Consequently the career of the League was checkered; but the idea, and in some cases the local clubs themselves, lived on, and associations to distribute radical pamphlets and spread radical opinion played no small part in preparing the way for disunion. But again the radical was too far ahead of the crowd for great success. He was as yet a voice crying in the wilderness. Some might be content with that, but Ruffin had a weakness for real audiences and human approval.

Although he had opposed the resolutions favoring the opening of the slave trade at the Montgomery Convention, Ruffin had done so on the grounds of policy, not principle. His belief in the benefits of slavery to both the negroes and their masters soon altered the old feeling that the slave trade was "in the same category with piracy and murder." He began to ascribe the horrors of the business to its illegal character, and he saw in the demand of the South for cheap labor to match the white hordes pouring into the North another force that might be used "strongly to promote secession." That put the slave trade in a new light. He did not urge the reopening of the business; he merely viewed it from a new angle because the North was so certain of its wrongs.

The more positive note that was creeping into the Southern voice, as the superiority of its ways and institutions was asserted, brought with it a demand for expansion. Although not impressed by the filibusterer Walker, Ruffin accepted the conquest of Central America and the Isthmus of Panama as desirable objects, to be delayed if possible until after secession, but to be carried out at once if necessary. Like slavery, "the conquest of any of these mongrel and semi-barbarous communities, by any civilized power, would be a benefit to the conquered and to the world." The Southern mind was indeed in a paternal mood in this period. Slavery had colored the whole outlook.[16]

Meanwhile, agitation to arouse the people went on without respite. Through the columns of *The South* Ruffin dinned the certainty of a "Black Republican or Abolition" victory in 1860. The slight division that had prevented the election of Frémont would "not occur again, and their absolute and relative numbers and strength in the North" was increasing every year. The next candidate would be a real leader, "most probably Seward," and then would come new amendments to the Constitution, the end of slave representation and of the surrender of fugitive slaves, a remodeling of the Supreme Court, and the destruction of all minority rights. How could the Southern people "exhibit as much unconcern and apathy as if there was no impending danger to [their] dearest interests and rights and the existence of slavery?" If Seward or any other abolitionist were elected in 1860, there would remain "no prospect for safety, no hope for the very existence of the South." [17]

And the Democratic Party, in truth, offered little more. Its last two conventions had been forced to nominate Northern men because they alone could secure Northern votes. If these leaders had been chosen because of superior qualities, there could be no complaint; but in both cases they were weaklings offered to the voters because no Southern man could bring success to the party. The leaders of the South were thus as effectively barred from office as if by constitutional provision. The Democrats were divided absolutely in opinion and principles; the open disruption of the party was in order. Then each group might find its true associations and honesty be restored. It was time to face realities, time for Southern politicians to serve their section and cease yielding principles in the vain hope of office.

Now and then the zeal of the grim old sectional patriot came near the point of humor. Once when a New York paper hinted that the British Government had designs on the State of Maine, he enthused over the benefits to the nation if all of New England were seized or purchased by

England. "This absolute and final removal of New England from the American Confederation of States," he wrote, "would be much the most effectual means for quieting all existing and growing evils." He was certain that the Southern states could well afford to pay $500,000,000 for such a favor.

On another occasion, when he read of a "Free Convention" held in Rutland, Vermont, he commented on the fact that "nowhere in the world except New England could such an assembly have met or persons . . . have uttered such doctrines." There were ministers of the gospel, Shaker elders, woman's-rights advocates, and spiritualists denouncing the Bible and the Constitution and revealing all the freakish turns that a free society was inclined to produce. He hoped there would be many like it.

Ruffin may have smiled when he made these comments on New England, but there is all-seriousness about his attitude toward Ohio's refusal to obey the fugitive-slave law. "The state government . . . is arrayed against the lawful jurisdiction and constitutional power of the Federal Government," he wrote, "and I correctly hope may push the opposition to the extent of treason and rebellion. New York, Massachusetts, and some other of the Northern States have also made like enactments, to nullify the fugitive slave law. I trust that all, like Ohio, may have an opportunity, and that they will also put their theory of opposition into practice. It would be a capital move if one or more of these fanatical northern states would begin the operation of secession from or resistance to the Union." Treason and rebellion! Fanatical states resisting the Union! Southern virtues were evidently vices when they got away from home.[18]

As the summer of 1859 drew to a close, Edmund Ruffin grew weary of life and labor. It was a hopeless task to bring a people to face realities. They loved their illusions, and hope for better things colored the grim facts about them. The average man thought that all was well, arguing that the repeal of the Missouri Compromise, the Dred Scott decision, and the Administration's attitude toward Kansas had placed slavery in a safer position than it had occupied since an early day. They were at least certain that agitation did not make for comfort and prosperity, the two really essential things in life. Meanwhile Northern conservatives assured their Southern friends that Seward's radical speeches had ruined him and that if his "party should nominate him, they . . . [would] thereby dwindle to a mere sectional faction and become an easy conquest." They insisted that "we may look forward without much anxiety" and reported "a healthful change in the public temper . . . sectional animosities . . . subsiding and National feeling resuming its ancient sway over the popular heart." One of them declared that "a large proportion of the Republicans are dissatisfied with their position. They are growing weary of the endless 'rub-a-dub' about slavery, and desire to enter the next Presidential contest on fair national issues. Many of them openly advocate a union with the old Whigs and conservatives of the South on a just national basis." [19]

Even Hammond did not favor radical measures just then. In August, 1858, he had written Ruffin saying that he would not oppose the League of United Southerners but sharply condemned raising *"false issues"* such as "Kansas and this African Slave Trade." "We can whip them in the Union," he said, "and the attempt to do it, will only the better prepare us to kick them out of it, if we fail. . . . But for

Kansas what would they have had to gnaw these four years past? . . . We have them now dead. Nothing but filibustering can prevent us from putting an end to the whole Abolition movement, which is about to expire of inanimity." [20]

Ruffin found that in Virginia "talk of secession would ruin any man with political aims." He knew of "no candidate for office who . . . [did] not think he would be ruined by such avowal," no publisher or press that would dare to support it. Leading citizens refused to join his League or to take "any prominent or active part to stir up the South for preparation or future action." He could count "scarcely a dozen men in Virginia who . . . [would] now [1858] even speak openly, much less act, in defense of the South to the extent that was avowed very generally a year or two ago." He decided to give up the effort "to establish associations of United Southerners or in any such manner to separate and identify our true and bolder view." It seemed that all the leaders were "bribed by their entirely vain hopes, either to openly and actively go into the service of our enemies to buy northern votes (as Douglas, Wise and Jefferson Davis had done) or otherwise, like Hunter and others, to remain silent and inactive, for fear of offending the North." Even Orr and Keitt of South Carolina had become conservative. There was but one course open—to give up the ardent struggle, continuing "from time to time . . . to proclaim resistance through the newspapers," and to wait for the campaign of 1860 to bring the South to its senses by showing that no Southern man or issue could win even in the Democratic Party.[21]

And then, as if Fate had planned his complete undoing, personal misfortune was added to public defeat. Death had stalked through the family with unrelenting tread in the years since 1854, leaving the father with but one unmarried daughter upon whom to shower all the devotion of a lonely heart. In the autumn of 1859 she revealed to him her engagement and plans for a marriage which would take her to far-off Kentucky. It was a staggering blow. Her residence at "Marlbourne" had made it still his home in spite of withdrawal from active control. She was his confidante, his hope in declining years. Grief settled down upon him as, hiding his true feelings, he dutifully gave his approval. But to his diary he confessed the pain that swept his soul and caused him to remain constantly at home so that the world might not know his sorrow. "If I had died five years ago, how much of unhappiness would have been escaped," he moaned.

As the day of the wedding approached, he felt "wretchedly" but strove "to put the best face on things," asking but one last evening about the melodeon to hear the old songs which had become to his mind the symbol of the family fireside. On the evening of October 18, when all was over and he sat alone at his desk, he wrote: "Already I feel it disagreeable to make any exertion to seek either pleasure or employment though I know it to be more necessary than ever before. I have lived long enough—and a little more . . . of. such unused and wearisome passage of time will make my life too long."

*　　*　　*

Two nights before Ruffin had penned these words, and yet unknown to him, a little band of silent, determined men swung down the dark road from the Maryland side toward Harper's Ferry. They carried arms hidden under their long gray shawls, and an old farm wagon, creaking down the grade ahead, bore a load of long, hand-made pikes recently fashioned in a New England blacksmith shop. At their head strode a grim and gaunt old man, Kansas battle-scarred, who carried, according to Wendell Phillips, "letters of marque from God." He had come to turn slaves into freemen and to awaken the Northern people from their lethargy. He had also come to answer the prayers of the downhearted and discouraged Southern radicals.

CHAPTER VIII

A PROPHET IN HIS OWN COUNTRY

ON the morning of October 19 news of John Brown's raid on Harper's Ferry reached the forlorn and dejected Edmund Ruffin. Details were vague and uncertain, but out of the confusion he caught one stirring fact: abolitionism had at last reached a logical climax. "All the actors are Northerners and new comers, even the few negroes," he wrote. "And as incredible as it seemed at first . . . it really seems now most probable that the outbreak was planned and instigated by Northern abolitionists and with the expectation of thus starting a general slave insurrection. I earnestly hope that such may be the truth of the case. Such a practical exercise of abolition principles is needed to stir the sluggish blood of the South."

Later information seemed to confirm his suspicions. When radical Northern newspapers failed to condemn the raid and Northern abolitionists began to talk of a martyrdom comparable with that of Christ on the Cross, Ruffin was fully convinced that this attack was merely the premature thrust of a general drive which was soon to follow. Brown was but more bold and honest than his fellows. "He is as thorough a fanatic as ever suffered martyrdom," he declared, "and a very brave and able man. . . . It is impossible for me not to respect his thorough devotion to his bad cause and the undaunted courage with which he has sustained it through all losses and hazards." Edmund

Ruffin could understand John Brown's spirit if not his deeds.

The reactions that came out of the North showed that men there also understood. Ruffin noted that the abolition papers and speakers justified and applauded the attempt "for everything except its rashness and impudence," and he held this as certain proof that they would have "rejoiced at its success even if ever so destructive to the whites." It showed beyond question "that the great mass of the people of the North . . . [were] enemies of the South . . . [and] of negro slavery," that they would "sympathize even with treason, murder and every accompaniment of insurrection . . . to overthrow slavery." This was what he had been insisting upon for nearly a decade. Perhaps now men would listen to him.[1]

At once the old spirit returned, and personal troubles were forgotten. Within a few days he had drawn and was circulating a petition to the legislature for "Aid and Defense of Trade and Industry, and Proprietary and Political Rights of the People of this Commonwealth." It bewailed the loss of Virginia's formerly large trade with Europe and the growing power of Northern agents and carriers. It declared that "the greatest injury and danger to Virginia . . . [was] the hostile and incendiary action of the abolitionists of the North . . . sustained by their State Governments, in operating for the weakening and final destruction of the labor system and rights of property . . . of the Southern States; and that their power to endanger and inflict evil . . . [was] mainly due to the numerous facilities afforded through the possession and virtual monopoly of the Northern States of numerous branches of Southern trade and supply." The remedy lay in developing local agencies of commerce and thereby checking all intercourse between negro slaves and the Northern abolitionists. John Brown had shown the necessity for direct trade with Europe; the fears he had stirred must be used to forward that movement.

A few days later, noticing that even the most conservative people, who had heretofore been "submissive to Northern usurpations and aggressions" and who would have clung "to the Union under all circumstances," were saying that "something must be done by the South," he revamped his petition under the title, "Harper's Ferry Memorial," and carried it down to the Richmond meeting of the Southern Rights Association. To his surprise the newspapers published it with favorable comment, and the Association gave it hearty approval.[2]

In its new form the petition stressed the "all importance" of maintaining the "institution of negro slavery, with the due subordination of slaves to masters, and of the inferior black to the dominant white class." It declared that "the great and most operative cause of the corrupting of the habits and morals of slaves and of the infusing into their minds of discontent and the spirit of insubordination" was the "unlicensed selling of intoxicating liquors" and other articles by "vagrants or temporary sojourners" who were, in fact, "hired emissaries of Northern associations and individuals." It urged legislation by which all Northern interests would be barred from Southern trade and all Southern negroes would be cut off from Northern contacts.

To the Southern Rights Association he also presented a set of resolutions for the purpose of stirring the public mind to the highest pitch over the Harper's Ferry attack. He openly charged that "the late outbreak . . . [was the result] of a long-concocted and widespread Northern conspiracy for the destruction by armed violence and bloodshed of all that . . . [was] valuable for the welfare, safety and even existence of Virginia and the other Southern states." He labeled it "malignant, atrocious and devilish," yet believed that it had served a good purpose, "proving to the world the actual condition of entire obedience and general loyalty of . . . [the] negro slaves." Furthermore, it had revealed the true character of Northern men and their willingness to lay waste the South by fire and sword. It had opened the eyes of many who "had trusted to the justice and forbearance of the majority of the Northern people" and made it evident that "the only safeguard from the insane hostility of the North" was secession.[3]

With new zeal he pleaded that "every State and every man of the South" should "act promptly and effectively for the defense of . . . [their] institutions and dearest rights;" that "the Legislature of Virginia and . . . of all other . . . slave states . . . [should] consult and deliberate [upon] all past aggressions of Northern usurpation and hatred, and devise suitable and efficient measures for the defense of the Southern people . . . from the unceasing hostility and unscrupulous assaults of Northern enemies, fanatics and conspirators."

His words were hard, his proposals drastic. Yet the newspapers reported that "regard for the stability of the roof or walls of the building probably deterred the President from requesting those in favor of the resolutions to respond with the usual 'aye'."

With lip service completed, the rejuvenated agitator turned towards Harper's Ferry and Charleston (Virginia), where John Brown awaited execution. The entry in his

[174]

diary for November 26 reads: "6:30 A.M. On the cars and on my way to the 'seat of war'." Deep in his heart he hoped that the abolitionsts would attempt to rescue Brown and that every one connected with the move would be "put to death like a wolf." But, more important, such an attempt, "successful or not . . . would be the immediate cause of separation of Southern and Northern States." He would like to be on hand when the first blows of secession were struck.

The quaint little village of Harper's Ferry which ever seems dwarfed to miniature by the heights and rapids of its setting, was strangely astir in those late November days. Curious visitors clustered about the arsenal and the engine house, inspecting broken doors and windows and pointing out the scars made by rifle balls. Troops from different parts of the state gave color to the scene and by their differences revealed with startling effect the sectional character of the Old Dominion. There were sturdy German boys from the Valley, "talking to each other in a foreign language"; upstanding sons of the best families of the tidewater, who retained their manners even when in uniform and saluted the venerable old gentleman as they passed; trim cadets from the Virginia Military Institute, in their scarlet flannel shirts crossed by two white belts and given dignity and maturity by their long gray overcoats. The atmosphere was tense. Rumors of Northern schemes to rescue "old John Brown," started out of hopes and fears, were repeated with increasing certainty as the guards, set at every approach to the town, gathered parcels of suspects and marched them to headquarters for identification.

It was a splendid atmosphere in which to agitate. Crowds gathered to listen whenever participants in the late

struggle told of their experiences or private citizens in the
streets lifted their voices above the usual pitch in excited
discussion. Ruffin more than once found himself the object
of interest in such a group as he gave expression to his radical opinions. He seized every occasion to advocate secession,
printing his petitions and resolutions in the Charleston
papers and seeking signatures for his appeal to the legislature in the public streets. At length he secured one of the
pikes that Brown had brought along for "changing slaves
into men" and carried it about bearing the label, "Sample
of the favors designed for us by our Northern Brethren."
It attracted much attention, and it seemed to the bearer that
his "opinions and precepts," which had been uttered "to
deaf ears heretofore," were now "likely to be heeded
and to stand some chance of being made part of the public
policy of Virginia."

As the day of Brown's execution drew near, Ruffin began
to make plans for seeing the event, which was supposedly
open only to the military guard. Catching the idea from
his friend Hugh Nelson, who, though sixty-seven years of
age, had come from Petersburg with the militia, he begged
permission to join the cadets of the Military Institute for
a single day. The request was granted, and on the morning
of December 2 he took his place in full uniform with the
color guard of that organization. "When I made my appearance," he later wrote, "I could see what was very natural
and excusable, that my position was very amusing, and
perhaps ludicrous, to the young men, and it required all
the constraint of their good manners to hide their merri-
ment." But the experience gained in the War of 1812
stood him in good stead, and from parade at 7:30 in the
morning until taps at night he carried out his part with

such precision and good humor as to win "the favor and respect" of his youthful comrades.

Before nine o'clock of that eventful day the cadets marched "without music or even a tap of the drum" to the execution field. After some two hours of waiting John Brown, sitting on the coffin with his arms closely pinioned at the elbows, was brought from the jail in a light open wagon. As he passed the gallows, he looked at it intently and then ascended the scaffold "with readiness and seeming alacrity." "His movements and manner gave no evidence of his being either terrified or concerned, rather giving the impression of being a willing assistant instead of the victim."

From the lines of the cadets the stern old Virginia agitator watched John Brown intently and with something of admiration. Not a movement escaped him. He saw nothing of cruelty in the event, simply justice. Only the military escort that returned with the body was out of place—it seemed too much "like offering . . . respect and honorable attention to the atrocious criminal." Yet the grim old Southerner, awkward in his "long gray overcoat" and "plain parade cap," confessed in his diary that:

> The villain whose life has thus been forfeited possessed . . . one virtue (if it should be so called) or one quality that is more highly esteemed by the world than most rare and perfect virtues. This . . . [was] physical or animal courage, or the most complete fearlessness of and insensibility to danger and death. In this quality he seems to me to have had few equals.

It was an interesting comment, as revealing of his own inner self as of the qualities of "old John Brown." Edmund Ruffin would have died like that for an ideal.[4]

When John Brown had passed into history, Harper's Ferry surrendered its place in the public eye. The troops and visitors soon departed, leaving the sleepy little village to fall back into its accustomed ways amid the beauties of early December on the hills and rivers. Not again until weary boys in blue or in gray should alternately swing through Nature's gateway to the South or North would her streets be disturbed. Only the restless soul of "old John Brown" was astir.

*　　*　　*

Edmund Ruffin turned homeward by way of Washington, carrying with him the pike that had been used so effectively at the Ferry. Before leaving he had arranged to acquire enough of these pikes to send to every slaveholding state, and he now proposed that the legislature of Virginia should carry forward the scheme. On the morning of December 4, 1859, the Richmond *Enquirer* carried the following letter signed boldly with the initials "E. R.":

> The pikes brought to Harper's Ferry by John Brown, which were devised and directed by Northern Conspirators, made in Northern Factories, paid for by Northern funds, and designed to slaughter sleeping Southern men and their awakened wives and children, were captured before being used and so diverted from their designed purpose. Still they may be put to another and most effective use, and that for the defense of the people of the South for whose butchery they were designed. It is respectfully recommended to the Legislature of Virginia, to order that one of these weapons shall be formally presented to each of our sister slaveholding states, and sent to their respective Governors, to be placed in the legislative hall, and exposed to the view of every visitor.

Each one of these will then serve as a most eloquent and impressive preacher, appealing in the most effective manner to the patriotism of the people, and urging their sure and perfect defense against all assaults from unscrupulous and measureless enmity of Northern Abolitionists. The pikes may serve well for patriotic purposes as did the drum made of old Zispa's skin, which was bequested by him when dying, to his countrymen, for this use, to rouse and encourage them, as did his voice when alive, and with even greater influence, to battle against their enemies and oppressors.

The legislature did not accept the suggestion, but Ruffin himself carried it out. To the governor of each of the slave-holding states he forwarded a pike bearing the label used at Harper's Ferry, with the request that it be placed in a conspicuous location where it might best preach its sermon. The letter of presentation to the governor of South Carolina will suffice to show the burning spirit that had once more found freedom in action:

Washington, D. C., Dec. 16, 1859.

To his Excellency W. H. Gist, Governor of South Carolina.

Sir: Permit me to present to the State of South Carolina, through you its Chief Magistrate, one of the pikes which were sent from the North to arm the negro slaves, and to be imbrued in the blood of the white South, in the designed and expected general insurrection which Northern Abolitionists had planned and recently and fruitlessly attempted to excite and commence the practical execution of at Harper's Ferry. It is requested that this weapon may be placed in some conspicuous position in the State House of South Carolina, there to remain and be preserved as abiding and impressive evidence of the fanatical hatred borne by the dominant Northern party to the institutions and the people of the Southern States and of the unscrupulous and atrocious means resorted to for the attainment of the objects sought by that party.

Very respectfully,

EDMUND RUFFIN of Virginia.

His purpose was clear. He believed that the invasion at Harper's Ferry and the "very general sympathy of the Northern people with murderers afforded the best practical grounds for [the] dissolution [of the Union] that the South had ever had, and that it ought not to be passed over." "We ought to agitate and exasperate the already highly excited indignation of the South," he said. John Brown's pikes, fresh from New England, could speak without the confusion that troubled their distributor. Perhaps the South might be aroused by their eloquence.

Conditions indeed were encouraging. John Letcher, governor-elect of Virginia, admitted frankly that he thought the Union would be dissolved "at no distant time." James A. Seddon found a tendency throughout the South "to spread the greatest excitement and indignation against the whole North," forcing the conservative, as Lewis S. Harvie said, to remain "very still and quiet of late."[5] Ruffin was certain that the people were well in advance of their legislators and magistrates. He had never seen them "so much aroused by Northern aggressions"; there had never been "such feverish excitement." Rumors of negro uprisings swept the countryside, and steps to establish an effective military organization were taken in response. On the morning of December 10, in the "Marlbourne" neighborhood, riders carried word of a "body of negroes, headed by several public men," who were about to march through the country. The women hurried to central homes for protection. The men, mounted and armed, gathered to meet the terrible hosts which never came. The old agitator knew that it would take little to turn both this fear and force against the North. Efforts must be redoubled.

The ever-busy pen went to work with new energy. It warned the people through the columns of the *Virginia Index* that only two alternatives were presented to them. They could either preserve the existing Union "with the subversion of the institution of negro slavery" and the certain ruin thereby implied, or they could separate from the abolition states and form a new Confederacy. "There is no other possible choice or result, whether of our action or inaction," he wrote. "The subversion of slavery, if the present Union continues, may be the speedy work of Northern conspiracy and lawless violence such as has just been attempted, or it may be the work of a somewhat longer time effected simply and necessarily by the faster-growing and final overwhelming political power of the North through constitutional enactments." But come it would. Only a "timely separation and independence" could save the South. The time for action was at hand. "An occasion more suitable" and "means more useful and efficient" for this only "safe, patriotic and honorable course" could not be found.[6]

The next few weeks seemed to justify the hope that had been raised. For the first time in two years, leaders were ready "to keep V [irginia] . . . at the head of the South, and not at the tail of the North . . . for the purpose of getting broken victuals to feed her hungry politicians." Under Governor Wise's leadership there was a general tendency to hold the "whole Republican party" responsible for the Harper's Ferry raid and to make "these infamous felons grand political criminals." The conservatives called it "swaggering and bullying" but recognized the fact that the radicals were now exercising an influence far out of proportion to their numerical strength. The men who in 1850 had counseled secession were beginning to appear in the light of prophets.[7]

Passions cooled considerably during the winter of 1859-60, but the tension did not entirely yield again before the final break. From this time forward the radical remained in a favored position. Rhett and Yancey came back with new strength and Ruffin, in his lesser way, found his fellow men more respectful and his opinions more respected. Even the more conservative political leaders began to widen the gap between the sections by demanding new affirmations of Southern rights in the territories—rights which supposedly had been sufficiently guaranteed by the Compromise of 1850, the Kansas-Nebraska Act, and the Dred Scott decision. Jefferson Davis introduced resolutions on the subject in Congress, and the more radical leaders carried the new demands to the Democratic Convention at Charleston. The politician also was playing into the hands of the radical.

"It is the very foolishness of folly to raise and make prominent such issues now," declared Robert Toombs to Alexander Stephens. "Hostility to Douglas is the sole motive to movers of this mischief," was his conclusion. But the damage had been done and, there were men at Charleston "ready to risk *everything* rather than fail in obtaining a *direct* affirmation of the power and duty of Congress to protect their rights within the Territories." When Yancey voiced their demands, George E. Pugh of Ohio flung back the only answer a Northern Democrat could give: "Gentlemen of the South, you mistake us—you mistake us

—we will not do it." [8]   Thus all the irritation and all the apprehensions that the long struggle over the extension of slavery had raised in Northern minds were again thrust to the fore. The Convention went to pieces. The Northern radical accepted it as "proof" of a Southern determination to rule or ruin. It gave him new power. The sane conservative might see that there was "nothing at issue except abstractions," that principles had been brought forward to cover personal and political interests. But the leadership of sanity was passing. The radical had come to dominance in both sections.

Edmund Ruffin at home rejoiced at the split in the Democratic Convention. He had labored hard throughout the winter for the cause of secession, pleading with public leaders, distributing his pamphlets, and even encouraging the formation of "Ladies Shooting Clubs" to prepare the women of the South for self-defense in case their men folks were called away for larger service. He was gratified to find the Virginia legislature debating the different proposals he had earlier suggested for taxing or prohibiting Northern goods, for reënslaving free negroes, and for checking the opportunities of Northern traders to reach the slaves. He was gratified to find his popularity returning. When he went to the meeting of a Conference of Southern States, he was greeted with enthusiasm and forced to make a public speech. Then Rhett began republishing his articles on secession, and C. C. Memminger, sent by South Carolina to confer with the legislature of Virginia, sought him out for conferences as a man of influence. The tide was running in a new direction.

Under such conditions the Democratic quarrel at Charleston seemed the beginning of "the final struggle." The staunch support given to Douglas and his squatter-sovereignty doctrine furnished ample proof that "few Northern Democrats . . . [were] really sound on the slavery question [but were] inclined more to the views of the moderate abolitionists." It showed that no Southern man could ever again obtain high office through the Democratic Party. Seward "or some other abolitionist" would be elected in 1860 to begin the rule of a section over a nation. The end of the Union was in sight.

Alive with hope, Ruffin, dressed "in a full suit of cheap clothes manufactured in Virginia," went about urging the withdrawal of the remaining Southern delegates from the new Democratic Convention called to meet in Baltimore. He hurried to Columbia, when the Democrats of South Carolina met to choose their delegates to the Richmond Convention, anxious to see what was "the disposition as to secession of the cotton (or any of them) states from the Union." He was gratified to find himself invited by that body to take a seat on the platform with the officers, but it pained him to discover elements of discord which indicated that there were "not more avowed advocates for secession . . . [in South Carolina] than there were in Virginia." [9] Loitering home by way of the Thomas Ruffin estate, he joined the delegates from the Lower South on their way to Baltimore and found opportunity to urge secession upon them. He followed them to the convention city, stopping off at Washington to confer "on the present prospects and doubts" with such friends as Elwood Fisher, A. P. Calhoun, Lawrence Keitt, and James M. Mason. But he did not remain until the Convention adjourned. Disgusted with the Douglas flavor there so evident, he turned back to Richmond, where the "rump Convention was as-

sembling" and where he found "many agreeable acquaint-
ances" who appreciated his "fellowship and sympathy with
them highly."

Meanwhile, news of the Republican Convention had
come. Ruffin was disappointed. They "had not nominated
Seward, as expected, or Bates, or Banks or Chase or Cam-
eron, or Wade, who had been spoken of as the probable
alternative choices, but Lincoln of Illinois, inferior in ability
and reputation to all—and whom no one had mentioned
before." He was sorry they had not nominated "their
ablest man . . . and so made their success more probable."
He agreed with his friend the Reverend John Bachman,
of Charleston, that the nomination meant that the Republicans would put an ass into the presidential chair and then
allow Seward to "lead or drive him." [10]

As the summer wore on, Ruffin grew disheartened over
the prospects in his own state. It seemed that "old Virginia want[ed] another John Brown raid to wake her up
to a sense of danger." Too many persons were willing "to
swallow black republicanism, nigger, tariff and all." The
state had "kicked the descendants of their Patrick Henry
and the list of patriots and heroes out of the school house
and was conning over the spelling books of submission." [11]
Even Lincoln wrote in August of a letter received from
Virginia containing "one of the many assurances . . . from
the South that in no probable event . . . [would] there be
any very formidable effort to break up the Union." Ruffin
contemplated moving to Florida in order to escape "the
prospects of abolition supremacy in the Federal Government and the submission of Virginia." He was pained by
the thought but certain that safety for slave property was
hopeless in his native state. [12]

With these forebodings he started for a visit to his daughter Mildred at Frankfort, Kentucky. He stopped in late August at White Sulphur Springs, where over 1,650 other visitors, mainly from the Southern States, had congregated and where conversation "among the men" was mainly regarding the approaching election. "I find myself alone as an avowed disunionist *per se*," he wrote, but added grimly: "I avow that opinion upon every occasion." The gay life about him passed unnoticed—the dancing, the music, the flirtations, and the small talk which the rural South had reduced to an art. He was too busy for such things, conferring on public affairs with such men as Henry Burgwin of North Carolina, Senator Chesnut of South Carolina, or Governor McWillie of Mississippi. With Burgwin, Dr. Tabb, Philip St. G. Cocke, and James Lyons he formed a "Publication Society," each member agreeing to give one hundred dollars annually for three years for the publication of books and pamphlets, the best calculated to sustain the rights of the Southern States. It was the first of September before he left this congenial atmosphere and turned south and west toward Knoxville on the next leg of his journey.

Ruffin found Kentucky so moderate in its opinions that he was surprised, even though he had been warned of the fact. His son-in-law, Burwell Sayer, was what would have been termed a "conservative" or "Union man" back in Virginia, because he would have submitted to much wrong from the North rather than destroy the Union. Ruffin secretly classified him as "a submissionist." Yet, since he would not yield all, the Kentuckians looked upon him as almost a disunionist. Their great planters were willing to sacrifice their slaves or give up any other right in order to preserve the Union. Secession was hardly thought of as a possibility.

It was a bit hard on the old radical, especially as he was a guest in the community. But he strove earnestly to avoid arguments, and when callers such as ex-Senator Crittenden or Charles S. Todd forced him to express opinions, he did so "in a joking sort of way, so as to offend no one." There was comfort, however, to be derived from the thought that his "very odious" reputation as a disunionist had preceded him and that among these "unionists and submissionists" he "must be deemed a sort of speculative Benedict Arnold, a traitor and enemy of the country in wishes and design, though not yet in action."

Only Governor Magoffin, of all the politicians he met, seemed to be "decidedly southern" in his avowed opinions. This fiery leader freely discussed the refusal of Ohio to act on the matter of abducted slaves and delighted Ruffin with his declaration that if Lincoln were elected and should send an army through Kentucky to attack the Southern states that might secede, "he as governor would make every night's encampment a grave yard." But even *he* believed the election of an abolition president followed by some overt act was a necessary antecedent to secession.[13]

The return trip to Virginia carried Ruffin through a portion of Ohio, where for the first time a comparison could be made between the farm lands in free and in slave territories. Northern writers had long dwelt upon the better farming and the superior industry manifest on the northern banks of the Ohio, but Ruffin, viewing conditions from an equally prejudiced angle, could see no farms equal to those of Kentucky. He concluded, therefore, that this claim, like most other things Northern, was false and un-

sound, and he came back to Virginia more certain that
a superior Southern civilization was facing a crisis in the
coming election.

During the stay in Kentucky long letters had been sent
back to the newspapers of the seaboard states, and on his
return Ruffin found that his volume, *Anticipations of the
Future,* had come from the press. This, his most pretentious contribution to the cause of secession, had been written
during the preceding spring and had been published in part
in the Charleston *Mercury.* As now issued, it formed a
book of over four hundred pages of clever propaganda.

Taking the idea from a sketch called "Wild Scenes of
the South," the author had attempted to prophesy the
course of events in the United States in the period from
1864 to 1869, in a series of letters purported to have been
written by an English visitor to the London *Times.* The
purpose was to show how causes already at work, if un-
checked, would ultimately affect the nation; how a "Northern sectional party" would soon rule and, without exercising
any constitutional power or committing a single "overt
act," would produce "the most complete subjection and
political bondage, degradation, and ruin of the South." It
pictured Lincoln's election in 1860 and the triumph of
Seward four years later; the abolition majorities amending
the Constitution so as to abolish slavery; protective tariffs
passed, high enough to satisfy the most rabid manufacturing
interest; and, in the end, a South dwindling to such ruin
that secession was accepted. Then followed the imaginary
course of events in which the border states, holding off
until the Confederacy was firmly established, joined the
new nation in protest against Northern troops crossing
their borders to attack the offending states. A short but

ruinous war was imagined to have ensued, in which the South suffered from a blockade but the Northern merchants were ruined and their cities torn to pieces by mobs of "undigested foreigners." The West took little part in the struggle but ultimately, driven by commercial interests, broke with the North and joined the South, now on its way to prosperity through the development of its own industries and the establishment of direct trade with Europe.

It was a glorious picture of ruin turned to prosperity; of a people suffering because they had delayed taking steps which in the end proved to be necessary; of a majority, drunk with power, blundering forward to ruin and forcing a minority to defend its superior social-economic system; and, in the end, of urban-industrial things bowing before the superior merits of agriculture.

To enforce the indirect arguments of his imaginative work Ruffin appended an earlier pamphlet, "Causes and Consequences of the Independence of the South." Here in direct form he reasoned out the same sequence of events but expressed serious doubts as to whether the North would resort to war in case of Southern secession. He was making sure that even the most stupid would understand his arguments.

As election day drew near, the possibility of Lincoln's election and of South Carolina's secession grew greater. Governor Ellis of North Carolina told Ruffin of a letter he had recently received from Governor Gist of South Carolina, urging the calling of a convention in case of Lincoln's election, and of assurance given that the Palmetto State would secede alone if others refused to act. The nervous old Virginian then began to worry lest the recently manifest conservative attitudes of the Lincoln faction might

drive the radicals away and thus prevent a Republican victory. Or, perchance, the Southern conservatives might be
won over to await "the overt act." It was horribly discon-
certing to read in the Richmond *Daily Whig* that "Virginia
will *not* unite . . . in resistance to the mere Constitutional
election of Abraham Lincoln." [14] What could be done to
arouse the passions of men to whom peace and Union
seemed so dear?

Ruffin lay awake at night pondering this question. Another golden opportunity was slipping away, and only
South Carolina showed signs of taking the impending
Republican victory seriously. At last a plan evolved—a last
desperate stroke to be made. He would write Yancey in
Alabama, urging him to step forward again and stir the
people as Patrick Henry had done of old. The weakness
of the Southern people for oratory might turn the tide.
The Lower South might be persuaded to support its old
leader.

"Within a few days after this letter can reach you," his
appeal ran, "the popular vote will have been given in the
presidential election, and the result will be known to you.
According to all present indications the result . . . will
give the election to the avowed abolition candidate. . . . I
cannot doubt that you will view this result as I do, of the
clear and unmistakable indication of future and fixed domination of the Northern section, its abolition policy . . .
and the beginning of a sure and speedy progress to the
extermination of negro slavery and the consequent and utter
ruin of the prosperity of the South. I cannot doubt that
you see the one passage for escape from this impending
and awful danger and calamity by secession of some . . .
of the Southern states from the Union . . . which has

changed from the former bond of fraternal love . . . to a yoke and manacles on the South—the instrument of our oppression and destruction in the hands of our northern enemies and prospective masters." He pleaded with Yancey to swing through the South preaching a crusade. "You are the man for this great work," he urged. "Will you be the Henry for this impending contest? Move in it at once, and I would stake my life on the venture that your success will not be less complete and glorious than that of your great example." [15]

How Ruffin longed for the gift of stirring a people! How his own services dwindled as he thought of what the orator might accomplish! "I do not urge on you," he continued, "what I would not attempt myself, if endowed with your peculiar power as a public speaker . . . instead of being, as I am, entirely destitute of all such talent. . . . Already, and for years past, in a different and far less effective mode, I have labored by writing and publishing my views to influence the public mind in favor of this great object, but with such small success as might have been expected from my obscure name and position and limited powers." Yet he pledged the best efforts of mind and body "for the very short remainder" of his life to assist Yancey in "earning imperishable fame," in "establishing the rights and freedom and security of the South." It was the picture of his own dearest dreams—the expression of longings unfulfilled.

Meanwhile, through letters to the Charleston *Mercury,* Ruffin pressed on South Carolina the necessity of action in case of Lincoln's election. The domination of the "Abolition party . . . over all the interests and rights" of the Southern states must meet with resistance. "One state will be enough to begin the movement," he urged. "South Carolina will not fail." [16]

On election day the determined old leader cast his ballot for John C. Breckinridge, in order "to avert the disgrace of Virginia giving a plurality to Bell," and hurried off to South Carolina where the zeal for secession seemed greatest. He wrote in his diary on that morning:

> This is the day for the election of electors—the momentous election which, if showing the subsequent election of Lincoln to be certain, will serve to show whether these Southern States are to remain free, or to be politically enslaved; whether the institution of negro slavery on which the social and political existence of the South rests, is to be secured by our resistance or to be abolished in a short time as the result of our . . . submission to Northern domination.

When the returns of that day were in, Abraham Lincoln had been elected president of the United States. The victory had not been decisive. He had secured but forty per cent of the total vote cast, and his combined opponents had secured over a million and a half votes in the free states. Nor had the South spoken with assurance. Breckinridge lacked 136,875 votes of having a popular majority in the slave states, and Bell had carried Virginia, Kentucky, and Tennessee, and Douglas, Missouri. The radical both North and South might well stop and consider. The great mass of the people were surely not of his temper.

* * *

As Ruffin rode southward toward Columbia, where the South Carolina legislature was about to issue its call for a convention of the people to consider "the value of the

Union," he scattered broadcast the tracts and pamphlets
that the Charleston Association of 1860 had furnished. He
had been "sowing" these in the "sterile Virginia soil" for
the past months, and his spirits rose as he passed out of the
equally barren North Carolina and into the land where a
"universal secession feeling appeared." Soon men entered
the train wearing the "blue cockade" of the "minute men,"
and enthusiastic demonstrations were staged at towns along
the line. His pamphlets were now in demand. He began
to feel at home "in a strange land." [17]

In Columbia all was astir. Enthusiastic crowds filled the
streets and public halls. Bands marched about and, prominent men, when they were recognized, were forced to
speak. The fiery little stranger, with his long white hair,
was soon noticed, and such friends as Rhett, Bonham, Palmer, and Yeadon crowded about in the lobby of the old
Congaree House to ply him with questions as to the conditions in Virginia. He paused to speak with Bishop
Lynch, the Catholic leader of Charleston, and as the conversation turned "upon the all-absorbing topic," a crowd pressed
in close to hear. The good bishop feared the consequences
of South Carolina seceding alone. He thought the Federal
Government would hold the forts within the state and
with an armed squadron of ships compel all vessels entering
the harbors to pay duties. He would wait until other
states were willing to act. Ruffin answered him firmly,
though a bit uncertain of his ability to meet an antagonist
of such potency, and in the end declared that "if all the
dangers and losses feared were . . . certain, it would still
be proper to meet them" rather than to submit or delay.

At these words the crowd broke into "a storm of applause," enabling Ruffin to withdraw gracefully with a re-

mark to the bishop that though His Honor had the best of the argument, the sympathies of the hearers seemed to be with the weaker party. Later in the evening a serenade began before the door of the hotel, and Ruffin's name was called loudly until he appeared and spoke. To his surprise he was self-possessed and his speaking effective. He declared that the independence of the South had "been literally the one great idea" of his life and that it could now be realized through the action of South Carolina.

The great crowd cheered as he spoke of the danger in which he had come to join them and of his belief that "the first drop of blood spilled" would bring Virginia and every other border state to their side. He had come here, he said, because he was certain that if anything were to be done at this time, it would be done by South Carolina. He had faith in her people. He hoped their legislature would act at once so as to give courage to the timid outside and to strike fear to the North.

The crowd approved, and confidence and new energy surged through the straightened form of the old sectional patriot. That night he wrote along the side of the narrative of the day's events in his diary these words: "A Prophet is not without honor but in his country and among his own kin, and in his own house."

The next weeks were tense and happy. Articles from his pen found space in the Charleston papers, and the citizens of Columbia paid respectful attention to his opinions. Now he made light of the danger from Northern resistance to secession, pointing out the inadequacy of the regular army and the large number of Northerners who believed that secession was a right; again he argued that the sacrifice of Southern blood by men defending their homes against invasion would bring to their assistance thousands of brave men from every state south of Mason and Dixon's Line. Even Virginia would not stand aside and see her sister state attacked. He called attention to the influence that a declaration of free trade with Europe would have in bringing the sympathies of foreign nations to a seceding state. He admitted the danger from a Northern blockade but brushed it aside by reminding men of the importance of cotton and rice to the peoples of the Old World. The blockade would be on paper; swift blockade runners would, in fact, keep the channels of trade filled with all essential supplies.

On the morning of November 8 a delegation of students from the College of South Carolina waited on Ruffin at his hotel and requested that he come and address the student body on the issues of the day. Lack of confidence checked an acceptance, but he obtained the gratification without the confusion of a formal appearance by promising an "informal" visit at noon the following day. Then, with pleasant visions of applauding youth in his mind, he hurried to the gallery of the House of Representatives, where the bill for calling a convention was expected to be introduced. Both houses by unanimous vote offered him a seat in their respective halls, enabling him to witness the passage of that momentous act and to feel that he had some share in what he believed to be the beginning of the great events for which he had so long labored.

When the last vote which made certain the convention had been recorded, he wrote in his diary: "Thus this great and important measure, which I have so long anxiously desired, is adopted; and on this hereafter glorious day, the 10th of November, is inaugurated the revolution which will tear the slave-holding states from their connection with the

Northern section and establish their separate independence."

Passing down the street, he persuaded the editor of the *South Carolinian* to haul down the Palmetto flag as the symbol of the state and to unfurl in its stead the banner that had flown over Fort Moultrie during its defense in the Revolution, as the symbol of "the expected Southern Confederacy." The period of separate state action was ended— South Carolina was acting for the oppressed of all the South!

Ruffin was in his glory. Never before had he been free. Writing to his sons on November 11, he declared: [18]

> The time since I have been here has been the happiest of my life, in which personal feelings and interests were not concerned. The public events are as gratifying to me as they are glorious and momentous, and there has been much to gratify my individual and selfish feelings. I have always heretofore been treated most kindly and respectfully by the people of South Carolina. But all previous did not compare with the present time. My coming was hailed as if a subject of public interest and rejoicing. I have been cordially and affectionately welcomed by both former friends and acquaintances and strangers and every respect and attention paid to me, both in private and public. . . . What a contrast to my position in my native state and among most of my countrymen! I know that much of the language addressed to me is mere compliment and in some cases flattery. But even in the latter case it is gratifying to me—as for example, when last night, a member of the legislature, before a stranger to me, told me that he was convinced that my presence here has aided the completion of the result of secession.

In the meantime Ruffin had joined the South Carolina "minute men," and Mrs. John Bachman had sewed the cockade on his hat. This step brought new publicity, and as he prepared to leave Columbia for Charleston, he was suddenly startled to find himself in demand as a public speaker. The citizens of Sumter requested an address at a public meeting called to forward the spirit of secession. Regardless of misgivings, he was forced to play the part that he had assumed. Public men in South Carolina were expected to speak on call.

When Ruffin reached the town of Sumter on November 14, he found a corps of one hundred and fifty minute men waiting to pay their respects and indulge in the inevitable serenade. The band blared and the cannon roared its welcome. Leaders made speeches, and Ruffin, the excuse for all the disturbance, replied carefully lest he spend the ammunition he had prepared for the great occasion on the morrow. The agitator had arrived; dreams were coming true!

The next day, amid an equal show of enthusiasm, the prophet away from his own country entered the crowded Court House and sat with becoming modesty while a state senator and three representatives made short preliminary addresses in favor of immediate secession. When resolutions had been passed to bind all delegates elected to the coming convention to that position, the chief speaker of the day was introduced.

The astonishing performance that followed is best described in the orator's own words:

> I spoke and without embarrassment after the beginning for about three-quarters of an hour, and then stopped, having forgotten to bring in some of my main points. I referred to no notes. I was greatly applauded, and, I believe, from what I was told afterwards, that my remarks and my plain manner of delivering them, gave

much satisfaction. Indeed some have so far complimented me, both here and at Columbia, as to declare
that they thought my presence in this state has operated
to strengthen and forward the action of secession.

He had succeeded as a public speaker. The man and his
section were moving forward to a new freedom.

Triumphs continued in Charleston, whither he went the
following day. No sooner was his presence discovered in
the city than a group of townsmen, headed by "Mr. Carlisle,
editor of the *Courier*," called and announced that a serenade was about to be offered in his honor. They expected
him to answer with a short address. They, too, assumed
that agitators were ready speakers. Ruffin could not escape.

As he stepped forward to face the crowd which filled the
street, enthusiastic cheers greeted him and the ladies who
filled the balcony of the old Charleston Hotel waved their
handkerchiefs to his consternation. He suddenly realized
that he was entirely out of place. Yet he could not turn
back. Forces that he had set free were driving him help-
lessly forward. He began to speak in a low voice, apolo-
gizing for the failure of his own state to move toward
secession. "If Virginia remains in the Union, under the
domination of this infamous, low, vulgar tyranny of Black
Republicanism and there is one other state in the Union
that has bravely thrown off the yoke," he declared, "I will
seek my domicile in that state and abandon Virginia forever. If Virginia will not act as South Carolina, I have no
longer a home, and I am a banished man." And then, as
if abashed by his own boldness, he brought his speech to
a sudden close with a declaration of his willingness to sacrifice his all for the success of the cause.[19]

He was disappointed, certain that he had not done him-

self "as proud as before." The applause had been given as
a matter of form. He had failed. Even the wild cheers of
the cadets at the Citadel the next day did not entirely restore his spirit. If only he might act instead of being forced
to talk!

Anxious to be near and play some part in the Southern
movement where it was most alive, Ruffin now went on to
Georgia, in company with Barnwell Rhett, to attend the
session of the legislature then discussing the calling of a
state convention. The radical element welcomed them.
There was need for assistance where leaders still kept hopes
that "our rights may be maintained and our wrongs be re-
dressed in the Union." The visitors were given seats in the
Senate chamber and later in the House. Their evenings
were spent with such men as Judge Benning, General Wil-
liams (speaker of the House), Colonel Hardee, and others,
discussing the "present crisis" and ways and means of
accomplishing secession. They brightened the prospects
with champagne "drunk in great moderation," and
even the temperate Ruffin "committed the unusual excess
of drinking half a glass to the most speedy secession of
Georgia."

But prospects for radical action were poor. It was evident that Georgia would not lead in the movement, perhaps
would not even follow if South Carolina took the initiative.
Such powerful leaders as Alexander Stephens and Benja-
min Hill resisted immediate secession, though professing
to advocate resistance to the North, and the temper of the
state was decidedly moderate. Ruffin took his disappointment out in condemning his "travelling trunk" as a miser-
able Yankee cheat and purchased another which was "said
to be of Southern production." The next day he was on

his way back to Virginia, musing on his recent happy
experiences.

As the wanderer neared his native state, he was pained
by the "mortifying reflection that at home, in his own country, in which . . . [he] had long lived and labored, and
had so much served and benefited," not only would "public
applause and appreciation" have been withheld, but enemies
would have depreciated and censured him. He found comfort again in writing in his diary the words: "A prophet is
not without honor, except in his own country." [20]

In the days that followed Ruffin defiantly wore about
Richmond the blue cockade of the minute men and scoffed
at the threats to "ride him upon a rail" for his recent
activities in South Carolina. He even thought he could
detect a slight change in the general attitude of the people,
many men expressing the belief that the Union was about
to be broken and that Virginia "ought to go with the Southern fragment." Reports came from distant counties of
"life-long Unionists clamoring for secession," of gentlemen
binding themselves into a new unity against "the class of
overseers and the like" who were openly declaring that
"they would not lift a finger in defense of the rights of
slave holders."

Yet the leaders counseled delay, and the conservatives
were everywhere in control. Moderate men were working
feverishly for a "compromise and settlement" between the
sections, and prominent Northern leaders, such as Edward
W. Bates, were giving assurance that Lincoln was "as true a
conservative, national Whig as . . . [could] be found in
Missouri, Virginia or Tennessee," that he would "endeavor
to restore peace and harmony" and avoid "all those exciting
subjects which . . . [had] so mischievously agitated the

country" for the past few years. Some men were even asking: "What is there in common with South Carolina and our proud old State but slavery? The one an empire of men strong in all that constitutes the force of manhood, the other the only oligarchy of our country. . . . Where . . . would a man as Letcher and the thousands who, like him, have done honor to their state by their talents and industry, find themselves in this landed aristocracy? F. F. O.'s must soon go down with the last of the cocked hats. The new Virginia race takes their position, willing and able to cope with the men of the North and East in all that constitutes manly toil and hardihood." Virginia was a long way from being a radical's paradise.[21]

But within three weeks' time Ruffin was back in South Carolina to witness the secession of the state from the Union. Again they gave him a seat in the convention, and on the evening when the ordinance was to be signed they invited him to stand by the side of ex-Governor Manning in the center of the hall as one after another "the first rebels" attached their names to the document. The galleries were crowded, and the suppressed enthusiasm which now and then had brought cheers and clapping during the two hours of signing broke into pandemonium as the last signature was affixed and the president waved the parchment above his head, "proclaiming South Carolina to be a free and independent community." Far into the night the old man tossed on his pillow as the "distant sounds of rejoicing, with the music of military bands" went on with "no thought of ceasing." He would have preferred to have been in the streets where the boys lighted their bonfires and fired their salutes. But his body and his spirit were of different generations.

A week later he was in Florida, ready to telegraph back to Governor Pickens the news of another secession. The convention invited him to occupy a seat in their hall, and a few days later requested that he address them on the issues in hand. Without embarrassment he pleaded for "immediate action," pointing out the necessity for a solid block of Southern states in open defiance before the fourth of March. He felt that he had played a small part in turning the tide when shortly afterward the resolutions for immediate secession passed with but five dissenting votes.

He would have hurried on to Georgia to lend a hand if he had not already overtaxed his strength and become ill. Reluctantly he turned back to Charleston, "to commit a little treason" by shoveling dirt for the strengthening of Fort Moultrie, and then continued homeward to work for the coming convention in his own state.

At home the prophet found his neighbors still a bit stingy with their honors. The citizens of the Prince George and Surry district refused to elect his son Edmund to represent them in the convention and showed marked attachment to the Union. It was a personal affront as well as a "demagogue and submission triumph." The son had suffered because of the sins of the father. Again Ruffin was forced to recognize "the dislike" which he had "always succeeded in acquiring wherever . . . [he] resided" and to contrast it with the "evidence of very high appreciation, respect and applause" which had been given by strangers. Anger and disgust filled him. He would carry out the threat he had made at Charleston.

A bit of consolation, however, came a short time afterward when *Leslie's Weekly* published his portrait, describing him as a secessionist who must have "imbibed with his mother's milk the desire to break up the compact that binds this great Confederacy together." It pictured him as "laden with years, and having the air of a partriarch," but "not yet by any means" at "the doddering state"; "his form . . . not bent nor . . . his step slow or uncertain; his hair . . . perfectly white, hanging in frosty locks over his shoulders." "On the left side of his hat," it concluded, "he wears the ever present cockade, and so with this symbol of resistance hoisted at the peak, the old man goes about from Convention to Convention, a political Peter the Hermit, preaching secession wherever he goes." [22]

It was notice that was welcome. The enemy felt his blows and understood his spirit even though his neighbors were dumb. "It is a coarse and bad picture," was Ruffin's comment, but he clipped it and pasted it with evident pleasure on the pages of his diary. His observations on prophets were all the more in order.

*　　*　　*

Meanwhile, out on the prairies of Illinois, Abraham Lincoln, president-elect by the sectional vote of a minority of the people of the nation, prepared to depart for Washington to assume control of the crumbling government. To the radical Southerner his election meant not only the end of Southern influence in national affairs, but the ultimate destruction of all that was "peculiar" in Southern life. The shrewd political maneuvering by which the abolitionist had been gathered to the Republican fold, the clever linking of Western interests in cheap lands and home markets with the struggle to preserve American democracy, and the apparent acceptance of court decisions and constitutional rights but with words and conduct that implied the later use of "legal" means to make them accord with "higher laws," all indicated that Lincoln was at war with all that the South held dear. The moderate man would await some "overt act" to justify secession in self-defense; the radical could see no reason for further delay. On this conviction six states had followed South Carolina into secession and on February 4, 1861, at Montgomery, Alabama, had assembled to launch a new nation.

When Virginia, with sincere purpose to save the Union, refused to accept the radical view, Ruffin shook her dust from his feet. "I will be out of Virginia before Lincoln's inauguration," he wrote, "and so . . . avoid being, as a Virginian, under his government even for an hour. I, at least, will become a citizen of the seceded Confederate States, and will not again reside in my native state, nor enter it except to make visits to my children, until Virginia shall also secede. . . . This result, though now postponed by the trick and fraud of assembling the 'Peace Congress' cannot be delayed long." A little bloodshed, he was certain, would drive her to her "natural allies." In less than a year, he was convinced, his Confederate citizenship would make him again a citizen of his native state.

The long process of creating fears and hopes was nearly ended. The radical had triumphed in the Lower South. That great divergent region had begun to draw together. The "united South" that the politician had urged to gain his ends, the "slave power" that the abolitionist had imagined, that "superior civilization" which the radical had conjured up, these as realities now stood forth to defend their rights. A confident people contemplated the cost of nationalism.

CHAPTER IX

THE WHIRLWIND

I F [the Black Republicans] beat us [next year] I see no safety for us, our property and our firesides, except in breaking up the concern. I do not think it wise for the South to suffer a party to get possession of the government whose principles and whose leaders are so openly hostile not only to her equality but to her safety in the Union, and my present opinion is that if such a calamity should come, we should prefer to defend ourselves at the doorsill rather than await the attack at our hearthstone. . . . They have already declared war, and if the North elect them it is endorsing the declaration." [1]

Thus Robert Toombs, from the ever moderate state of Georgia, expressed the Southern understanding of what the election of Abraham Lincoln on the Republican ticket implied. It was not the viewpoint of a fanatical Southern nationalist, for Toombs, as a Whig, had given aggressive support to the Compromise of 1850 and had swung over to the Democratic ranks only when such a course seemed best to serve the cause of Union. It represented, in fact, an honest Southern evaluation of Lincoln and his party, born neither of groundless fears nor of diabolical schemes. Toombs and his kind were merely practical leaders who saw in the Republican triumph the threat of all that was later to be carried out *under Republican rule,* in the days of War and Reconstruction. They saw both the radical element and the political necessity that worked within the party. They realized that, regardless of immediate purposes and leadership, this group was fundamentally at war with what Southerners called a "superior civilization." [2]

The Republican Party in 1860 was composed, like most successful political parties, of many diverse and complex elements. Born with the Kansas-Nebraska Act, it had early gathered to itself a large part of those idealistic, democratic forces which had already found expression in the Loco-Foco movement, the temperance crusade, and the Liberty and Free Soil parties. They represented an element which had long confused the Constitution with the Declaration of Independence and had thought of both as intended to establish a social order in keeping with the Puritan interpretation of the Scriptures. They offered a fertile seed bed for the doctrine of "higher law" as it was to come from the coarser mind of the politician Seward; they could understand Lincoln's talk about saving democracy. The party had also caught the first scattering Whigs as they forsook their old allegiance and had profited by the questionable, if not openly dishonest, "Appeal to the Independent Democrats" which Chase and his colleagues had hurled at Douglas—groups which gave a more practical turn to the party but did not at first greatly change its advanced character. When it appeared before the country in 1856, it well deserved the appellative "radical" with its statement of faith in the Declaration of Independence, its denunciation of the "crime against Kansas," and its more material demands for a central railway to the Pacific and for river and harbor improvements that would benefit the Northwest.[3]

In the next four years the more conservative and politically minded element gained control. A western railway interest nearly equal to that which looked to Stephen A.

Douglas for political favors turned to the new party for support; the foreigners responded to the talk of more favorable immigration laws and homestead legislation; and the manufacturing interests of both East and West found a carrier for their programs in the Republican advocacy of protective tariffs. Whig practices were being brought forward under a banner inscribed with Jeffersonian ideals. By 1860 the party represented the hope for political office and political advancement of the majority of Northern men who were outside the Democratic fold. It was, in a very ordinary sense, a *political* party, with aims similar to those of its opponents and with leaders capable of playing the usual political game.[4]

And the significant thing about it all was that both the conservative-interest group and the radical-idealistic group had been bound into a working unity, each certain that the new party promised it definite returns. Only the extreme abolitionists of New England, who had ever lacked faith in political action, stood aside. The suggestion that the Dred Scott decision could be altered by changing the complexion of the Court made its opponents stanch partisans, awaiting the time when Republican lawyers would draw fat salaries on the bench and achieve holy ends by new decisions. The absolute prohibition of slavery in the territories, confining it to the old limits and setting it "on the road to ultimate extinction," satisfied the average enemy of "that institution" and also guaranteed the Northern home-seeker a free hand with western lands. "You do not seem to consider that the permission of slavery [in the territories] is in ordinary cases a greater prohibition to the mass of Northern men, than its exclusion is to Southern men," wrote Robert Littell to Wyndham Robertson in 1854.

"Capital being on the side of the slave labor, the Northern men must go somewhere else," he added, forecasting Lincoln's own declaration that slavery must be kept from the territories so that they might become the homes of free men.[5]

Moreover, in order to gain greatest political support in the North, Democratic Party rule had been constantly charged with being "slave-power" rule. The false idea that the Democratic Party was purely sectional had been fostered so long that Republicans could not understand the peculiar sectional threat that their own party carried in 1860. Even Edward Bates, as late as November 3 in that year, was answering the objection to Lincoln as a sectional candidate by saying, "You seem to forget that it would be equally objectionable that Bell or Breckinridge should be elected by the slave states." Wyndham Robertson complained bitterly of this unjust assumption, declaring that: "The possession of the power of the Federal Government by the Democratic party . . . furnished the pretext . . . to confound the whole slaveholding interest as absolutely identical with Democracy, and thus to turn and direct opposition, for whatever cause, to the policy and acts of the Democratic party, into apparent opposition to the slaveholding interests. This ruse . . . fused . . . and united in a common line of policy, some who merely opposed the administration on political grounds, with its opponents on the slavery issue." He recognized it as an old trick, but a decidedly dangerous one.[6]

In like vein Samuel J. Tilden saw the political strategy that had been used to elect Lincoln and declared that the election was not a "verdict of the Northern States on the theoretic questions urged by the Republicans," but a movement of the "masses" going for "Lincoln from habit and association, as a lineal succession from Whiggism . . . mere opposition to the Democratic party and from all the causes which gradually operate to make a revolution between the Ins and the Outs." But he did understand, regardless of the reasons for the vote, that Republican rule "would be in substance the government of one people by another" and a shock to the Southern social order which would bring "a pervading sense of danger to the life of every human being and to the honor of every woman." He pointed out that "sectionalism of parties [had] *hitherto* been founded in differences upon subjects comparatively unimportant, but that sectionalism [was] . . . *now* founded upon differences of opinion reaching to the very structure of civil society in fifteen states." He believed that the final result of such a development would be disunion.[7]

The Republicans, however, absorbed in obtaining a political victory, could not understand this point of view. They had to hold their divergent elements together, making such appeals as would satisfy all groups. They had to abide firmly by every tenet on which agreement had been reached and could yield no more than the most radical element in the party was willing to concede. Their leaders were, as Judge R. B. Curtis said, under the necessity "of adhering to their party platform which constituted their only claim to popular support," and Lincoln, in spite of vague assurance given to the South, was forced in 1861, for party's sake, to reject every suggestion of compromise and to choose the use of force as the last means of satisfying the Union sentiment he had stirred as party cement in the border states and in the southern portions of the Old Northwest.[8]

It was also necessary constantly to minimize the danger involved and to interpret the Southern move as a Democratic Party affair. "I am grieved to find that you seem to be of that large and amiable class of patriots—true genuine patriots—of which my venerable friend Mr. Crittenden may be considered the head, who have allowed themselves to be scared into the belief that the existence of the Union is in danger," wrote Bates to Robertson in November, 1860. "I do not participate in that fear," he continued. "I know that even small factions, by putting on an air of desperation may stir up troubles. . . . I knew that the Democracy would struggle hard to retain its long abused power to misgovern the country, and that, whenever the crisis should come, it would die hard." He assured his friend that: "If anything like justice is done to Mr. Lincoln and he is allowed, quietly, to organize his administration and make a fair start, I have no doubt that he will act . . . in a mild and conciliatory spirit. His character is marked by a happy mixture of amiability and courage, and while I expect him to be as mild as Fillmore, I equally expect him to be as firm as Jackson." [9]

Under such conditions, as a matter of fact, the radical element in the Republican Party held the balance of power. As the price of its adherence the more extreme attitudes on slavery had to be accepted, and whatever threat that element carried to the South became the threat of the party. Freed from the restraints that a Southern wing would have imposed, the Republicans had unconsciously become more and more antagonistic to the South in their efforts to control the North, offering an economic program which satisfied the more conservative and adopting an attitude on abstract questions which was satisfactory to the radical. To gain the anti-slavery element they admitted the moral evil in slavery, thereby inadvertently pledging themselves to use every legal means for its destruction in a government where numbers could alter the fundamental law of the land. They had become, in spite of a majority which "would not interfere with slavery," the party of freedom; they had accepted radical obligations.

Moderate Northern men had seen this drift, and some had made positive efforts to check it. In 1859 Washington Hunt had called "the Republican organization the most serious impediment in the way of Union." He had seen the party shaping its program to catch a wider sectional support and had sought to give it a national appeal. "If that party as now organized were to modify its avowals and assume a more national tone," he had asked of Wyndham Robertson, "would it be practicable for you in the South to join in their support?" His plan had been to capitalize the Whiggish character of the Republican platform and to build a Southern wing among the former members of the Whig Party in that section. But he had failed. The party leaders had chosen to woo the Northern radical, not the Southern conservative. The sins of Brooks and Yancey were to be visited upon all their people alike.[10]

The South, therefore, in 1861 could take its choice between revolution and ultimate subjection to the most advanced of those who held in their hands the unity of the Republican Party. The slavery issue could not be cast aside; it must be kept alive or the party would perish. Tilden understood this when he said in January, 1861: "Lincoln's administration must necessarily go utterly to pieces, when it comes either to present affirmative measures or to distribute its patronage." But he did not see the alternative. He believed that there was "a larger and stronger party capable of doing the Southern States full justice"—meaning that they would be permitted "the natural expansion of their industrial and social systems." But he was wrong. The Republican Party, not the Union, was to go on undivided. And that unity was to last until every vestige of the "peculiar civilization" was in ruins and the proud masters had bowed before the black freedmen.

The course of events had thus been determined beforehand. The Republican Party would hold fast to its sectional program. "Entertain no proposition for a compromise in regard to the extension of slavery," wrote Lincoln to his aides, meanwhile proposing the "sending of supplies, without an attempt to reënforce" Fort Sumter, in order to provoke the citizens of Charleston to begin an attack. "He himself conceived the idea," wrote Orville Browning shortly after he had come from a conference with Lincoln, and then added: "The plan succeeded. They attacked Sumter—it fell, and thus did more service than it otherwise could." Lincoln had shifted the issue to one of saving the Union. A little blood had been spilled. The Republican leaders and their party were, for the time being, certain of their power.[11]

* * *

Edmund Ruffin, voluntary exile from Virginia, had anticipated events. He had been as anxious for the "letting of blood" as were his opponents, and for the same reason. In January, 1861, he had written that the "bloodshed of South Carolinians defending their soil and their rights, or maintaining the possession of their harbor . . . will stir doubly fast the sluggish blood of the more backward Southern States into secession and intimate alliance." He had eagerly watched the building of fortifications about his adopted home, refusing to venture far from the city of Charleston lest Lincoln begin hostilities in his absence. In March he did go to Goldsboro, North Carolina, to speak for secession, but only because the prospects "had become still more faint." But he hurried back to the city certain that Lincoln would carry out the "previously designed plan or policy, dictated by anti-slavery fanaticism," of rejecting any "plan for adjustment" and would provoke a war. He wanted to be on hand when the struggle began.

Ruffin became even more anxious for the fatal stroke when ex-Governor Richardson, who had been a member of the Montgomery Convention, informed him that it was supposed by the delegates there that a majority of the people of every Southern state except South Carolina was indisposed to the disruption of the Union, and that if the question of reconstruction of the former Union were referred to a popular vote, there was every probability that it would be approved.[12] He was alarmed. Further delay might bring a settlement of difficulties. But he did not despair, for the attitudes of both Lincoln and the people of Charleston were in his favor. The former in his speeches, sprinkled along the road from Springfield to Washington, was manifesting "enough of party feeling and Northern blindness and fanaticism to show clearly that he . . . [meant] to yield nothing of the . . . precious policy of his party," while the latter, at first reluctant to take the initial step, had now begun to feel that there had been enough of forbearance. The troops, gathered from the plantations about, were becoming restless. "They had come to defend South Carolina and fight." While such service seemed in near prospect, "they had disregarded all hardships or personal considerations." But waiting, even though "watchful," was irksome. Both troops and civilians were "becoming feverishly impatient for the reduction of

Fort Sumter." An excuse for "justifiable action" could hardly be wanting for long.

While Lincoln and Seward, working on cross lines, confused the Federal purposes in regard to Fort Sumter, Jefferson Davis held the restless Southerners in check. But the task was growing more difficult. Almost at the same moment that Lincoln decided to cut the Gordian knot, Roger Pryor, representing a group who had determined to bring popular pressure on the government at Montgomery for the same end, came to Charleston to urge the willing troops to "strike a blow." He declared to "an immense and enthusiastic audience" that in case of conflict Virginia would secede "within an hour by Shrewsbury clock"—Virginia the mother of states, which had called a peace congress and given eager support to every effort at compromise! [13] It was a prize for which many hands were ready to coöperate in precipitating a crisis. Lincoln was to have his way.

Local supplies for Fort Sumter had been cut off on April 6, with the expectation, based on assurance from Seward, that Major Anderson would quietly evacuate on April 15. Lincoln's move altered the entire situation. On the 8th Governor Pickens informed his aides that Captain Talbot had brought word from Washington that supplies were already on the way from the North and that resistance to landing would mean war. Wild rumors of an impending attack on the rear of Morris Island spread through the city. Volunteers poured into the ranks of the defending troops as hotheaded leaders prepared to make the most of the new situation. Pryor and Ruffin were also to have their way!

Having learned of the impending clash, Ruffin hurried to the Citadel, where the young men had so recently acclaimed him, and obtained the loan of a light musket. He then boarded the little steamer that made a daily trip to the forts in the harbor, in the hope that Major Anderson might open fire upon her, coveting "the distinction and éclat" that would thus be acquired. But the guns of Sumter were silent. They frowned at the old warrior on the deck, but did not speak. He was disappointed, but came back to Charleston with a new plan of action.

The next morning at daybreak an old man with long white hair might have been seen making his way along the wharf, a musket in one hand, a carpetbag in the other, bound for the boat that ran out to Morris Island, where rumor said the Northern troops would attack when the supply ship arrived. A stir ran through the crowd that had gathered to see the new volunteers depart for the forts as the stern old patriot joined them, his purpose plainly written in every look and action. Strangers crowded about with words of praise. The soldiers-in-the-making accepted him as one with themselves and accorded him the place of honor. Dressed in his suit of plain Southern homespun, he seemed to represent something of the devotion that men believed was to be given to the cause of a new nation. So completely did he become the center of interest, both at the wharf and on the boat as it crossed the harbor, that he later noted in his diary the shame he felt at such exaggerated commendation for the very small effort or sacrifice he was making.

As the boat neared the shore of the Island and the soldiers gathered to welcome the new recruits, some one spied the picturesque old figure on the deck and set up a cheer. When he landed, the officers of the various units descended upon him with invitations to attach himself particularly to their respective troops and to become a member of the officers' mess. After due deliberation he chose the Palmetto Guards, commanded by Captain Cuthbert, to which was attached the Iron Battery under Major Stevens who had pointed the cannon that was fired on the *Star of the West.*

The soldiers accepted the new recruit as something of an ornament, but Ruffin took the matter very seriously. He had come to fight. In fact, his decision to become a member of this particular company was due to his belief that its position was such that it would be in the thick of any struggle that developed. He asked no favors save that when the flag of the Confederacy floated over Sumter, his term of enlistment should be ended. He slept in the open tents with the men, and when, on the evening of April 10, word came that the attack was about to begin, he marched with his musket to the batteries along the shore, ready to do his part.[14]

But the order was premature. President Davis still hesitated and hoped to avoid an open break. His orders to General P. G. T. Beauregard, who commanded at Charleston, were conditional, and that officer, acting in the same spirit, sent Roger A. Pryor and three other aides to secure, if possible, definite assurance from Major Anderson regarding the surrender of the Fort. It was a move dictated by caution. Yet it was, in the light of Pryor's avowed desire for a break, a most dangerous one. Out of it came the firing on Sumter. Though Anderson gave assurance that he would yield his post on April 15 unless he received supplies or orders to the contrary, Pryor refused to consider the answer satisfactory and, without consulting superior authority, gave the orders to the artillery commanders to open fire on the morning of April 12.[15]

On the evening before the struggle was to begin, Captain Cuthbert sought Ruffin out and informed him that the company had chosen him to fire the first shot of the fight. "I was highly gratified by the compliment, and delighted to perform the service," wrote the man who more than any other had longed for this event. That night he lay down on his cot without undressing, lest he miss the great opportunity on the morrow.

Before four o'clock the drums beat for parade. Ruffin hurried to his post to await the signal gun from Fort Johnson across the harbor. At exactly 4:30 the signal flashed, and the old Southerner struck his first blow at the enemy. The shell hit the fort "at the Northeast angle of the parapet," and the other guns took up the battle. Sumter did not reply. Two hours passed, raising the fear that nonresistance might "cheapen the conquest of the fort." Then Anderson opened fire, and Ruffin was more than gratified. He wanted a clean-cut triumph over the Yankee resisting with all the ardor the Yankee could muster. An inglorious surrender, though perhaps fitting, would not satisfy.[16]

All day long Ruffin remained at his post, watching over the parapet to call out to the gunners the effect of their shots in order to correct defects in aim. Not until evening did he seek his tent to refresh himself for the later struggle. Even then he went reluctantly, and he lay awake far into the night watching the shells cut the darkness as they rose and fell in flaming arcs across the dark waters of the harbor. He was out again with the dawn directing the gunners at their work.

As Sumter showed signs of distress, his spirits rose. He could not keep under cover as the bursting shells set fire to portions of the Northern defenses. He stood forth to shout as the flagstaff burned and the flag of Washington and Jefferson fell from view. He crowded close when Wigfall came back from the Fort after a conference and stood in the boat waving his hat and shouting the news of unconditional surrender. It seemed that all the bitterness and fury that raged in his heart had at last been cooled; the world was becoming a place in which he could find satisfaction complete. His enemies were falling.

The next day was Sunday. The Palmetto Guards paraded at ten o'clock, Ruffin proudly carrying the company flag, and then embarked on a steamer which moved out and anchored off Fort Sumter. Near the close of the day, when the last remnant of the Union garrison had filed out of the ruins that Confederate guns had made of a once imposing fortress, the Guards landed and raised their flag and that of the Confederate States of America upon the staff that had recently carried the emblem of a once glorious Union. Ruffin was among the first to set foot within the fortress. He wandered about amid the débris, slyly cutting a piece from the first flag to float over conquered territory, gathering fragments of shells to send to his friends at home, and then set off for Charleston and the applause of a triumphant people.[17]

The next few days were glorious. The fact that an old man who had already earned the right to rest from public service had brought to a climax his long struggle for secession by firing the first shot for Southern independence furnished a touch of the dramatic which the Southern movement needed. The Southerners had entered into a serious business; they could make use of all the glamor that could be found. The Charleston papers told of the "venerable Edmund Ruffin" hurrying to battle and dwelt on the "fadeless wreath of honor" that the "chivalric Virginian" should wear. A Mobile writer called it a "sublime spectacle," thanking

God that the spirit of Washington and Henry still lived on in the children of the Old Dominion. He compared the conduct of the venerable Virginian with his musket and knapsack to that of Cincinnatus and placed him in "the niche of fame" beside the illustrious Roman. The Northern press added its bit by suggesting that "a piece of the first hemp . . . stretched in South Carolina should be kept for the venerable and blood-thirsty Ruffian."

Popularity grew in the next few weeks with the rising tide of war spirit. Photographers discovered that his photograph had a commercial value, and perfumed letters poured in from all over the Southland. President Davis acknowledged a "memorial of your recent conflict" and expressed his "best wishes and grateful acknowledgment of your heroic devotion to the South, of truth and Constitutional Government." From Tibbee Station in Mississippi came word that a body of troops had been christened "The Ruffin Rangers," while in the General Assembly of Georgia one vote was cast for Edmund Ruffin as president of the "Southern United States." [18]

General Beauregard thought the deeds of the old patriot of sufficient importance to be mentioned in his official report of the firing on Sumter. He wrote: "The venerable and gallant Edmund Ruffin of Virginia was at the Iron Battery and fired many guns, undergoing every fatigue and sharing the hardships at the Battery with the youngest of the Palmettoes." Perhaps General Beauregard too felt that the example might be of value back in Virginia, where men still hesitated and talked of Union. The stirring tale of native valor cast into the scales that tilted back and forth between the sections might, in these days when compromise failed, throw the Old Dominion to the Southern

side. "The neighbors" might be led to accept their prophet
and end his exile.

*　　*　　*

The struggle then on in Virginia was indeed bitter. The
eonomic forces that had given her a new agricultural life
and diversified her efforts in trade and manufacturing drew
her both North and South, but with an added tug toward
the former. Her markets had shifted in that direction, and
her politicians had formed combinations with leaders in
New York and Pennsylvania which gave them a more national outlook than was possible to the men of the farther
South. For the first time in many years the Virginia politician had aspired, with some hope of success, to the great
offices that amid the sectional struggles had been so often
filled by men from the more neutral middle states. In
1860 both Hunter and Wise had been thought of as possible
candidates for the presidency on the Democratic ticket,
while the Ritchies, for their editorial work in Richmond,
had received national recognition. Only slavery and tradition pulled southward. But they were mighty forces in
those troubled days.

Virginia leaders, with more to lose by a break-up of the
Union than most others, had striven valiantly for compromise. They had labored in Congress and in the Peace Conference for some adjustment that would prevent an open
break between the sections and as late as February 2, 1861,
had persuaded the people to choose delegates to a state
convention who were overwhelmingly opposed to immediate
secession. The avowed Union group was large and active.
Many of them, especially those who had been Whigs in the
old days, kept in close touch with Northern conservatives,

urging them to curb the rabid demands of their section and
to give them assurance of the good intentions of the great
masses in the North. Their friends had responded with
confidence, expressing such opinions as enabled them to
check the radical tide at home and to influence other waver-
ing states. Their later embarrassment and helplessness in
the face of secession sentiment can be understood only in the
light of these assurances and the use they had made of
them.[19]

The correspondence of ex-Governor Wyndham Robertson with Northern men and his reaction to Lincoln's program in regard to Fort Sumter will help us to understand
the quick change of sentiment in Virginia in April, 1861,
and the immediate reasons why the exile of Edmund Ruffin
was so suddenly ended. Robertson, long prominent in the
councils of the Whig Party, had joined with such men as
John Minor Botts, Alexander H. H. Stuart, and William C.
Rives, in the effort to save both Southern rights and the
Union. He had early turned to his Northern friends for information about Lincoln's purposes in regard to the South
and had received, almost without exception, replies which
inspired confidence and justified opposition to radical action.
Edward Bates told him that if Lincoln were permitted to
organize his government and thus satisfy party demands, he
would then adopt a conciliatory policy. As for himself, he
was "an advocate for liberal compromise, for mutual concessions, for friendly settlement of all quarrels among the
States and sections." He thought this "was the only mode
by which violence and war . . . [could] be prevented
among States and Sections which differ[ed] about their
respective rights and yet . . . [had] no common and au-
thoritative arbiter between them." Winfield Scott had writ-

ten as late as February 19, 1861, that "the idea of coercing
any seceded state by an army in the field . . . [would] be
eschewed by the incoming administration." He had "a
lively hope—a reasonable expectation—that the new Cabi-
net, in less than three months, probably in less than a
month . . . [would] openly support a plan of conciliation
or compromise . . . as liberal as Crittenden's Resolutions."
Washington Hunt assured his Southern friends that all
but a few "zealots and ultra partisans" thought Seward's
"idea that the free states and the slave states . . . [could]
not coexist side by side . . . but . . . [were] to wage a
hateful warfare until the institutions of one section . . .
[should] be overthrown by the other" was "a stupendous
fallacy alike mischievous and absurd." He declared that
such ideas were so far in advance of public opinion in the
free states that they would be immediately fatal to their
author. For such utterances Seward, like his party, would
soon be "politically dead." Samuel J. Tilden thought the
great majority of the Northern people were "conservative
at the bottom" and that even the few who had been led
astray would soon be back on sound ground. R. B. Curtis
was not so confident that trouble could be avoided, but was
positive that only the "blows of Brooks' cane returned to the
Senate the very unfit subject of them" and that the "present
state of Northern action and opinion . . . [had] not grown
out of permanent and necessary differences between the
South and North." He declared that if war should come,
he would "die in the belief that . . . dissensions . . .
[were] wholly unnecessary—that they . . . [had] grown
out of the bad passions and narrow views and selfish wishes
of a few persons." [20]

Small wonder, with such statements from prominent

Northern leaders, the Virginia conservatives had laughed at the fears that timid folk felt when Lincoln was elected. They had expected compromise—peace without question. They had staked their all, risked their standing among their neighbors, on the patient, conservative leader of a party seemingly growing Whiggish in principles.

The effect of Lincoln's move at Sumter on such men is revealed in a letter written by Robertson to his son at the University of Virginia on the day after Edmund Ruffin set the guns at Charleston roaring: [21]

Yesterday was a day of intense excitement here [he wrote from Richmond]. The knowledge that actual war—bombardments and strife—were in progress between our own brethren could not but intensely excite the public passions. The Convention without acting on the question was yet a scene of some very excited debate. In the evening the town was all ablaze with tar barrels and torches, and shaken for hours with the firing off of cannon and of speeches. I did not, as you may suppose, attend, or take part in the *hullabaloo*. I see nothing in Civil War to rejoice over, let who may be victor. Yet I consider Lincoln's course utterly infamous, as well as wholly unwarranted by Law and wish all confusion and defeat to his counsels and his plans. His silence and stillness has been like the tiger's preparatory to his leap. I feared it, and called attention to it, in the *Whig* of last Saturday . . . and urged sending a commission to Washington to demand to know his purposes. The same evening resolutions to that effect were offered in the Convention and Commissioners sent—but they were already too late, and orders and troops, now engaged along our Southern coast, were already on their way, the whole country being kept ignorant of the scheme. What an idea of a Government to steal on its own people like a thief in the night, just by the way as he stole into the

Government, and perhaps means still to carry it on in the dark.

The conservative was thus disarmed. Lincoln's call for troops to crush the "rebellion" begun at Sumter completed the rout. A few days later an "exile" on the streets of Charleston received word that the Virginia Convention had adopted an ordinance of secession. A dream had come true. His diary for the day reads: "I departed from my usual abstinence so far as to drink a glass of ale, and another of wine." The time for restraint had passed, all along the line. Back in Virginia Wyndham Robertson, grieved but determined, was offering his services to the Confederate States of America.

* * *

The day after the news of Virginia's action reached Charleston, Edmund Ruffin wrote: "The formal act of secession and withdrawal from Lincoln's government terminates my voluntary exile." Shortly afterward the papers announced his departure. In spite of drawbacks Virginia was his native state, and she had now come to his position. Perhaps she might yet receive her prophets and find a place where they might serve.

On the way home, crowds gathered at different stations to demand a speech, and in Richmond the venerable leader found himself welcomed "by very many who were strangers before" and congratulated as having "alone upheld the honor of Virginia abroad." He found a "complete and wonderful change" to have taken place in the state—all the people in earnest for secession and "a friendly and favorable" appreciation of himself which approached that of Charleston. The bands serenaded the hotel, the crowd demanding "an address" and listening "with marked attention and respect." For once he refrained from saying anything about prophets.

But with the Confederate administration things were moving all too slowly to suit his taste. Public officials were allowing Northern ships to load tobacco at the wharves, and although the "invasion" of Maryland had already begun, no effort was being made to send aid. Nor did they quite as yet understand the character of the foe who threatened. Had they not seen the clipping from the *West Chester Democrat* (Pennsylvania), then going the rounds of the Southern press, in which Northern volunteers were urged to remember that Baltimore had "always been celebrated for the beauty of its women" and that "the fair were ever the reward of the brave"? The Lower South had already learned the value of propaganda; it was time for Virginia to fall into line.

But Ruffin could not afford to become too active. He was now in favor, and to speak his mind would again drive fickle popularity away. It was a price too dear to pay for the privilege, so he turned away from the city to "Beechwood," where his sons would listen to his opinions with approval. A parting shot in the *Examiner* at Governor Letcher was unsigned. He would keep his silence and his place in the public favor. In fact, he felt that for his own future place in the regard of his countrymen it would be best for him to die at once. He was certain that in death he could hold his tongue—the one member most responsible for all the suffering he had endured in days gone by.

How heavy the price he had decided to pay really was, he did not at first realize. A few days in the country made it clear. Desperately he took over the management of plan-

tation affairs when his son Edmund went off with the
troops to eastern Virginia, venturing into the city only for
a brief visit with the men of the Palmetto Guards as they
passed on their way to the front near Alexandria. Day after
day he plodded over the fields, following a reaper which
insisted on breaking at all inopportune times, inwardly
chafing at this "exile" which was not entirely voluntary.

At length he could stand it no longer. "I hope to obtain
a leave of absence," he wrote—a hope which turned in less
than a week's time into a threat "to decamp." On the first
of July he was in Richmond, purchasing blankets, cheese,
and crackers and completing his plans to join his recent
comrades at the front. The next day he was on his way to
Manassas Junction, a barrel of crackers and a whole
cheese at his side. The Guards had pushed forward to Fairfax Court House, but he did not hesitate. In spite of the
torture that a new pair of shoes inflicted, he set out on
foot along the dusty road that supply wagons had beaten
from the station to the front lines. His comrades welcomed
him with the same enthusiasm they had shown at Charleston and made much of the reputation he had given them by
his former services. They allowed him to share their
tasks and to believe, at least, that he was enduring their
hardships. With a ground shovel, "such as . . . [he] had
used for throwing up marl," he took a hand in digging
trenches; he marched with them on expeditions when his
ancient feet permitted; and for a period of over two
weeks he cherished the delusion that he was serving his
country as a private in the ranks.

As he mingled with the soldiers, he caught the rumors
of Yankee atrocities that had marked the few brushes between the gathering armies. He concluded that the strug-

gle was being waged by the North "on a system of brigandage and outrage of every kind." Property had "been stolen or wantonly destroyed" near Hampton; houses had been burned, fields laid waste, "and slaves invited to flee." The South was not to fight against "an honorable enemy, carrying on honorable and legitimate warfare," but one so vile that they "should be treated as robbers, incendiaries and murderers." Ruffin thought that every Yankee soldier "whom it . . . [was] not easy and certain to make prisoner . . . should be shot." Guerilla warfare under the black flag was all that the North deserved. They were already beyond the pale of civilization.

As his opinion of Yankees declined, his estimate of the Southern soldier improved. Ruffin found the privates perfect in respect for their officers when on duty but permitted the equality and freedom of conversation of civil life at all other times. It was an army of gentlemen. Outside the requirements of military efficiency all members remained on an equal basis. He became enthusiastic in his descriptions, almost poetic:

> After dark and before 9 P.M. (when the fires and lights are put out, except at officers' tents) clusters of men are collected around the lights at various tents, in conversation. Merry laughter is often heard from some distant group. Last night there was some good singing, in harmonized parts. The lights and the surrounding groups of soldiers, under the trees, presented a very pleasing scene and great variety of changing lights and shadows.

Ruffin was still in camp on April 17 when news came that the Northern army had broken the quiet along the Potomac and was moving forward. The Palmetto Guards, well to the front at Fairfax Court House, received hurried orders in the night to retreat toward Manassas Junction, where the defensive stand was to be made. The march was rapid, much of it at first in double-quick time, which forced the old man to run as fast as he could to keep his place in the ranks. For two miles he held on, then, sadly out of breath, fell behind, seeking a chance to ride lest he fall into the hands of the advancing enemy. The men of Kemper's light artillery picked him up and gave him a place on one of the caissons, letting him down at Centerville, where his company had halted. He was a sad but no wiser man when he took his place in the ranks hastily drawn up in the fields outside the little village.

But the preparations for battle were not over. A second retreat found him again on the caisson, jolting over the rough roads toward Bull Run, his back aching for lack of support and his arms weary with clinging to his precarious seat. Just before dawn he found his company halted at Mitchell's Ford, where they remained under arms all through the day, moving out across the stream after a time to take part in the preliminaries of what was to be the first great battle of a long, bitter war. Ruffin did not follow them. He was too weary even to fight Yankees. When twilight came, he stirred from his place to join the company on the higher ground which had been taken in order to guard against a night attack. He would be ready for the morrow.

Rain had now begun to fall, and Ruffin was soon wet to the skin. His baggage had been lost in the retreat, and all that he had was the old homespun suit he had worn so proudly at Charleston. A comrade forced him to accept the loan of an overcoat, and he lay down upon the wet ground for a few hours of troubled sleep. But he was awake before eleven o'clock, chilled and hungry, with only a "few gingerbread nuts" to satisfy his wants. The rest of the night seemed an endless misery.

When the morning came, he found the food that had come up for the troops too hard for his poor teeth, but he refused to leave the field. His hands and feet were numb and his face pinched and worn. Friends urged him to go to the rear for rest and nourishment, but he kept his place throughout another day, while the armies maneuvered, and slept that night on his arms. He had determined to stand on duty with his comrades, even though he "could not run with them, whether it was towards or from the opposing enemy."

On the morning of the 20th of July, haggard and old, he yielded to the wishes of his younger companions and journeyed back to Manassas Junction in search of his baggage and essential food and rest. He evidently remained there overnight, for the next morning he was writing in his diary when the heavy roar of cannon caused him to shoulder his musket and hurry back to his company. He did not intend to miss the fight after all it had already cost him.

But the battle did not come his way. His company was largely idle, while the struggle raged with increasing fury on the ridge to the left. He climbed a hill near at hand to get a better view and then, musket in hand, made his way toward the point where the fighting seemed most intense. As he passed through the woods, he found a body of skulkers who had drawn back from the fury of the struggle. Rage swept over him. Lifting his gun above his head, he shouted his indignation at their cowardice and pleaded with them to follow him back into the battle. But they would not stir. War to them had become a reality, and the impression was strong that the Southern army was hopelessly defeated. Ruffin went on alone, determined that his body should be left upon the field when the victors swept southward.

As he trudged forward, Kemper's battery suddenly swung down the ridge—falling back for a period of rest after heavy fighting. The weary men caught sight of the determined figure pressing eagerly forward and broke into a cheer. A rider drew his horses to a stop, and young hands lifted him to a place upon a gun carriage. There he clung as the battery plunged forward into position to shell the Federal retreat down the road toward Centerville. When the halt was made, the old man, who had slid forward to a position astride the cannon itself, climbed down amid the shouts of the soldiers and accepted the honor of firing the first shot at the ragged line of blue that had begun to run back in disorder from the field of battle. The shell fell squarely amid the troops that crowded the approach to the Suspension Bridge over Cub Run and checked the flow from both the turnpike itself and the Sudley's Ford road which joined it there. The whole retreat was suddenly blocked. A barricade of cannon, caissons, ambulances, wagons, and struggling horses cut off the one way of escape from a victorious enemy. Men fled in every direction; drivers abandoned their wagons and horses; soldiers threw their arms into the creek; panic seized men and beasts; the retreat became a rout. The guns of the battery swept the scene of confusion, and Edmund Ruffin, his efforts ended, stood by, conscious of having had some part in a new nation's first victory over its foes.

The next day the old warrior rode over the battlefield.

The dead and wounded of the Union army, scattered over the open ground, "lay quiet and motionless." He approached a wounded man and, dismounting, pressed a cup of water to his lips. He spoke "in compassionate tones," assuring him that the work of caring for the Confederate wounded was nearly completed and that the Northerners would soon be taken care of. He stopped to rebuke a group of his fellow soldiers who questioned a wounded man as to why he had come to invade the Southland. He confessed that no one more bitterly hated "the Northerners as a class" than he, or "would be more rejoiced to have every invading soldier killed," but declared that all his hatred was "silenced for the wounded, seen in this long continued and wretched state of suffering."

He was particularly eager to visit the bridge where the shell he had fired had done its work of destruction. He wanted to see and count the dead—his dead, his contribution to the cause! He found only three bodies. "This," he wrote a few hours later, "was a great disappointment to me. I should have liked not only to have killed the greatest possible number but also to know if possible which I had killed and see and count the bodies." He wanted the assurance of his service. Tangible proofs had too often been lacking in his career. His worth had too often been without the measure that common men could read. But dead Yankees constituted a new kind of contribution to a great cause which could not be mistaken.

There is something pathetic in the old man searching the field for his dead. His eagerness for numbers lay not in a love of bloodshed. His attitude toward the wounded denies the charge. It came, perhaps, not even from a hatred of Yankees. Deep in his very nature was the old longing for public approval never quite granted. He was so eager to serve in a way that was acceptable to his fellows, to free himself from those restraints and foes which seemed to deny the full expression of his real worth. Violence against an accepted foe seemed at last to afford opportunity and satisfaction. He was free by service.[22]

Months afterwards, through persistent inquiry, he learned "from several trustworthy eye-witnesses, that there were about seven dead bodies" found lying in the road where his shell struck immediately after the battle. His list had begun a growth which was to continue until, in the end, he had convinced himself that fully fifteen Yankee soldiers had been either killed or wounded by his shot. In time he had even sought out the peculiar construction of this shell to explain its unusual effectiveness. There could be no question as to his services to the newborn Confederacy!

On July 23, certain "that this hard-fought battle would be virtually the close of the war," Ruffin went back to Richmond, and then to his adopted home at "Beechwood." His strength was nearly spent. Weeks passed before he recovered from the suffering and exposure of the campaign. His hearing, already bad, had suffered permanent injury from remaining too close to the guns at Sumter and Bull Run. He could no longer hear the sermons at church, which did not greatly pain him, or even the conversations carried on about him in the household. Reading was his only consolation. But even here a new difficulty had arisen. The book supply, both from the North and from abroad, had been completely cut off, leaving him with only the newspapers for entertainment. This mattered little, however, for the war occupied all his attention and constituted the subject matter of both his reading and his conversation.

As physical difficulties increased, he longed for death, caring only to live that he might know the outcome of the great struggle into which his people had entered. There seemed little now that he could do. The burdens of battle had proven too great for his frail body; the work of agitation was ended.

And so a summer of rural routine passed. A few articles went off to the newspapers, but even he now read only the stories that came from the front and passed by the articles, signed and unsigned. It was but a way of killing time. "If only a cannon-ball at Bull Run" had been the means of "a sudden, unexpected and painless death," he would have considered it "the most desirable termination" of his life. But the soldier's ending had been denied. He must live on in inaction while the struggle for Southern independence stretched out into the years.

Meanwhile, across the borderland to the North, Abraham Lincoln, already learning the troubles that the radical element within his party could raise, stood aghast at the realities of the war his actions had loosed. His judgment had been sound. Sumter had given his party wide support and produced a surprising degree of sectional unity in the North. Even the mayor of New York City who had so recently been threatening the formation of a city-state had declared that parties had ceased to exist and that all true men stood by the government. The battle of Bull Run had completed the task. Soon Northern papers were printing such articles as the following: [23]

> Nothing in all this war has more deeply stirred the heart of the community than the dreadful barbarities inflicted by the rebel soldiers upon our fallen men in the retreat from Manassas. Every report confirms the shock-

ing fact that they bayoneted our wounded soldiers all along the road for miles, cut them in quarters, kicked about their severed heads in fiendish sport, tied them naked to trees, tormented them with knives, and many other such barbarities never before heard of in a civilized community. . . . This worse than Fiji manner is attributable to the barbarism of slavery, in which and to which the Southern soldiers have been educated. May the war end in annihilating slavery and in restoring to the nation a civilized South.

CHAPTER X

A SOUTHERNER AND HIS NATION PERISH

ALL wars in modern times are defensive wars, waged against foes so unrighteous that each struggle should, by all the rules of a just universe, be brief. After Bull Run Edmund Ruffin confidently expected, even feared, an immediate peace. He would have welcomed the "cessation of aggressive and offensive operations of war," but the possibility of a renewal of "former business connections and commercial vassalage" to the North was another matter. It might be well for justice to delay a little.

Even at the end of the year he had not lost hope, but he admitted "that in the last two months most of our people have been lowered in their sanguine hopes of signal success over our enemy and a speedy and triumphant end of the war." He hastened to add, however, that there were "no indications of discouragement or doubts of final success." Even the "previous submissionists and late professed converts to secession" were confident, or at least did not dare to appear otherwise. What amused him most was the attitude of the Yankees, "who in all their views seemed to be demented"; they were foolish enough still to dream of success, deeming Southern "subjection or voluntary submission a certainty." But there was no accounting for Yankee ideas! [1]

When the campaigns of the second year opened with every prospect of continued fighting, he was somewhat surprised but still sure that peace and victory were near. Admitting the superiority of the North in numbers, naval power, and "the present means of applying force," he relied on "the higher moral and intellectual grade of the Southern people, the superior principles by which they . . . [were] actuated, and the holy cause which support[ed] their patriotism and courage." Men fighting for their "dearest rights, their property, their families" against a foe impelled by the desire to rob and "glut their fanatical hatred in blood" could not be defeated. The patriot, "clothed in the armor of a just cause," was superior to "banditti and pirates."

The crushing victory of the new ironclad *Merrimac* over the wooden ships of the North at Hampton Roads in March, though anticlimaxed by the arrival of the *Monitor,* served to strengthen his confidence. He was prepared for a series of unbroken triumphs when Grant's rude thrusts in the West, culminating at Shiloh, and Farragut's capture of New Orleans forced a new understanding. For the first time he entertained "the possibility of the subjection of the Southern States, and the ruin to their cause." It stirred thoughts of Cromwell in Ireland and the barbarians in Rome. "I would prefer that our despotic ruler and master should be any power in Europe, even Russia or Spain," he wrote, as thoughts of negro domination and Yankee plunder filled his mind.

The calling out of the entire militia of Virginia to resist the threatened invasion by McClellan and the appearance of Yankee gunboats on the James within sight of "Beechwood" brought closer home the fact that Northern men were in earnest about Lincoln's Union. In the middle of the summer, as the Army of the Potomac swarmed onto the Peninsula to begin its ill-fated campaign, the fear of capture seized the old Virginian. For a time he thought himself an especial

object of quest and hurried off to Richmond. There illness
overtook him, rendering him "too weak to fight or to flee."
But he could still criticize. The troubles into which the
Confederacy seemed to have fallen had resulted from two
things, "West Point and red tape." "O! that our President
had never studied at West Point," he cried. "I honestly
wish that our Civil and military affairs were in the hands
of leaders who knew nothing of either." It was not the
first time or the last that such sentiments were expressed.
But steps to resistance were not hurried, and the remaining
occupants of "Beechwood," as well as those at "Marlbourne,"
soon packed the few things they could carry with them and
abandoned their houses, lands, and slaves to the advancing
enemy. Jem Sykes had not waited for this. He and his
most valuable fellows had already fled eastward to meet the
new-found friends of all black folk.

When the Mayor of Richmond proposed to enlist all
persons exempt from military service because of age or
infirmity, Ruffin considered himself eligible on both counts
and joined the company. He also subscribed the sum of
five hundred dollars for the building of an ironclad to
defend the city. And then, as the fighting broke along the
ridges and streams below the city, he climbed the stairs of
the Capitol to catch a "whiff of battle." The range was
too great, so the next day, astride a horse procured in the
city, he made his way toward the smoke and roar along
the Chickahominy. Through the mud and horrors of the
battleground, scarce a day old, he went, until he came to
where the shells still fell and death lurked. The soldiers
caught sight of the familiar figure and gave "Three cheers
for Edmund Ruffin of Virginia." He lifted his hat and
bowed. A soldier hurried up to inform him that his grand-

son, Julian Beckwith, had just been killed. Like the men in the storybooks, he only voiced the regret that he did not have more of flesh and blood to give. It was a paltry price to pay for the salvation of the capital of the Confederacy.

A few days later, as the enemy fell away, he ventured back to "Beechwood" and wandered through the deserted rooms, recalling the happy days spent there in what now seemed the long, long ago. As the shadows lengthened, he sought the plot of sacred ground where those who had toiled in other days now rested, and fell to his knees. "And here I addressed to God my customary daily prayer and added others for the welfare of my family and country; the restoration of that prosperity and happiness recently enjoyed or available . . . and which has been so much reduced by the conduct of our vile public enemies."

The ebbing tide of the Peninsular campaign left the fields below Coggin's Point and across the river at Berkeley farm filled with Union soldiers, wagons, and tents. Northern boats, their decks plainly visible from the bluff above, filled the river, and the noise of distant fighting came up, now loud, now dim, with the shifting currents of air. The haze of battle hung over the forests; the summer sun whitened the canvas on wagons and tents, flashing back, here and there, from burnished bits of metal, the temper of the god of war.

Ruffin remained about the farm through the first days of July, watching the enemy from the cover of vegetation on his high lands and chafing a bit when on the morning of the Fourth the boats below him on the river sent the valley echoing with salutes to "their flag." "What a farce," he exclaimed, "the Northerners thus glorifying the Declaration of Independence, which was the declaration of the rights

[238]

of every oppressed people to assert their independence and separate nationality."

As he watched, day by day, with growing bitterness, a plan took shape in his mind for planting cannon on his bluff which would sweep the river and force the vessels to retire. Shortly afterward, acting on this suggestion, the local military commander placed his guns with the guidance of the old man and his son and in the dead of night launched an attack which was effective enough to produce a second raid on the neighborhood and the scattering of its people.

Not until the middle of August were the Yankee troops withdrawn so that Ruffin could go back to "Beechwood" to learn something of the vengeance that soldiers, regardless of time and place, may take upon the helpless civilians of an invaded region. As he entered the fields, he found them stripped of grain and lying bare. The yard of the mansion was scattered over with rubbish—"broken chairs and other furniture, broken dishes, plates and other crockery, feathers emptied from the ticks of feather beds and different other filling materials of mattresses. The doors of the house were all open, and many of the windows broken in, glass or sashes." Within the house conditions were even worse. All the mirrors were either broken or carried off; the rooms were filled with "rubbish and litter, produced by the general breakage and destruction of everything that could not be conveniently stolen." Every article of furniture, without exception, showed material damage which could have come only from "wilful and malignant design." The library had been frightfully pillaged, several thousand books having been stolen and the doors of the bookcases torn from their hinges. The old harmonicon, which Ruffin loved so much, had yielded up its glass panels; the pictures on the walls were gone or hanging from their frames in ruin; his valuable collection of shells and fossils, gathered on his agricultural expeditions or sent by friends from all over the world, was scattered about or carried away with other small valuables to become souvenirs in Northern homes for years to come. The walls of the mansion were covered with tobacco juice or defaced with names or filthy expressions written in charcoal or excrement. "This house belonged to a Ruffinly son-of-a-bitch," one read; "Old Ruffin, don't you wish you had left the Southern Confederacy go to Hell (where it will go) and had stayed at home," read another. Most were too obscene to be reproduced.[2]

But what hurt most was the loss of all his private papers, many having been carried away, the rest torn and scattered about in such a way as to render it impossible to restore his files. Nearly as painful was the wanton girdling of his great oaks, which had no other purpose than to cause their death and to inflict a wound on the very physical South. These were losses which made insignificant the carrying off of all his mules and cattle and all the grain that had been stored for their use. Ruffin estimated his material losses and those of his son at not less than one hundred and fifty thousand dollars. His more vital losses could not be measured. It was a thorough job of plundering. Even the Germans in Belgium, with vastly superior technical equipment for doing damage, could hardly have improved upon it.

The old man wandered about amid the ruins with nothing of the terror and desire for peace that such vandalism is supposed to inspire. Rather he thought of vengeance. He would send a band of raiders into Pennsylvania to plunder the property of the rich and to incite the laboring element to rebellion. Every town would be sacked and burned, unless ransomed, and the countryside laid waste. All prisoners would be shot, and the lawless element in every community would be organized for the more efficient plundering of their own neighbors. The South would proclaim it retaliation, to be ended only when the North had decided to abide by the laws of humanity in warfare.

The remainder of the summer was spent in the work of restoration and the task of saving something from the fields for the winter ahead. A few disillusioned slaves in time drifted back to the farm, the surplus to be sold off to the Lower South at the first opportunity, the remainder to take up their accustomed ways and work. Ruffin found much to do. He worked in the fields as his strength permitted, but lived mostly in the past with his remaining books and the familiar trees and shrubs which had become more dear to him through their threatened destruction. He seldom left "Beechwood." A new danger had come to him and his cause in the wake of the late invasion.

The disloyalty not only of the blacks but especially of the poorer whites in the lower portion of the state had come as something of a shock to the loyal people. It presented a new problem. Ruffin had known from the beginning that there were many men without property in the section, envious of their wealthy neighbors, who were "too ignorant to know the value of [Southern] institutions and of African slavery even to the poorest citizens." His friend Willoughby Newton had told him of such disaffection in the Northern Neck, where common men had declared "that the object of secession and war . . . [was] to protect the negroes of the rich men, who own all the negroes and all the good land." They had early insisted that they had no interest in fighting or opposing the North. But the actual conduct of these people in the face of Northern invasion had revealed more of disloyalty than Ruffin had expected. The foundations of the new nation were not as solid in all parts as the patriot might wish.

But there was another side to it. These simple folk, now deserted by the Northern army, found themselves worse off than they had been before. They began openly to complain of those who had brought on the trouble. Some of them declared that they would seize Ruffin, whom they believed to be "the whole and sole cause of the war," and hang him for the crime. He soon found that such men, forced into the Southern army and now stationed in his neighborhood, were stealing the "Beechwood" fruit, breaking into the barns, and in general acting "like Yankees." By the end of the summer conditions were so bad that his son decided to purchase a small farm in Amelia County, to which he could send his remaining slaves, and to move the family to "Marlbourne," where the danger, for the present, was not so great.[3]

Although the battle of Antietam in September brought discouragement, Lincoln's Emancipation Proclamation restored the balance. It was better for the Southern cause that the Northern "future policy" should be known, that Southern men should learn the price they must pay—and would have paid if they had not seceded—if they submitted or their arms failed. The disguise was now off. The Republican program had at last been made clear. It portended a social revolution which should send a "shudder of horror throughout England and France" and double the efforts of Southern men to escape the fate prepared.[4]

But the people did not respond as Ruffin had hoped. Their morale still rose and fell with victory and defeat on the field of battle or with the economic pinch that soon began to run from the common people up toward the higher levels as the winter turned to spring and the summer's fighting began. The shifting fortunes of war that marked the campaigns of 1863 gave new cause for worry. The fall of Vicksburg, which seemed "incredible," followed by the defeat of Lee at Gettysburg, produced a dull sense of impending disaster which was made more real by the sharp thrusts of Yankee cavalry delivered at intervals in the neighborhood of "Marlbourne." Once Ruffin was forced to hide in the fields when Union riders entered his yard and inquired for the "damned Ruffin men" whose heads they "were bound to have."

As the summer wore on, Ruffin began to "fear that Mr. Davis . . . [was] far from being the right sort of a leader" for the country in its present difficulties. He heard Rhett speak "in strong terms of condemnation of the dilatory and otherwise improper conduct of the President," and though he felt there might be an added sharpness because Davis in his appointments had passed by most of the *"earliest and staunchest movers of secession"* in favor of "eleventh hour laborers," he was certain of "sufficient grounds for such censure." He noted that during the great reverses of the Confederacy, President Davis had been engaged in seeking to save his own soul and had recently been confirmed a member of the church. He was quite inclined to believe that "it would have been much better for his administration and the public service if he had . . . completed this individual and private duty before he began his presidency. . . . To the morbid tenderness of conscience of a seeker of religion" Ruffin ascribed "much of the imbecility" of the president in dealing with prisoners, deserters, and spies. He concluded that Davis was hard-headed and soft-hearted while Lincoln was soft-headed and hard-hearted.[5]

"The coldness or disaffection to the Southern cause, produced or increased by [the] late disasters and gloomy prospects," especially disturbed Ruffin. In North Carolina W. W. Holden, editor of "the most able paper of that state," had long been uttering "sentiments and doctrines opposing the cause of the South and the prosecution of . . . defensive war, and evidently but plainly enough, advocating peace by submission and reconstruction of the Union." And what was more disturbing was the assurance that Holden was supported in his nefarious course by "many men of position" and by "some county meetings." Rumor also reported like discontent in parts of Georgia and Mississippi, while the calm acceptance of Yankee rule in certain conquered districts revealed there the lack of the unyielding determination that dwelt in Ruffin's heart.

He could not escape the feeling that something was decidedly wrong in Richmond. The distorting of news for the upholding of morale, as had been done after Gettysburg and as had been done recently in regard to the loss of General Bragg's wagon train, was unpardonable. "The silence as to our defeats and deserters," he moaned, "is without excuse. . . . When it is understood to be the course of government thus to endeavor, by studied silence to conceal altogether, the effect will be the reverse of what is expected. . . . The truth of all disasters will be magnified . . . and the reports of . . . advantages will be distrusted." And then, to even matters a bit, he added: "This system of silence to conceal disagreeable truth is but little better than the direct lies of the Yankees."

Even worse than administrative blunders was the unrelenting pressure of economic conditions. Prices were soaring. On the 1st of January, 1863, brown sugar sold for a dollar per pound and molasses at from $7.50 to $8.00 a gallon; bacon and fresh beef cost $1.10 per pound; corn, $4.50, and wheat, $3.50, per bushel; chickens, $2.00 apiece; and sweet potatoes, $12.00 a bushel. Ruffin, still certain that the South would "not fail in resolution, constancy or courage, nor in soldiers, arms or money," began to "lose hope of [the] Confederacy being able to carry on the war much longer, with such high prices and the increasing scarcity of the necessaries of life." [6]

Moreover, the most fertile lands in the Old South lay in the river valleys, apparently wide open to Yankee plunder —one harvest intended for Southern support already having been gathered by the invaders. Defensive warfare might have some advantages, but the effect of invasion on material and spiritual forces was something which could not be lightly measured. Then there were the losses from the plantation type of agriculture when slaves ran away to the enemy and masters and overseers were called from the fields to fight. Ruffin spoke from the sad experiences at "Beechwood" and "Marlbourne" when he declared that a place thus left in the hands of Southern women, old men, and decrepit negroes "must soon come to nothing." More than half the farms in Virginia, he thought, were thus struggling along, headed for certain destruction. "If our struggle was only in fighting an enemy, even with all their superiority in arms and munitions of war and of naval means," he wrote, "I should not entertain a shadow of doubt of our triumphant success. But sanguine and confident as I am, some fears for the result darken my view of the future in reference to our great disadvantages in commercial and economic matters." An urban-industrial world had some advantages in war, at least, over rural-agricultural simplicity.

Economic conditions grew worse as the season advanced. In April, with corn selling at $11.00 a bushel, a bread riot broke out in Richmond, and a mob of what Ruffin called "low men and women" broke into the stores and plundered them of provisions. He saw them scurrying to their homes, their arms filled "with bacon and other supplies," and was forced, in order to save the goods he had just procured, to send his wagons out of the city through the back streets. He was despondent. Such events were of "more awful portent than the loss of a bloody battle. . . . And these crimes . . . openly committed in the principal business streets of Richmond, the capital of Virginia and the Confederate States . . . without opposition from the police or danger to the criminals!"[7]

News of other riots of the same kind in Petersburg (Virginia) and in Salisbury (North Carolina), where soldiers' wives were the chief actors, added to his fears. The transportation system of his rural world was evidently breaking down under the stress of war, and the capacity of the great Southland to produce foodstuffs was availing her little in the face of hostile invasion. He could only turn against a government which relied "almost exclusively on emissions of treasury notes to finance itself" and left its people to struggle along with depreciated currency and high prices. It was the only evil that the Southern people could not bear up under; it was a system which *might* compel the Confederacy to yield to its enemies.

One further condition caused alarm. The South, before the war, had depended largely on Kentucky and Tennessee for its supply of horses and mules, the plantation product seldom running beyond immediate needs. Furthermore, the character of Southern soils and climate had always made the growing of grasses difficult and rendered the section to some degree weak in transportable forage. Consequently, as the war took its enormous toll of cavalry horses and the enemy overran the western basin of supply, the efficiency of an important branch of the army was greatly impaired. Then to scarcity of horses was added the difficulty of securing hay, even at the unheard-of price of $25.00 per hundredweight which was reached early in 1863. Men were constantly falling out of the ranks, their mounts too weak to carry them, and leading their emaciated horses from place to place in search of pasture lands. In August, Ruffin's grandson Thomas, who was with Stuart's cavalry, was home with his "broken-down critter," hoping to exchange it at the farm for another. But the Northern raids had depleted the supply, and the lad was forced to return with an animal totally unfit for the work required.

"It seems to me," wrote Ruffin on April 11, 1863, "that our country and cause are now, for the first time during the war, in great peril of defeat—and not from the enemy's arms, but from the scarcity and high prices of provisions and the inability of the government in feeding the horses of the army, which is even much more difficult than to feed and support the men. In the cavalry brigade to which my grandson belongs, the horses have rarely had any feed but corn for some months—and are generally without any hay or other long provender, and for weeks together. . . . As might be expected, the horses are reduced very low in flesh and strength, and many are dying and more failing entirely." It seemed to him that the *eyes of the army* were growing dim, to say nothing of the sad condition of the patient beasts that dragged the artillery. Unless something was done the cause would be lost.[8]

Under such conditions Ruffin set logic to work, as he had done so often in days gone by when realities were unsatisfactory. News of the powers that the Northern Congress had conferred on Lincoln, to call into service the whole or any part of the population between the ages of twenty and forty-five, to suspend the right of *habeas corpus,* and to command the whole credit of the government for a fixed period of time, led Ruffin to believe that revolution would soon follow. The people of the North would not "submit to these regulated and formal unconstitutional enactments and measures for the complete submission of all freedom, individual rights and state powers." Base and abject as Yankees were, they would not make this "low-minded and narrow-minded man" as much "a master of government, country and people as (was) the Czar of Russia."

Even if New England submitted, surely Governor Seymour of New York would "check the draft . . . and even recall the troops out now in service." And if New York failed, the Northwest, drawn by every tie of interest, would step forward. He had thought before the fall of Vicksburg that the Southern government should offer the Northwesterners a separate peace, insuring free navigation of the Mississippi River, the profits of Southern markets, and the benefits of European goods imported under free-trade conditions. It was too late to do this now, but fundamental interests still remained. The advantages of being joined with their agricultural brethren instead of being tied to the selfish industrial East must already be apparent to every man in the valley of the Mississippi. Did they not realize that even if the North were victorious, the farmers of the nation would pay the bills while manufacturers gathered in new wealth behind protective-tariff walls? If only reason had its way, the Southern cause was in no great danger.

But reality crowded out what might have been. The Yankee raiders, seemingly unconscious of what Governor Seymour and the Northwest should have been doing, kept sweeping out from the river toward "Marlbourne" until Ruffin decided again on flight, this time to "Ruthven," the home of his son Julian not far from "Beechwood." Then the Confederate levy took Julian into the service and left the father again to struggle feebly with problems of farming which were far too difficult and prosaic for his waning strength. To make matters worse, "all of Governor Seymour's pledges and threats" came to nothing, and even the peace Democrats of the Northwest seemed ready to support the war if the early defeat of the South impended. Ruffin felt ill and broken. His weight had fallen to a scant hundred and twenty pounds. Life held little save the ebbing hope for his country's triumph.

Then came news that the Yankees had been shelling Charleston. Eagerly he followed events, speaking often of that city as the scene of his "public services" and manifesting each day more impatience with the "private duties" that now engaged him. At length the chance stationing of his son's company in the neighborhood of "Ruthven," where he could again supervise its affairs, gave the much desired excuse. On September 21 Ruffin was on his way to the beloved South Carolina city, feeling fit for any adventure.

For three months he remained in and about Charleston, leading an active life and regaining much of his former spirit. He visited the offices of the *Courier* and learned that his exploits since Sumter had been reported regularly in the press to an interested public. Charleston had rejoiced in his deeds at Bull Run and noted with pride his continued zeal for the cause in the days of distress. A citizen had seen him on the field of Seven Pines, "armed and ready, as at Sumter" or on "the memorable field of Manassas, to face danger, whenever there [was] likelihood of striking at Yankeedom or for Southern independence." It made him feel like doing more for his country! [9]

Hence, when he found a group of Charleston residents, too old or infirm for active military service, erecting a battery on the Cooper River, he enlisted in the regiment subject to call. He visited the various batteries about the city, accepting an occasional invitation to fire a gun at the enemy's defenses. Eagerly he awaited the great attack on the city, having come with the idea that the last desperate stand was about to be made and that he might have a chance to share in the glory of saving his friends from the despised invaders. To pass the time he fraternized with the soldiers, finding a companionship which well suited his notion of himself and the service he was rendering. Out to Sumter he went, remaining to make a series of sketches, later completed through spyglasses from the shore, so that he might follow day by day the damage done by the enemy's fire. It gave him new confidence to discover that the constant pounding of Yankee shells only left the Fort more certain of its ability to withstand any attack. Charleston would not know the humility of surrender.

When the intermittent shelling of the city began, he seemed to be actually delighted, rushing about with his body servant, digging fragments of the missiles from the ground and retaining them as relics. "Huzza!" he wrote on November 20, "more glory for Fort Sumter. Another assault was made last night and repelled." But the great drive did not begin, and the winter set in with Charleston yet safe from Yankee control. He could not delay longer if Christmas was to be spent with relatives. The beloved city could, at least for the time, spare him and his services.

On the way home he went to Columbia to revisit the scenes of other "public services" and was surprised to receive a set of resolutions passed in the Senate, referring to him as the "distinguished Virginian, who has identified himself with the struggle in which we are engaged, from its commencement on the soil of South Carolina," and inviting him to a seat on the floor of their chamber. One suspects that he felt he had not taken this roundabout way to Virginia in vain.

Back home, Ruffin rounded out, on January 5, 1864, his allotted span of three score years and ten. He noted that in spite of a feeble body he had attained an age greater than any of his progenitors since the great-grandfather for whom he had been named. Yet he was sensible of growing weaknesses; his hair was becoming thinner, his hands trembled, and his memory failed; he tired quickly—though he hastened to add that in Charleston he had walked much and without fatigue. Everything seemed to indicate that death could not be far off, a conviction which was not distressing or even painful. The extension of life was desirable only in order to witness the successful termination of the war, the glory and the prosperitv of a new nation among the peoples of the earth.

The year that thus opened was to be filled with sorrow. It had scarcely begun when a message, long delayed, brought word of the death of his daughter Mildred on the foreign soil of Kentucky. He was stunned. The cup of grief, already full, could not run over. The tired heart of the old man seemed numb to pain—perhaps age and suffering had "paralized [his] affections and dried up the sources of parental love and of all deep feelings," leaving him scarcely able to grieve "for the death of her his best beloved child." It was well, for the blows had only begun to fall. The cause of the Confederacy, more dear than life itself, was entering its darkest hour.

As Sherman started his drive on Atlanta in February and Grant began pounding at Lee in the wilderness Ruffin took from his income a sum barely large enough to purchase the food required to sustain life and sent the remainder to the Confederate Treasury as an example which others must follow if the South was to be saved. He sensed the seriousness of the threats, crying out for a "Stonewall Jackson to command the army" against Sherman and enough of "patriotism and vigor to lay waste the country ahead of him." He would have gone himself if the tired old body had permitted. But a great "weariness" had settled down upon him, taking away even the inclination to walk or ride about. The days weighed heavily as the supply of books ran low and left him much of the time with only the Bible and its uncertain authority to puzzle over. If only there were some useful task he could perform, some service to render his suffering people that lay within the reach of an active mind that was chained to a feeble body. But war thrives on youth and mixes iron with its blood. He could only stand and wait.

As the summer came with the fighting which showed clearly that numbers and resources were to have their way, and as prices rose to new heights, Ruffin understood the meaning. Illness and depression had already brought him to the point where death seemed near when the most cruel blow possible fell: his son Julian was killed in battle at Drewry's Bluff. On May 23 the trembling hand wrote:

> It is less than two hours since the mail brought, both in telegram and letter, the astonishing and woeful intelligence of the death of my son Julian—killed in battle on the 16th. My mind cannot take in the momentous fact, nor my perceptions approach to the measure of the reality. As I had before reasons to know by experience, and to deplore, it seems as if age and decay have withered and dried up my affections and sensibilities and hardened my heart so that I can neither love as formerly, nor feel grief for the death of the most beloved. I have not shed a tear. Yet it was impossible for any father to esteem and appreciate more highly a son for his rare merits, as a son, and as a man, than I did this one person. Yet, I have received the unexpected announcement of his sudden death, with as little evidence of grief and of feelings as some years past would have been caused to me by the death of any ordinary but valued friend, or intimate acquaintance.

He was to learn in the weeks that followed, however, that grief slow born is more real and enduring, that age deprived of its own has lost the reason for being.

But grieving is a luxury not long permitted to those beneath the heel of war. Already the jaws of the great Union vise were closing in, one body of troops actually occupying the "Marlbourne" farm late in May, which sent the family hurrying to the little farm purchased the year before in Amelia County. The New York *Herald* boasted of headquarters set up in the house of "the old rebel who fired the first gun in the present war" and commented on the well-tilled fields and the remains of a splendid library of agricultural works. Ruffin's only answer was that "when these marauding scoundrels leave, I do not suppose there will be any 'remains' or anything else for the next comers to destroy." He had already had experiences with Yankees.

A few weeks later a letter from the grandson Thomas, recently out of a Northern prison, described "Marlbourne" as he had found it after the enemy had gone. Every window in the house was broken, all the fences destroyed, the trees cut and burned, the drainage ditches dammed to furnish water for the horses, and everything of value in the house and outside stolen and carried away. Moreover, Grant's refusal to accept defeat as a reason for turning back brought the whirl of battle intermittently into the neighborhood and made the return of the family impossible. Ruffin was never again to dwell at his beloved "Marlbourne." Before long he was even contemplating the dismal prospect of further flight before the determined foe.

Realist that he was, Edmund Ruffin knew that the fate of the Confederacy was sealed as the summer of 1864 came to a close and winter set in with Sherman sweeping through Georgia and Grant entrenched before Petersburg. He was willing, however, to resort to the last desperate measures to prolong the struggle and to accept extinction rather than surrender. He knew that "almost every man of ordinary military age and very many beyond its limits" were already in the service, and that if the ranks were to be filled, negro slaves must be used as soldiers. Although that was a fatal policy, making an end of slavery and thrusting forward the race problem that the South had gone to war to avoid, it was preferable to the "greater evil of Yankee subjugation and domination."

He was willing to turn to England and implore her to accept the Southern states back as colonies, preferring to yield to a monarch rather than to Lincoln and Seward, the elect of the "vilest and most malignant people . . . in Christendom." He longed for a dictator to gather the South together for one last effort and to give efficient direction to her forces. The time had come when harsh measures must be taken to check desertion, to bring those on leave back to the fighting lines where they might force Grant to pile his "fodder" higher. The "tender-hearted Davis" had pardoned deserters before they could serve as examples to others, and his speech in Macon, Georgia, in September revealed the fact that two-thirds of the Southern soldiers were absent—some "sick, some wounded, but most of them absent without leave."

From his dwindling fortune Ruffin sent in March, 1865, the sum of seven hundred dollars, representing nearly all the cash in his possession. Confederate bonds to the value of eleven hundred and fifty dollars followed a few weeks later, and then the family plate and even his gold watch. "Contribute everything that can be spared to defend us from the enemy," he pleaded with his children, and avowed his own purpose to retain only enough to prevent dependence on others whose burdens were already too great.

But in his heart he knew that it was hopeless. Forebodings filled his mind. He pictured Richmond fallen and every part of the state subjected to devastation and the people to "oppression, insult and outrage." A few might flee across the Mississippi, dragging the widows and aged with them, there to continue the struggle for a time but ultimately to join their fellows in prison and torture. "In such event," he wrote, "the fate which I would most desire for myself would be to be shot dead in giving my feeble aid to some of the last defenders of our country against its assailing foes. But there is no probability that my then locality, wherever it may be, or my feebleness of body will permit my then finding so honorable a death. May God grant that my much earlier occurring death, by natural decay or accidental fatality, shall preclude me from the necessity of choosing my course, when such dreadful alternatives only be available!" [10]

But the thin gray lines that lay across the paths of Grant and Sherman did not stiffen that spring. Instead, they seemed, at times, fairly to melt away, offering little shelter to the helpless old Southerner and the young nation he had helped to found. On April 2 fears turned to realities. Lee informed Davis that he could no longer maintain his lines and that the capital of the Confederacy must be abandoned. By midnight his army was marching off toward the south and west in the vain hope of forming a juncture with Johnston's troops, leaving the proud capital to its fate.

In the dim light of the following morning, haggard and worn from pain and loss of sleep, the old exile in Amelia sat at his desk and wrote:

> Richmond was evacuated last night. All Virginia, and this eastern part certainly and speedily, will be occupied or over-run by the vindictive and atrocious enemy. . . . Every proprietor and resident must now choose between flight and remaining to suffer every insult and indignity added to impoverishment if not destitution. And very few can flee, or have any safe . . . place of refuge, or . . . means of support. . . . And as to funds, I suppose that the bonds and treasury notes of the Confederate States will lose all credit and currency. My whole remaining capital is vested in public stocks yielding here-

tofore . . . a fixed interest . . . and all of the former, except $500.00, is in Confederate State Bonds. The before close approaching and expected result of my utter ruin I, therefore, suppose is now completed. My son and my daughter-in-law . . . are now but little better off, their remaining property not yielding any income, being also chiefly in stocks. For myself, I am without any resources either of property or escape left. . . . Even the dependence on one or the other of my two sons and their wives . . . must now fail, because they will be stripped of everything. I cannot consent to live a pauper on the charity of strangers abroad, or of impoverished children and friends near our present home.

When, on April 12, the shattered remnant of Lee's once glorious army, in "swinging route step," passed before the "men in blue" to lay down their arms, the old man sat again and wrote of another April day exactly four years before when the guns had turned on Sumter. He knew that the Confederate States of America had come to the end of its stormy life. He knew also that an "old South" of which he had been a part had run its course. The men in tattered gray who were turning their tear-stained faces southward were going back to begin all over again.

That such was to be their fate became clear almost at once. With the assassination of Abraham Lincoln the radical Republican element in Congress entered upon a ten-year course of Southern "reconstruction" which in severity has never been matched in modern society by the terms that a victor has imposed upon a fallen foe. Before they had finished, civil rights were to vanish before arbitrary military rule; native leaders were to be thrust aside to make place for grasping "carpetbag" adventurers; the social pyramid was to be upturned and negroes, just out of slavery, given dominance;

the whole economic order was to be destroyed because Northern men had never understood the part that the plantation system played in Southern life and thought that slavery made up the whole relationship between the races. The South was to be subjected to an effort to make it over into what the abolitionist group thought it should be. All that had been feared by the most extreme Southern alarmist from the beginning was to be carried out in detail.

As Edmund Ruffin saw the negro drifting from old moorings, disregarding old ties, and revealing a total unconsciousness of obligations in his new status, he knew that the South had started down this dark road. The planting of crops to feed a destitute people seemed of less importance to Northern officials than the securing of the outer evidences of a contrite spirit and a broken heart. Only humiliation and starvation were in the offing. As his sons and grandsons gathered up the few horses and implements that were left and started down the roads that led toward "Beechwood" and "Marlbourne," he turned back to his room blinded by grief and anger. The old bitter struggle had returned to its first battleground within his heart.[11]

The studied pages of the broken Southerner's diary tell the story of those last days. Fear of death, offense to God, grief to those he loved—these did battle with the stern old mind where logic held sway. The shortening of a life useless to its owner for the relief or service of others could not be condemned. A man without a country was already dead! If the God of Battles had overlooked one of his tired soldiers on the field, might he not hasten on to join his comrades without further waiting? To be wrapped in a blanket and "buried as usually were our brave soldiers who were slain in battle" was his only wish.

But one parting shot at the foe:

> I here declare my unmitigated hatred to Yankee rule—
> to all political, social and business connections with the
> Yankees and to the Yankee race. Would that I could
> impress these sentiments, in their full force, on every
> living Southerner and bequeath them to every one yet to
> be born! May such sentiments be held universally in
> the outraged and down-trodden South, though in silence
> and stillness, until the now far-distant day shall arrive
> for just retribution for Yankee usurpation, oppression
> and atrocious outrages, and for deliverance and venge-
> ance for the now ruined, subjugated and enslaved
> Southern States! . . . And now with my latest writing
> and utterance, and with what will be near my latest
> breath, I here repeat and would willingly proclaim my
> unmitigated hatred to Yankee rule—to all political, social
> and business connections with Yankees, and the per-
> fidious, malignant and vile Yankee race.

The ink had scarcely dried. The sound of a carriage on
the road died in the distance, announcing the departure of
the morning's guests. A shot rang out. The weary old
soldier had gone to join the comrades of a lost cause.

NOTES

CHAPTER I

1. J. G. Nicolay, *The Outbreak of Rebellion*, p. 62.
2. Charleston *Daily Courier*, April 13, 1861.
3. *Collections of the Virginia Historical Society* (New Series), X, p. 380.
4. *American Farmer*, VII, p. 293; W. P. Cutter, *Year Book of the United States Department of Agriculture, 1895;* H. G. Ellis, *John P. Branch Historical Papers of Randolph-Macon College*, III, No. 2, pp. 99-123.
5. *DeBow's Review*, XI, pp. 431-36.
6. Diary of Edmund Ruffin. Manuscript in the Library of Congress. The personal material in this study is drawn largely from this Diary which begins in 1855 and closes in 1865 a few minutes before his death.
7. In addition to the works that will be discussed at the appropriate time in this study, there is in existence a second manuscript diary, a large amount of correspondence, a series of personal reactions to important events, and a large number of newspaper articles of minor importance which in manuscript form run into thousands of pages. In addition to these, many papers, journals, and personal letters were destroyed by the Union troops in 1863.
8. Ruffin to J. H. Hammond, September 7, 1845: Hammond Papers, MS., Library of Congress.
9. Ruffin Diary, January 20, 1863.
10. Because of the picture of Ruffin given by Thomas Dixon in his *Man in Gray,* this extreme moderation in personal habits needs emphasis.
11. Statement made in letter found on body of a soldier killed in the second battle of Bull Run.
12. Ruffin Diary, January 6, 1858.
13. *Ibid.*, March 21, 1857.
14. *Ibid.*, January 8, 1858.
15. *Ibid.*, February 25, 1858.
16. Coggin's Point lies east of Petersburg on the James near the present town of Hopewell.
17. Marlbourne Farm Journal, MS., the Virginia State Library, Richmond. "Marlbourne" is located just east of Old Church on the Tappahannock road.
    The Farm Journal here referred to begins on January 1, 1844, and runs to September, 1851. Combined with the correspondence between the father and his two sons, it gives an excellent picture of progressive methods used in this period in Virginia.
18. Ruffin's improved methods for teaching are contained in a long communication addressed to Mr. Charles Campbell of Petersburg, January 16, 1864, offering his services to a committee of the teachers' convention in preparing a better *Primer* for elementary education.

CHAPTER II

1. John Coleman, *Life of Devereux Jarratt.*
2. W. M. Gewehr, *The Great Awakening in Virginia;* F. J. Turner, *The Frontier in American History.*
3. Julian Ruffin to Edmund Ruffin, December 7, 1849; Edmund Ruffin to Julian Ruffin, December 12, 1849.
4. Ruffin Diary, September 19, 1859.
5. *Ibid.,* December 16, 1858, June 1, 1859, June 18, 1863.
6. *Ibid.,* February 24, 1864.
7. *Ibid.,* June 2, 1859.
8. C. H. Ambler, *Sectionalism in Virginia, Thomas Ritchie—A Study in Virginia Politics;* A. O. Craven, *Soil Exhaustion as a Factor in the Agricultural History of Virginia and Maryland.*
9. *Journal of the Senate of the Commonwealth of Virginia, 1823-1826.*
10. Ruffin Diary, January 20, 1863.
11. *Ibid.,* November 12, 1857.
12. *Ibid.,* July 20, 1857, October 9, 1858, May 14, 1863.
13. *Ibid.,* November 1, 1864.
14. Richmond *Enquirer,* June 13, 1823; beginning a series of articles, signed, *"A Farmer."*
15. A sixteen-page pamphlet signed by Richard Field, President, and Edmund Ruffin, Secretary.
16. Edmund Ruffin to John Tyler, January 29, 1841; *Farmers' Register,* IX, p. 253. It should be noted that Ruffin became an ardent admirer of John C. Calhoun at the time of the Compromise of 1850. He declared at the time of Calhoun's death that he "never felt so much sorrow for the death of any one not of his own family."

CHAPTER III

1. *Calendar of State Papers, America and West Indies, 1696-1697,* p. 643.
2. J. D. Schoepf, *Travels in the Confederation, 1783-1784,* II, p. 32.
3. A. O. Craven, *Soil Exhaustion . . . in Virginia and Maryland,* pp. 72-121.
4. *Farmers' Register,* II, pp. 382-83, 577-80, 685-88, 762-64; III, pp. 233-36, 685-88; VII, pp. 659-67; Craven, *op. cit.,* pp. 122-26; *American Farmer,* VII (4th Series), p. 293.
5. *DeBow's Review,* XI, p. 432.
6. *American Farmer,* III, pp. 313-20.
7. W. P. Cutter, *Yearbook of the United States Department of Agriculture, 1895,* p. 493. *An Essay on Calcareous Manures* went through five editions, the last published in 1853.
8. *An Essay on Calcareous Manures* (1833), pp. 29-30.
9. *Farmers' Register,* VII, pp. 609-10; *Southern Planter,* XII, pp. 289-305; "An Address on the Opposite Results of Exhausting and Fertilizing Systems of Agriculture," a paper read before the South Carolina Institute, November 18, 1852.
10. *American Farmer,* III, p. 314.
11. See Supplement to Volume I of *Farmers' Register* for list of subscribers.

NOTES

12. *Farmers' Register*, X, pp. 383, 489-90; *Southern Planter*, XII, p. 258; Craven, *op. cit.*, pp. 142-61.
13. Committee to Julian Ruffin, December 18, 1843; Resolutions of Farmers of Prince George County, October 10, 1843, Peyton P. Bolling, Chairman.
14. See *Farmers' Register*, IX, pp. 163-66, 618-19, etc.
15. The *Bank Reformer* began publication on September 4, 1841, and continued for at least a year and a half.
16. Letters with these telling attacks printed upon them are found in the papers of J. H. Hammond as well as in the papers of Ruffin himself. He evidently used them on all correspondence over a period of some two years.
17. See *Journal of the State Board of Agriculture*, First Session, Monday, December 6, 1841.

CHAPTER IV

1. For details on Charleston's story see: Mrs. St. Julien Ravenel, *Charleston, the Place and the People;* H. H. Ravenel, *Eliza Pinckney;* W. A. Schaper, "Sectionalism and Representation in South Carolina," *Report of the American Historical Association,* 1900, I, pp. 230-463; Verner Crane, *The Southern Frontier;* D. D. Wallace, *Life of Henry Laurens.*
2. U. B. Phillips, "South Carolina Federalists," *American Historical Review,* XIV, pp. 537-39.
3. *Register of Debates in Congress,* VIII, Pt. I, pp. 80-81.
4. Hammond Papers, MS., Library of Congress; E. Merritt, *James Henry Hammond.*
5. MS. oration in Hammond Papers, Library of Congress. See also J. H. Hammond, "Address Delivered before the South Carolina Institute, at its First Annual Fair, on the 20th November, 1849."
6. Merritt, *op. cit.*, pp. 65-77.
7. *Farmers' Register,* VIII, p. 244.
8. Hammond to Ruffin, February 5, 1843.
9. "Report of the Commencement and Progress of the Agricultural Survey of South Carolina for 1843"; MS. journal of work as surveyor in Ruffin papers.
10. For details of this agricultural revolution see A. O. Craven, *Soil Exhaustion . . . in Virginia and Maryland,* pp. 122-61.
11. Ruffin's detailed description of the drainage plant at "Marlbourne" (MS.) is a masterpiece and deserves the notice of all students of ante-bellum agriculture.
12. See also "The Westover Journal of John A. Selden," *Smith College Studies in History,* VI, No. 4, July, 1921; Willoughby Newton to the Virginia State Agricultural Society, February 19, 1852.
13. Ruffin to Hammond, May 17, 1845; October 24, 1845: Hammond Papers; Richmond *Enquirer,* May 24, 1845.
14. *DeBow's Review,* XI, pp. 431-36.
15. "Incidents of My Life, 1853. In Memoriam, 1855." (MS.) Under this title Ruffin gives in detail the story of his return to public life, sprinkling his pages with clippings from the newspapers to "document" and justify his course; *Journal of Transactions of the Virginia State Agricultural*

Society, from Its Organization to the Close of the First Annual Exhibition of 1853, I, p. 118.

16. Ruffin to Hammond, December 3, 1853, February 26, 1854: Hammond Papers.

17. Ruffin Diary, January 20, 1863.

18. "Statement of the Alarming Scenes of the Life of Thomas Cocke. Feb. 25, 1840." (MS.) An eleven-page description with horrifying details of his friend's suicide. Ruffin's own death in 1865 was accomplished in almost exactly the same way, with scarcely any variation in a single detail.

CHAPTER V

1. Irvin S. Cobb, "No Damn Yankee."

2. A. O. Craven, "The South in American History," *Historical Outlook,* XXI, pp. 105-09.

3. *Proceedings and Debates of the Virginia State Convention of 1829-30,* pp. 76, 306, 389, 858; C. H. Ambler, *Sectionalism in Virginia; Proceedings and Debates of the Convention of North Carolina, Called to Amend the Constitution of the State* (1835); H. W. Connor to John C. Calhoun, January 12, 1849: *Report of the American Historical Association, 1899,* II, p. 1188.

4. U. B. Phillips, "The Central Theme in Southern History," *American Historical Review,* XXIV, pp. 30-43.

5. C. E. Persinger, "The 'Bargain of 1844' as the Origin of the Wilmot Proviso," *Report of the American Historical Association, 1911,* I, pp. 189-95; C. B. Going, *David Wilmot, Free-Soiler,* pp. 117-41.

6. Elwood Fisher to J. C. Calhoun, December 2, 1846: "Letters to John C. Calhoun," *Report of the American Historical Association, 1899,* II. How completely sectional hostility had been aroused, especially after Polk's veto of the River and Harbor bill, is shown in an editorial published in the Chicago *Daily Journal,* August 19, 1846:

   "The lives and property of the freemen of the North, her free laborers, sailors, and those passing to and fro upon her great Lakes and Rivers, are of no concern to the Government. They live and labor in a portion of country which is out of the pale of its care and protection. . . . Three times already has the whole policy of this Government been changed at the command of the South, all its business broken up and deranged, because the slave-owner was jealous of the prosperity of the free States. They were rising in prosperity, growing rich in commerce, agriculture, manufactures, and great in intelligence, whilst the South, with the curse of slavery upon her, was standing still or going backward. And shutting their eyes to the real cause which produced such results, they attributed it all to what they pleased to call partial legislation, and they have demanded a change, and every change has brought the same results, and ever will, until slavery be at an end, and the energy of free hands and minds shall raise this country to that position for which Nature intended her.

   "All other pretenses of objections to the Harbor Bill are idle and vain. . . .

"The North can and will be no longer hoodwinked. If no measures for protection and improvement of anything North or West are to be suffered by our Southern masters, if we are to be downtrodden, and all our cherished interests crushed by them, a signal revolution will inevitably ensue. The same spirit and energy that forced emancipation for the whole country from Great Britain will throw off the Southern yoke. The North and West will look to and take care of their own interests henceforth. They will . . . see . . . that the power to oppress shall not again be entrusted to men who have shown themselves to be slave-holders, but not Americans. . . . The fiat has gone forth—Southern rule is at an end."

(This editorial was called to my attention by one of my students, Mr. Chester Destler.)

7. Alexander Stephens probably to George W. Crawford, December 27, 1848; Joseph H. Lumpkin to Howell Cobb, January 21, 1848; Robert Toombs to John J. Crittenden, January 3, 1849; John H. Lumpkin to Howell Cobb, November 13, 1846: all in *Report of the American Historical Association,* 1911, II; *Works of John C. Calhoun* (Cralle), VI, pp. 290-313; Hilliard M. Judge to John C. Calhoun, April 29, 1849: *Report of the American Historical Association,* 1899, II, p. 1195.

8. B. M. Palmer, *Life and Letters of James Henley Thornwell,* June 14, 1845; Henry L. Benning to Howell Cobb, July 1, 1849: *Report of the American Historical Association,* 1911, II, p. 169; J. H. Hammond to John C. Calhoun, March 5, 1850: *ibid.,* 1899, II, p. 1210.

9. *Farmers' Register,* IV, p. 49.

10. Ruffin to Hammond, July 6, 1845: Hammond Papers; *ibid.,* September 7, 1845.

11. *Farmers' Register,* I, p. 36; IV, p. 4.

12. Ruffin Diary, January 20, 1863.

13. "What Will be the Result of Northern Abolition Action?" was the title used for the articles in the Richmond *Enquirer,* the last one dated March 28, 1850.

14. April 27, 1845: *Report of the American Historical Association,* 1899, II, p. 1032.

15. N. W. Stephenson, "Southern Nationalism in South Carolina in 1851," *American Historical Review,* XXXVI, pp. 314-35; E. Merritt, *James Henry Hammond,* pp. 94-108; Lieber to Hilliard, October 18, 1851 (Huntington Library MS.).

16. "The Armed Truce," Charleston *Mercury,* November 7, 1851; Richmond *Examiner,* Nov. 11, 1851; Ruffin to Hammond, November 11, 1851: Hammond Papers; *ibid.,* November 13, 1851.

17. Ruffin obtained his "information" regarding Ritchie and the Compromise from Elwood Fisher. It is interesting to note that at this time both Ruffin and Hammond were reading and praising John Taylor's *Inquiry into the Principles and Policy of Government in the United States.*

CHAPTER VI

1. *Annals of Congress, 16th Congress, 1st Sess.,* pp. 259-74; Edwin C. Holland, *A Refutation of the Calumnies Circulated against the Southern*

and Western States Respecting the Institution and Existence of Slavery among Them; Edward Brown, Notes on the Origin and Necessity of Slavery; Thomas Cooper, On the Constitution of the United States, and the Questions that have Arisen under it; C. C. Pinckney, "Address to the South Carolina Agricultural Society"; for Miller's statement see Charleston Courier, November 28, 1829.

2. Thomas R. Dew. Review of the Debate in the Virginia Legislature of 1831 and 1832, Richmond, 1832 (133 pages).

3. See The Pro-Slavery Argument for Harper, Hammond, Simms and Dew; George Fitzhugh, Cannibals All and Sociology for the South; Thornton Stringfellow, Slavery, Its Origin, Nature and History, and Scriptural and Statistical Views in Favor of Slavery; J. H. Van Evrie, Negroes and Negro Slavery; J. C. Nott and George R. Gliddon, Types of Mankind; George D. Armstrong, The Christian Doctrine of Slavery; John Fletcher, Studies in Slavery; A. T. Bledsoe, An Essay on Liberty and Slavery.

4. E. A. Pollard, The Lost Cause Regained, p. 141. One of Ruffin's relatives had written in September, 1811, regarding the sale of a slave as follows: "My man Vall I am about to sell and I adopt this mode for him to choose a master, by allowing him the liberty of looking out; he appears to be pleased with you, if you are disposed to purchase my price is $400. I suppose I could get more than that at public sale but am anxious to humour him as he has been a faithful servant to me—he is an excellent house servant, horseler, gardener & tolerable good weaver, & his character stands unblemished as respects honesty &c." (MS., Huntington Library.)

5. Ruffin Diary, April 17, 1858, May 20, 1864.

6. "Political Economy of Slavery," pp. 3-8; "Slavery and Free Labor Compared," p. 8.

7. Ibid., pp. 9-10.

8. Ibid., p. 9.

9. "African Colonization Unveiled," pp. 17-32; "Political Economy of Slavery," pp. 15-20.

10. Nott and Gliddon, op. cit. (Morton, S. G.); Van Evrie, op. cit.; S. D. Baldwin, Dominion; J. L. Cabell, The Testimony of Modern Science to the Unity of Mankind; John Bachman, The Doctrine of the Unity of the Human Race Examined on the Principles of Science; Medical Life, 35, pp. 485-504; Two Lectures on the Natural History of the Caucasian and Negro Races, by Josiah C. Nott, M.D. (Mobile, 1844)

11. John Tyler to Edmund Ruffin, February 15, 1860 (MS.); Ruffin Diary, July 2, 1858; The South, July 2, 1858, article on "The Free Negro Nuisance and How to Abate It."

12. "Slavery and Free Labor Compared," pp. 9-28.

13. "The Influence of Slavery, or of its Absence, on Manners, Morals, and Intellect," pp. 25-31; Ruffin Diary, August 28, 1862.

14. "Political Economy of Slavery," pp. 20-22.

CHAPTER VII

1. John Slidell, to Howell Cobb, January 28, 1852: Report of the American Historical Association, 1911, II, p. 276.

NOTES

2. Henry L. Benning to Howell Cobb, September 2, 1852: *ibid.*, p. 319.
3. Cleo Hearon, *Mississippi and the Compromise of 1850,* p. 213; Hammond Diary, May 25, 1851; Columbus *Sentinel* in the Charleston *Mercury,* January 23, 1851 (quoted in R. H. Shryock, *Georgia and the Union in 1850,* pp. 344-45).
4. Elwood Fisher to R. M. T. Hunter, October 29, 1850: *Report of the American Historical Association,* 1916, II, p. 120.
5. The materials on which this discussion of the Northeast is based are too extensive to be listed here. A few secondary works of value are: S. E. Morrison, *Maritime History of Massachusetts;* D. R. Fox, *Decline of Aristocracy in the Politics of New York;* A. B. Darling, *Political Changes in Massachusetts, 1824-48;* F. Byrdsall, *History of the Loco Foco Movement;* W. R. Waterman, *Frances Wright;* O. G. Frothingham, *Gerritt Smith;* J. A. Krout, *Origins of Prohibition;* H. D. A. Donovan, *The Barnburners, 1830-52;* J. P. Bretz, "The Economic Background of the Liberty Party," *American Historical Review,* XXIV, pp. 250-64; F. J. Turner, "New England, 1830-50," *Huntington Library Bulletin,* No. 1, pp. 153-98.
6. The relation of political attitude to economic stages in the Northwest remains yet to be worked out. Such studies of wheat growing as have been made by J. G. Thompson for Wisconsin and by Russell Anderson for Illinois indicate that the breaking of the home market was basic in shaping political attitudes.
7. "The Influence of Slavery, or of its Absence, on Manners, Morals, and Intellect"; "An Address on the Opposite Results of Exhausting and Fertilizing Systems of Agriculture," read before South Carolina Institute at its Fourth Annual Fair, November 18, 1852.
8. *Daily Crescent,* New Orleans, August 9, 1855, July 27, 1855. "Really, were the question of abolition of slavery left exclusively to Massachusetts and England, it would not carry. The People there like to indulge in the luxury of mourning over imaginary woes of others; of investing largely in sympathy that costs nothing; and of parading before the world the fact that they profess to be the most exquisite philanthropists extant! But touch their pockets—tell them that the dimes are in danger—that further indulgence in philanthropy will be ruinous—and they will pitch sympathy, 'Sambo,' and philanthropy, overboard in the shortest possible order."
9. *Ibid.,* November 11, 1856.
10. Articles in *Enquirer* between dates December 18 and 24; reprinted in *DeBow's Review,* issues of June, September, October, November, 1857.
11. These ideas were developed in a series of five articles published both in the Charleston *Mercury* and the *Virginia Index* under the title, "The True Policy for the Southern States."
12. Ruffin Diary, May 1, 1858; Hammond Papers, July 4, 1857; Herbert Wender, *Southern Commercial Conventions, 1837-1859,* pp. 27, 135, 209, 221.
13. *DeBow's Review,* XXIV, pp. 578 ff.
14. Ruffin Diary, May 10-14, 1858.
15. *Ibid.,* May 25, 1858; Richmond *Enquirer,* May 19-21, 1858; W. A. Grinted to Edmund Ruffin, August 27, 1858 (MS.).

16. Ruffin Diary, March 4, 1859, April 26, 1859, May 15, 1859.
17. *The South*, April 22, 1858, June 25, 1858; Charleston *Mercury*, July 16, 1859.
18. Ruffin Diary, September 11, 1858, January 19, 1859.
19. Washington Hunt to Wyndham Robertson, January 5, 1859 (MS.), January 8, 1858.
20. J. H. Hammond to Edmund Ruffin, August 17, 1858 (MS.).
21. Ruffin Diary, August 16, 1858, October 22, 1858; Laura A. White, in *South Atlantic Quarterly*, XXVIII, pp. 370-89.

CHAPTER VIII

1. Ruffin Diary, October 19, 20, 1859.
2. *Ibid.*, November 25, 1859.
3. *Ibid.*
4. *Ibid.*, December 2, 1859.
5. John Letcher to R. M. T. Hunter, December 9, 1859; *Report of the American Historical Association*, 1916, II, p. 275; Lewis E. Harvie to R. M. T. Hunter, October 18 (?), 1859: *ibid.*, p. 273.
6. "Subversion of Negro Slavery or the Dissolution of the Present Union, the Only Alternative for the South," *Virginia Index*, January (?), 1860.
7. Frederick W. Coleman to R. M. T. Hunter, December 21, 1859, James A. Seddon to R. M. T. Hunter, December 26, 1859: *Report of the American Historical Association*, 1916, II, p. 280.
8. Robert Toombs to Alexander H. Stevens, February 10, 1860: *Report of the American Historical Association*, 1911, II, p. 461; William W. Wick to R. M. T. Hunter, April 27, 1860: *ibid.*, 1916, II, p. 321.
9. Ruffin Diary, May 29-31, 1860.
10. *Ibid.*, May 21, 1860.
11. Rev. John Bachman to Edmund Ruffin, May 23, 1860 (MS.).
12. Abraham Lincoln to John B. Floyd, August 15, 1860, Jeremiah S. Black Papers.
13. Ruffin Diary, September 10-20, 1860.
14. *Daily Whig*, October 18, 1860.
15. Ruffin to Yancey, October 29, 1860.
16. Charleston *Mercury*, November 6, 7, 1860.
17. Ruffin distributed at this time two hundred copies of Townsend's pamphlet, "The South Alone Should Govern the South and African Slavery Should Be Controlled by Those Only Who Are Friendly to It."
18. Edmund Ruffin to Edmund Ruffin, Jr., and Julian Ruffin, November 11, 1860.
19. Charleston *Mercury*, November 17, 1860.
20. The story of Ruffin's visit in South Carolina is based on his Diary for this period.
21. Edward Bates to Wyndham Robertson, November 3, 1860 (MS.); D. H. Mahan to J. D. Davidson, November 1, 1860: Davidson Papers, MS., the McCormick Library.
22. *Frank Leslie's Weekly*, XI, p. 172.

NOTES

CHAPTER IX

1. Robert Toombs to Thomas W. Thomas, December 4, 1859: *Report of the American Historical Association,* 1911, II, p. 450.
2. U. B. Phillips, *Life of Robert Toombs.* Those who would judge the merits of Southern secession on the basis of Lincoln's personal attitudes miss the entire point. The South knew little of Lincoln and had formed its ideas of the Republican threat from Seward, Chase, Sumner, and such leaders. For what even a Northern man saw in Seward's attitude, see S. J. Tilden's letter to Kent in *The Writings and Speeches of Samuel J. Tilden* (Bigelow), pp. 289-330. See A. C. Cole, *American Historical Review,* XXVI, pp. 740-67.
3. J. L. Sellers, "The Make-up of the Early Republican Party," *Transactions of the Illinois State Historical Society,* Publication No. 37; W. E. Dodd, "The Fight for the Northwest," *American Historical Review,* XVI, pp. 774-88.
4. J. R. Perkins, *Trails, Rails and War,* p. 57; C. H. Ray to Lyman Trumbull, February 25, 1861: "We want this office [Postmaster in Chicago] not wholly for the money there is in it; but as a means of extending and insuring our business and extending the influence of the *Tribune.* We claim to have done as much for Mr. Lincoln and the Republican cause as any other agency in Illinois and we do not see why our claim should be denied": Trumbull Manuscripts; Joseph Medill to Trumbull, March 4, 1861: "To us the Post Office would be of great value. . . . If Mr. S. had it the country Post Masters of the Northwest would work to extend our circulation and while this would greatly help our firm it would benefit the party and promote the legitimate influence of our paper": *ibid.* I am under obligations to Mr. Tracy Strevey for these two letters.
5. "The Republican victory would be incomplete if it did not promise sooner or later to reform the United States Supreme Court. That bench full of Southern lawyers, which gentlemen of a political temperament call an 'august tribunal,' is the last entrenchment behind which despotism is sheltered; and until a national convention amends the Constitution so as to defeat the usurpations of that body, or until the court itself is reconstructed by the dropping off of a few of its members and the appointment of better men in their places, we have little hope for Congressional action in the way of restricting slavery": *Chicago Tribune,* March 4, 1861; Robert S. Littell to Wyndham Robertson, September 18, 1854 (MS.).
6. Edward Bates to Wyndham Robertson, November 3, 1861 (MS.); "Speech of Wyndham Robertson, Esq. . . . on the State of the Country," March 5 and 6, 1860.
7. S. J. Tilden to Wyndham Robertson, January 18, 1861 (MS.); "To the Honorable William Kent," New York *Evening Post,* October 30, 1860.
8. R. B. Curtis to Wyndham Robertson, December 24, 1860 (MS.). Some writers have argued that the passage of the Corwin resolutions, and the subsequent offering of the abortive "Thirteenth Amendment" by a Republican Congress, should have satisfied every honest Southern demand for the security of slavery. Such views overlook the fact that the South already had sufficient constitutional protection by the decision of the

Supreme Court and that it feared only sectional party agitation and efforts such as the Republicans offered. The insistence of the South on an open compromise and the refusal of Lincoln and his group to accept anything that would weaken the party's position indicate that both understood that this was the vital slavery issue at stake. See also *Memoirs of John A. Dix*, p. 354.

9. Edward Bates to Wyndham Robertson, November 3, 1860 (MS.).

10. Washington Hunt to Wyndham Robertson, January 5, 1859 (MS.).

11. Lincoln's Instructions to Hon. William Kellogg, December 11, 1860: Nicolay and Hay, *Abraham Lincoln*, III, p. 259; *Diary of Orville Browning* (Wednesday, July 3, 1861), p. 476; G. Welles, *Diary*, I, p. 13; S. W. Crawford, *Genesis of the Civil War*, p. 420, quotes letter of Lincoln to Capt. C. V. Fox (May 1, 1860): "You and I both anticipated that the cause of the country would be advanced by making the attempt to provision Fort Sumter, even if it should fail; and it is no small consolation now to feel that our anticipation is justified by the result." See also, H. G. Connor, *John Archibald Campbell*, for part that Seward played in creating the state of Southern minds.

12. Ruffin Diary, April 2, 1861.

13. Mrs. Roger A. Pryor, *Reminiscences of Peace and War*, pp. 120-21.

14. Edmund Ruffin to Julian Ruffin, March 9, 1861; Ruffin Diary, April 8, 1861.

15. Pryor, *op. cit.*

16. The question as to who fired the first gun at Sumter is one that has caused, and will cause as long as interest remains, a large amount of dispute. The evidence seems to show that Ruffin's claim is good, although the whole matter is one of deciding which battery opened fire first after the signal gun had flashed. Several batteries claimed the honor for the men who fired the first gun from their stations. In the excitement of the hour each man thought his shot reached the Fort first. On this basis much can be said for the claims of both Captain George S. James and Lieutenant W. Hampton Gibbes.

17. Ruffin Diary, April 8-12, 1861; Charleston *Daily Courier*, April 13, 1861.

18. Jefferson Davis to Edmund Ruffin, April 22, 1861 (MS.). The Ruffin Diary contains clippings from Charleston, Richmond, Mobile and New York newspapers describing Ruffin's part at Sumter.

19. A. F. Robertson, *Alexander Hugh Holmes Stuart; Interesting and Important Correspondence between Opposition Members of the Legislature of Virginia and Hon. John Minor Botts;* Wyndham Robertson Papers (MS.); B. B. Mumford, *Virginia's Attitude toward Slavery and Secession.*

20. Edward Bates to Wyndham Robertson, February 3, 1861; Winfield Scott to Wyndham Robertson, February 19, 1861; B. O. Tayloe to Col. E. T. Tayloe, January 25, 1860; Washington Hunt to Wyndham Robertson, January 5, 1858; S. J. Tilden to Wyndham Robertson, January 15, 1861; R. B. Curtis to Wyndham Robertson, December 24, 1860. These letters are in the Robertson Papers (MS.) in the University of Chicago Library.

21. Wyndham Robertson to Frank Robertson, April 13, 1861.

22. The story of Ruffin at Bull Run is taken from materials found in his Diary under dates from July 1 to July 22, 1861. See also Edmund Ruffin to Lottie Ruffin, September 5, 1862.

23. Cincinnati *Enquirer*, August 8, 1861.

NOTES

CHAPTER X

1. Ruffin Diary, July 31, 1861, December, 1861.
2. *Ibid.*, August 17, 1862. Ruffin's compass is in possession of the family of John Weidman of Lebanon, Pennsylvania, even today.
3. *Ibid.*, February 8, 1863.
4. *Ibid.*, September 28, 1862.
5. *Ibid.*, February 6, 1861, October 9, 1862.
6. *Ibid.*, June 19, 1862. These were prices Ruffin actually paid.
7. *Ibid.*, April 2, 1863.
8. *Ibid.*, August 13, 1863.
9. *Ibid.*, November 15, 1863. Ruffin copied from the Charleston newspaper files these comments from the pen of his friend Yeadon.
10. *Ibid.*, January 4, 1864. This is the first hint of a determination to destroy himself in case of defeat of Lee's army.
11. The negroes belonging to the Ruffin family deserted in large numbers during the war. Only a few worthless slaves were left to begin the experiment of free labor. "My son has two rich and large farms lying waste and abandoned. . . . But if he had hand labor at command and ever so cheap, these farms would still be destitute of teams, stock, implements, and machines of all kinds, provisions, and one of them with every house destroyed and the fences on all, and the owner without a dollar of current money." (January 5, 1865.)

    In early May Ruffin noted that "the negroes in the country in communication with Richmond, are very generally moving with their goods and chattels from their late masters' farms." On May 10 he said: "This day may be considered as to this family and our neighborhood the beginning of the practical operation of the new policy of free negro labor." Only five adults, all house servants, remained with his son.

    For details of Ruffin's death see: Edmund Ruffin, Jr., to his sons, June 20, 1865; *Tyler's Historical and Genealogical Magazine*, V, pp. 193‹ 95; *The Republic*, June 20, 1865.

INDEX

(1)